ken haley
emails
from
the
edge

A Journey Through Troubled Times

ken haley
emails
from
the
edge

A Journey Through Troubled Times

transit lounge

EMAILS FROM THE EDGE
First Published 2006 by
Transit Lounge Publishing
95 Stephen Street, Yarraville, Australia 3013
www.transitlounge.com.au
info@transitlounge.com.au

Design by Tim McQuiston
Maps by Ian Faulkner
Printed and bound in Australia by Griffin Press

National Library of Australia
Cataloguing-in-publication data

Haley, Ken, 1954- .
Emails from the Edge: a journey through troubled times.

Bibliography
ISBN 0-9750228-3-0

1. Haley, Ken 1954- . -Travel - Eurasia. 2. Journalists - Australia - Biography.
3. Paraplegics - Australia - Biography. 4. Eurasia - Description and travel. I.
Title.

070.92

*For my parents, without whom all this would have
been impossible, and I even more so.*

CONTENTS

PREFACE

The title of this book occurred to me upon awakening one mid-April day in 2001, shortly before I set out on the transcontinental journey it describes.

It was in my mind that if I were to send home a collection of newspaper articles from the countries en route they might cover such a range of themes that, as I would be using Internet cafés to deliver them, this would constitute a fairly new use of email which might somehow—precious thought—marry the staccato rhythms of that medium with the more sustained notes contained in news features.

So it was no coincidence that my irregular series of travel articles published in the Melbourne *Age* over the next two years was christened 'Emails from the Edge'.

In 2003, when it became clear that this book would be written not in Australia but in far-off Namibia, and that posting a hard-copy manuscript would be problematic, the title acquired a secondary, quite eerie, significance, because now the book itself would be sent to my long-suffering publishers in the form of emails from the edge of Africa.

At about the same time, when discussing with the publisher what form this memoir should take, I could see that to tell only of my outward journey and not of the inner one would be to tell half a story, or a kind of lie.

People, like continents, have edges. To cross one's own is a different voyage, undertaken with no obvious return ticket. But there are many roads back to a whole life.

At the time of going to print, self-exploration was free of charge and there was still no departure tax on flights of the imagination.

Chapter 1

LOWER, FASTER, FURTHER

In the path of verse, behold the travelling of place and of time!
The child of one night, the path of one year goeth.

A COUPLET BY HAFEZ (KHAJEH SHAMSEDDIN MOHAMMAD HAFEZ SHIRAZI),
14TH-CENTURY PERSIAN SUFI POET, FROM ANTHOLOGY *DIVAN OF HAFEZ*

CHRISTMAS 2001

Christmas is hardly the word for it, but unmistakable signs of the season were everywhere: there was no room at inn after inn, and tinselled trees sprouted in hotel foyers, welcoming Westerners to that part of the world where it all began.

They welcomed me to Manama, downtown Bahrain, an urban oasis wedged between the Arabian desert and opal-blue Gulf. At the commercial heart of this oasis, the Hotel Aradous beckoned me in from the unremitting heat of the street to the cool relief of its high-ceilinged interior.

This could have been a European grand hotel, from its glittering chandelier and room-key boxes at reception right down to the potted palms. But a glance outside would have cured anyone of such a misconception. From there emanated all the sounds and smells, the tingling, jangling and spicy aromas, that make up an Eastern bazaar.

On either side of the hotel's entrance were two shops: one a jeweller's, the other a moneychanger's, testament to the reign of commerce in this realm. In the alley that ran alongside the Aradous, I passed a tarpaulin-covered teashop, an airy refuge from the ceaseless hubbub of traders. A few metres further down the alley, I came upon a security door where, having made prior arrangements for entering

1

at ground level and avoiding staircases, I found an eager hotel porter waiting.

He unlocked the door, re-locked it at once, and led me through a warren of corridors that eventually brought me back to the foyer. Here I found myself asking yet again those questions that coming from any other guest would have sounded absurd: not only, 'Do you have a room for six nights?' but also, 'Could I have a look first to see whether I can get into the bathroom?'

All this arranged without too much fuss, we finally broached the question of the tariff—as important to me as to any budget traveller, and I still classed myself as one because, although this was no ordinary journey, I remained averse to paying gold-brick prices for base-metal accommodation. After Central Asia, where expenses could be kept within tolerable bounds, the Gulf had come as a rude shock to the wallet. In this region my usual ceiling, US$40 a night, was the basement.

There's no such thing as a cheap room in Bahrain's tourist quarter but the Aradous seemed the best option. So, as I waited for the reception staff to deal with other guests first, my mind wound back eleven years to 1990, when I had worked as a sub-editor on the national newspaper—and, anticipating the moment the duty manager's roving eye fell on me, I took the opportunity to beg a favour.

'May I use your phone for a local call, please?'

'Certainly,' he replied, idly pushing the device across the counter.

I picked up the receiver, checked my newly bought copy of the *Gulf Daily News*, and dialled.

'Could you put me through to the editor?' I asked, having noted in the paper that the deputy editor when I worked there had since been promoted. His familiar English Midlands accent came on the line.

'Ken Haley here. I'm back in Bahrain, for the first time since I was working here.'

'Oh, Ken,' he sounded slightly lost for words, 'how have you been?'

'Very well. Time heals, as they say.' A pause. 'I wouldn't mind seeing you … while I'm here.'

'That would be fantastic. Why don't you ring tomorrow? We'd be glad to see you. If you're staying in town, you could catch a bus out to the office.'

'Yes, well ... ' (the moment of revelation could not be deferred, as I knew the office layout well enough and the editorial offices were literally up stairs on the first floor), 'it would be fine to meet at the office but I have something to tell you if you have a moment to spare.'

'...Yes?'

'You needn't worry about this,' I began, a past master at imparting this fact to old acquaintances, 'but a few years ago I had a spot of bad luck and I should tell you that these days I'm in a wheelchair.'

Silence. I could have counted off the seconds, but took up the conversational slack after a handful had elapsed. 'There's really no need to worry, I've had a successful career since those days, and the fact I've just travelled all across Central Asia and Iran to get here will tell you that. So the office is out of the question, but somewhere in town perhaps?'

It takes more than a telephone to screen out the smell of fear. I could tell from this brief encounter that a meeting which should have provided resolution, a neat rounding off, to a very messy episode from a difficult time was now not going to take place. A chill dread had made that meeting—so imminent a minute ago—disappear. Even though to all the world I was the disabled one, all the pain would be weighing down his side of the ledger. What I looked to as closure would for him have been an opening—on to the worst of times.

So the next night I rang the editor's office back hour after hour after hour only to be serially fobbed off. In the end I tried to ignore the clenching of my chest, pocketed the indignity and steeled myself to look on it as something other than blameworthy, as nothing more or less than Fate.

Chapter 2

WHERE I'M COMING FROM

I know in my heart of hearts that it is a most excellent reason to do things merely because one likes the doing of them.

FREYA STARK THE VALLEYS OF THE ASSASSINS

I cannot plead anything particularly out of the ordinary in my childhood, except the child. The middle son of three, I was born into a conventional lower-middle-class family and raised on what lay near the edge of Melbourne's sprawling suburbia in the 1960s and is now a middle suburb. As it happens, my younger brother and his wife now live in that same, formerly weatherboard, house. I received a state-school education and probably had a more religious upbringing than most in secular Australia, owing to a devout maternal grandmother. My politics, though, I inherited from Dad, a traditional Labor voter.

In Australia 'tall poppies' are there to be cut down. Mum was, as she remains, an engaging mixture of egalitarianism and keeping up proper social standards. A certain woman down the street might be 'common' but a more heinous offence was to be 'a snob'. Somewhere in the great comfortable middle ground: that was where you belonged.

Except that I didn't. My rebellious spirit, combined with artistic inclinations, meant that when my grandmother bought me a piano for my sixth birthday I kicked against the discipline of strict morning practice hours but would then play—loudly and discordantly, it must be said—well into the evening.

Beyond boundaries, I became myself, felt free, grew wild.

While I was a loner, the gift of the gab (my part-Irish heritage?) made me quite a persuasive character, and, like most other teenagers, I craved the approval of my peers. But somehow the 'loner' and the observer within me proved stronger than the participant. As they shaped my personality I discovered that some of life's richest pleasures—though not happiness, damn it—are reserved for those of us who do our own thinking and imagining, who ask 'Why?' and 'What if?' more than is really good for us.

You would have described me as inquisitive rather than acquisitive—and this is a curse as much as a blessing. Somehow I survived high school, by talking my way out of trouble as often as I talked myself into it, and by concentrating on flight rather than fight (being on the move is nothing new to me, you see).

Cultivating individuality, refusing to follow the pack, served me well when I became a journalist, but there was a price to pay. No amount of planing off the social edges of your personality is going to make it anything but deformed. 'Know thyself,' said the Greeks. 'Be yourself,' say the moderns. They're both right, of course, but you can't really achieve the second until you've mastered the first—which takes decades, guaranteeing a bumpy ride along the way.

My curiosity got me into this life of journalism alternating with travel: it is the personal denominator common to both. The first news event that swam into my view was the flight of Sputnik. A half-formed image resides somewhere in my consciousness of being held aloft in the front yard, at the age of three, and seeing a pinpoint of white light streak across the sky.

The urge to break away, to disappear, kicked in quite young. I remember when, aged ten, I left my grandmother during a day's outing in the inner suburb of Richmond, to test a theory that if I went in a certain direction I could walk all the way home. That evening I knocked nonchalantly on our front door in South Oakleigh, 15 kilometres away, to be greeted with a welcome that was memorable enough but somewhat deficient in the congratulations I'd been counting on.

At 20 I went walkabout: up-country to the Murray–Darling basin, taking literally a great aunt's idle invitation to visit one day. 'Work' hadn't figured in my vision of what would follow but board was not going to be free so I adapted fast. In my ignorance, I had arrived at just the right season to pick up shifts as an orange packer in Coomealla, and when that ended I hitchhiked to Adelaide where I became a part-time piano player in a city pub. I even enrolled in an Arts course at Flinders University and stayed five days (and I'm glad of that because university experience always adds lustre to the résumé). But the sad truth was that my money reserves were getting perilously low so the dream of becoming a journalist and beginning a life's work could be put off no longer.

It was a profession that I, with my love of language and utter fearlessness when it came to asking dumb questions, took to like a duck to H_2O. One of the great attractions of being a reporter is that every day brings variety of experience and fresh ideas.

For my restless spirit, new experiences proved a satisfying substitute for new sights, although my wanderlust never slept for long. On weekends I would get into my battered old Torana and hare around the country. When reporting politics from Canberra for the Melbourne *Age*, I clocked up thousands of kilometres around New South Wales in my spare time.

A relish for solitude, added to a hunger for new views, meant that I could fairly claim to have 'seen' my homeland, Australia—all six states and both territories—long before I first set foot overseas, on New Year's Eve 1980. That trip took me to Australia's immediate northern neighbourhood: Papua New Guinea, Indonesia, Singapore and Malaysia. In later years, my journeys propelled me progressively farther afield.

Even the experienced traveller makes plenty of mistakes but the natural apprehensions most people feel at being a stranger in the crowd, or far away from home, never afflict me. There is just so much of interest in a fresh destination that until there is a clear and present danger my 'fear sensor' is almost always switched off, or at least turned way down low.

Bahrain, the first time round, set my sensor shrieking so alarmingly that it would be many years before I could face the idea of revisiting the scene of my psychic invasion. Like a GI returning to Normandy, I couldn't blot out the thought that something of my self had been left behind there—something irrecoverable yet, for all that, something that kept calling to me across the passage of decades, something embedded in the sands of time.

Chapter 3

STRAWS IN THE DESERT WIND

Hafez! Thou sawest that chatter of the strutting partridge;
Careless of the grasp of the falcon of Fate, he was.

Hafez, from the *Divan of Hafez*

1990

Early that year I was in London, scratching along as a freelance journalist in what was still known as Fleet Street, even though the term had been wrested from its physical domain years before by the likes of Rupert Murdoch and Conrad Black.

Rewind a few years. As happens with most people, I suppose, life had begun to take shape—to form a pattern—before I departed my energetic twenties for the let's-do-it-easier-now thirties.

With a sidelong glance, I recognised those who had overweening ambition to climb the office ladder and recognised that I wasn't one of them. Anyway, I felt the pull of a larger world. While working at the Melbourne offices of the *Age*, my secret dream was that one of my superiors would pluck me out of my generational pool and say, 'Boy, you're foreign correspondent material.' In the early 1980s I made my mark elsewhere, reporting politics in Canberra. But even in two years I started to see the same stories, the same rhetorical spittle, swirling round and round again. Self-mockingly, we journalists sometimes speak of the 'media circus': to me, it was more like a laundrette. The political cycle was becoming too predictable; I ached for novelty.

On one of my journeys back to Melbourne, early in 1984, I went for a drink with the news editor and asked him whether he could foresee the day when the paper would give me an overseas posting. My destination of choice would have been Beijing, its extreme otherness tantalising my curiosity, but Washington, London or Ouagadougou would have been equally acceptable. 'No' was his reply.

At least I was under no illusions: a short time later, I approached the editor and asked for a year's leave without pay. This wasn't a possibility just then, he said. So reluctantly, but with a pretence of fatalistic acceptance, I quit.

The editor must have sensed my unease for he said, 'Don't worry, there will always be a job for you at the *Age*.' He didn't add 'so long as I'm here' and I was too green to realise that such promises cannot outlast the tenure of the person who makes them. Still, his words warmed me.

Years later, only half joking, I would tell people I had retired at 30. But a new thought followed this, stemming from the action I had taken: 'If they won't turn me into a foreign correspondent, there's nothing to stop me becoming one on my own.' The 'plan' of my life, as it then unfolded, was to indulge two great passions, which can be summed up simply enough: to see the world, and to tell people what I saw.

In practical terms, combining those two passions meant alternating long periods of travel with equally long periods of intensive work—only it didn't feel like work, because previous travels had already taught me that in the absence of any other distraction I would write: obsessively, joyfully, cathartically. I'd lived long enough to discover that your vocation is what you choose to do when you don't really have to do anything.

To see the world certainly didn't mean endless sunbaking (my energy still needed channelling) but I would visit each country on my route thoroughly—a crossover trait from journalism. When money was running low, I found that sub-editing appealed more than reporting. To become a freelance writer would require staying in one place and building up contacts, which didn't sort well with the travel. Also, as I soon found, sub-editing suited my temperament and exacting approach to language. The craft had four great advantages: it was portable, profitable, always in demand and could be practised every day. 'They pay us to play with words,' I wrote home to a friend—and meant it.

8

In between my journeys throughout the late 1980s I learnt this craft, first in Athens, then in Oman, then in England (Cambridge); and now, in 1990, after an east-west crossing of Africa, I had finally 'graduated' to Fleet Street. This was a professional summit: some of the best newspapers in the world wanted my services—the *Times*, the *Sunday Times* and the *Observer*, to name three. Even now, if pressed for a career highlight, I would say that working on the *Times* foreign desk in the closing months of 1989 and early months of 1990—editing page-one stories about the fall of the Berlin Wall, the Christmas Day massacre of the Ceausescus and the triumphal release of Nelson Mandela—stands out as an imperishable memory.

Looking back, I can see how much I owed to luck: not only was I 35, seasoned yet still keen, but the economy was buoyant, near the end of the long 1980s bull run, so jobs for casual sub-editors were there for the asking. When applying to the foreign desk, it also helped that I could not only spell the names of far-off places but, by then, had actually visited many of them.

However, a pressingly practical reason—my visa status—dictated that, much as I felt at home in England, I could not stay there beyond April 1990.

Every Thursday a glossy weekly magazine, *UK Press Gazette*, appeared. The Omani job had been advertised in its pages. Now, right on cue, I saw the words, 'Wanted: Sub-editor, *Gulf Daily News*, Bahrain'.

There was an interview, conducted by an employment agency, in Croydon, on London's southern fringe. Within the space of a day I received offers, confirmed in writing, from Bahrain and Hong Kong.

Choices, how I hate them: you always make the wrong one or, rather, if you make one that doesn't turn out to be right you wonder whether the one you didn't make would have been better. Out came the feint-ruled foolscap, bisected with a dramatic vertical stroke of the biro: pros to the left, cons to the right. Every aspect was assigned points, the decision weighted according to the relative importance of urban amenity, social atmosphere, job satisfaction ... and everything came out line-ball.

In the end it was the lucre that lured me in. According to my calculations I could save twice as much by fulfilling a two-year contract in Bahrain as I could in Hong Kong and, since my aim was to work furiously until I had enough money to hit the road again for some more long-distance travelling, this tipped the balance.

Going out to the Gulf for a second time was an advantage, I felt. Cautions from a colleague—one who had worked closely with me on the *Oman Daily Observer*—I privately discounted. Knowing that he had split up with his girlfriend while working at the paper that now wanted me, I told myself, wouldn't that necessarily have coloured his view of the place?

It hadn't; the rationale behind his warning was twofold: Bahrain is a money-fixated city-state where the sense of social isolation can be very strong, and—he underlined this point—these were dangerous times. 'Just look at what has been happening to our stringer.'

I myself had been a stringer, or freelance correspondent, for Reuters during 1987–88, my time in Oman. For us newsgatherers the Iran–Iraq War was always just over the horizon, but the stories Reuters wanted from us tended to be about frankincense and camels. Farzad Bazoft was a stringer, too, for the *Observer*, but filed exclusively and far more regularly from the main theatre of action.

It was one of those pieces, involving acts of daring and daredevilry seemingly more at home in an Ian Fleming plot than the real world, that my colleague was using as a cautionary tale. Bazoft, who had befriended an Iraqi nurse, got her to drive him to the site of an alleged nuclear plant and scooped the soil outside it into a bottle. His idea was to test it later for radioactivity: no one in those days doubted that Saddam was striving after weapons of mass destruction. But Iraqi security saw Bazoft in the act, confiscated the bottle, arrested him and—by the time I was thinking of going to the region—had ignored pleas from the highest levels of the British Government to spare his life.

Yes, I agreed, these are dangerous times. But Iraq is not Bahrain. The war against Iran had finished eighteen months earlier and there was no imminent or obvious danger. So, all else being equal, I made up my mind to go.

A couple of weeks before my flight left Britain bound for the Gulf, Bazoft—convicted spy—was hanged. My colleague, normally a hearty well-wisher, fell silent.

So you couldn't say I wasn't warned. There were straws aplenty in the desert wind. I drew the short one.

On 10 April 1990, exactly thirteen years before Saddam's statue would be toppled in central Baghdad, a British Airways plane carrying me and my luggage touched down at Bahrain International Airport, Muharraq. It disgorged me but not my luggage which, due to a check-in error at Gatwick, flew on to Hong Kong without me. After an anxious 24-hour wait we would be reunited, but it was not an auspicious beginning.

In early April temperatures in the Gulf states begin the dramatic rise to their dizzy summer heights. No longer are people sunbathing in 30°C: they begin to absorb its merciless rays for ever shorter periods and avoid going out into the noonday furnace altogether.

A worker cannot see through a traveller's eyes. This time the bazaar was not a place to amble through but an obstruction to be hurried past on the way to the daily minibus that took us newspaper staff out to the publishing offices, halfway across the island in a designated industrial area. We would arrive hot and dusty. Of course there was airconditioning but the building itself was isolated from the commercial amenities that make office life in many cities bearable.

Isolation can be geographical or social: it took just a couple of days to discover that, working in Bahrain, I was in for the double whammy. Nothing in a workplace is more upsetting than being out of the loop. Since the job title for which I was explicitly being groomed was that of deputy chief sub-editor, it was naturally of the highest importance that I get on well with the person currently holding down that position. For whatever reason, we didn't click.

Perhaps I was too determined to experiment with my own ideas, perhaps he was right to consider me disinclined to learn the paper's established ways. It is, after all, a criticism made of me on some other newspapers where I have worked, so there must be something to it. For my part, I felt that unless I was seen to duplicate his way of doing things he was going to give me a 'bad report card', which is indeed what eventuated.

After all these years it amazes me how little I know myself. Even now I couldn't say for sure whether confessing to a lack of ambition is confronting the truth or avoiding it. At other times, when my self-esteem is battered, my thoughts go something like this: someone of my abilities should have been given more responsibility—even if I didn't seek it out—and the chance to show I had at least as much skill in people management as they tell me I have on the technical side of my craft.

So from the outset I was battling uphill: having to prove my worth to the incumbent deputy chief sub-editor, someone who was always hovering over my shoulder and who carried an immovable residue of disappointment that I had not measured up as his ideal successor. Small newspapers are like families, and here was someone a couple of years older than I, and actually less experienced in journalism, being called upon to exercise judgments that would affect not only my place in this clan but how long I could hope to retain it.

Journalists are often insecure creatures who mask their personal vulnerability by training the spotlight on others. Any office is a vacuum waiting to be filled by egos that establish a more or less settled pecking order. In my view, these facts taken together account for why newspaper offices are often hotbeds of jealousy, conspiracy, whispers and power struggles rather than co-operative endeavours bringing out the best in human nature. Add to this that one of the best assets a thrusting reporter can possess—a scepticism that extends to not being overawed by the high and mighty—becomes a liability when respect for authority is demanded by the office hierarchy itself, and anyone could see that Bahrain's overheated atmosphere extended to the office.

Adding to the volatility, the staff on this newspaper—as with all English-speaking media in countries where English isn't the native tongue—were an exotic mix. The subs' desk comprised two Englishmen, myself and half a dozen Indians, chosen partly because they would do equivalent work for far less than it cost to hire a Westerner, yet for amounts that appeared to them maharajahs' fortunes. Their vision was more in the nature of a mathematical equation than a mirage: a few years' unrelenting work in the Gulf would yield a relatively carefree life back home.

Somehow I always got on better with the Indians than with those in the driving seat, and before long this began to alienate me from management. Outside the office I didn't have time to develop any friendships. I was like a worm that has wandered out of the garden and finds itself inching across the tiled floor of a house, inexplicably cut off from the rich nutrients of its natural environment and condemned to a slow death.

My flat, in the inner Manama suburb of al-Adliya, was palatial but barren. It was a sprawling suite of rooms in a tower block where every neighbour was a stranger. A shopping centre was nearby, and my idea of radical good fun was to make a beeline for the Western food counter at the back of it, buy obscene amounts of ham (available only to the likes of us in this Muslim society) and take them back to the airconditioned fortress of the apartment, there to create and consume a modest mountain of ham sandwiches. From time to time I would breast the bar at the Londoner, an English pub on the edge of the city. But doing that every night never appealed, and I lived for the most part in a degree of social isolation that supplied ample scope for my office-based anxieties to fester.

So, almost four months into my second period of employment in the Middle East, my *Observer* colleague's forecast of unhappy times was being borne out. My future—insofar as it involved working in Bahrain—was on the line, and then one night at the beginning of August my world—and that of everyone I knew there—was turned upside down.

On the second morning of the hottest month of the year (which in the Gulf is really saying something) I awoke naked at seven o'clock in that clinically clean and cold cube in which I dwelt. Blanking out the thump of the airconditioning, I rolled the dial on my bedside shortwave radio, craving my first BBC fix of the morning.

At 2 am GMT, the newsreader intoned, Iraqi forces had invaded Kuwait and hand-to-hand fighting was reported in Kuwait City, the fiercest of it centred on the Emir's Palace.

When I reached the office, at the usual time, the excitement was palpable. After all, this is the type of occasion a journalist lives for. Editorially, the paper played it low-key. The tone was 'deplore' rather than 'condemn'. To foreigners, Arabs may be just Arabs but national consciousness cuts across ethnic lines everywhere in the modern world and Bahrainis, truth be told, regarded Kuwaitis with a mixture of envy and contempt because of their wealth and penchant for flaunting it.

While none of this altered the attitude of my fault-finding immediate superior, and I remained on notice that my work must improve or I would be for the high jump, those days did engender a greater feeling among the staff of 'we're all in this together' and that fed into a heightened sense of our work's importance. I think each of us knew that these were defining days for Bahrain, the Gulf and the whole Middle East. Cliché though it is, we were living through history.

But this was one story you couldn't confine to a box or leave at work. Outside, everyone was talking about it constantly, in tones of subdued fear. I recall more than one dinner spoilt that month by hearing restaurant staff, Indians who invariably had other sideline businesses to run (video shops, often enough), bemoan the invasion's ruinous impact on their livelihoods.

What did the locals fear might happen? That Kuwait might be just the opening skirmish in a rolling campaign that would proceed, like some unstoppable machine, wiping out more emirates as it gathered pace. At work we had a map on the wall, and anyone could see Bahrain was the next object in the juggernaut's path.

There was an element of overreaction in this, certainly, but the fear was regularly fed by Saddam's broadcasts from Baghdad which called on the Shia populations (70 per cent of Bahrainis are Shia) to rise up and overthrow their 'effete rulers', as Saddam termed them, in Bahrain, Qatar and the United Arab Emirates. It was a fear that we who worked at the newspaper knew had the Bahraini authorities worried. Within a week of the invasion, the Ministry of Information had installed censors in our offices, and every scrap of copy had to be vetted to ensure it gave Saddam no pretext for extending his destructive war to this tiny island.

Our cocoon of invulnerability to the events that made up our daily news diet had been violated. The outside came streaming in, and no one could ignore for long the fact that our neighbourhood was now the focus of an anxious world's attention.

Ever since my schooldays I had thought of myself as lacking in physical courage. Schoolyard fights fascinated me, but only as an onlooker: the idea of participation and, yes, fear of the pain of being punched senseless were repugnant to me. I would run a mile.

Here and now, for the first time in my life, fleeing offended my sense of moral courage and even my sense of professional duty. After all, whatever passed, my winding road had brought me to the brink of events that had a mesmerising effect on the mind, an irresistible attraction for the inquisitive intellect. The thought dawned only slowly that sitting this close to the fire of history might singe me, might cost me life itself.

For the first few days after the invasion, the tension between staying and doing my professional duty (strained as relations with the increasingly distant and preoccupied management were) and fleeing was no contest at all. Staying won hands down.

This was the first all-consuming emergency of my life. I can see that now; all I knew then was that, instead of disengaging myself from an obvious source of rising anxiety, I was indulging my inner 'news junkie', watching and listening to developments from all the available media eighteen hours a day. The obsessive seemed rational: the more one knew, the better protected one would be against irrational fear, I told myself. What I failed to take into account was rational fear, what must follow when the mind could no longer pretend this was happening only to others. I was being brought face to face with the prospect that I might be caught up in the drama myself, with all that could mean: invading and merciless troops, violence, capture, enslavement. My mind began to race, like an overheated car radiator, and I found that in these most abnormal of times the cost of being a loner is that just when you most need a support network no one is there.

Staying still seemed the right thing to do long before it seemed the choiceless fate of a powerless pawn. But I vividly remember the turning points, when an extra weight was dropped on the scales and fleeing became desirable in the exact proportion as the possibility of it receded. One such turning point was a phone call from home about five days after the invasion. Usually, conversation with my parents was a mixture of family news and the odd snippet of Australian politics. This time there was no small talk. Dad informed me that the Victorian Premier, John Cain, had resigned; and handed the phone to Mum, who—understandably but unnervingly—urged me to leave, saying that, from the TV news every night, she could tell how much danger I was in.

To hear from home that things sounded as dire as they looked to others across the sub-editing table rocked my complacency that all would turn out well in the end. My sense of peril was heightened, but I felt able to cope for as long as I could thrive on the adrenaline boost. So long as I could think of myself as a journalist in the midst of an exciting story rather than as an individual caught up in events that could change his life irrevocably, I could hold my worst fears at bay and keep a grip on reality.

The first essential was to remain busy. At work this wasn't a problem: there was no shortage of news and, with the censors now in-house, long-familiar procedures took twice as long. Outside, keeping my journalistic upper lip stiff, I saw a golden opportunity to maintain my standing with old contacts at Reuters and the *Observer* in London when I heard that the first survivors of the Kuwaiti invasion had made it overland to Bahrain and taken shelter in the Kuwaiti Embassy.

It must have been around 10 August, under a broiling summer sun, that I stood outside the embassy gates, eyeing a wary guard until the moment came when, taking refuge in close-packed numbers, I could enter the embassy reception room without arousing suspicions. At this of all times, you might be wondering how I could gain entry to such a sensitive area without being noticed by the guard and turned back. That was easy enough: I had taken care to dress myself in a traditional Kuwaiti outfit: red-and-white check *kaffiyeh* and snow-white *dishdasha* so that, in the confusion of milling Kuwaitis at the gates, desperate to meet their fellow nationals and, at least in some cases, missing relatives, all I had to do was keep my mouth shut.

Clutching my notebook and pen in the folds of the garment, I passed into a large, airy room where I saw three dozen or so Kuwaiti men—I noticed no women or children there—huddled together, conversing in agitated whispers. Seating myself at the end of a bench, I turned to the dignified gentleman on my right, asked whether he spoke English and, on receiving a nod, introduced myself as someone who could tell the world of his and others' reaction to the invasion of their homeland. Tentatively at first, and then like an unstoppable wave, word spread of my role. Admiring the effectiveness of my disguise, and still seeking an outlet for horribly pent-up emotions, the world's richest refugees spilled their stories with increasing lack of restraint, until in the end the only inhibition that clung to some was an unwillingness to let their names be quoted. With this I could not quibble: several told me their families remained behind, in houses where anonymity would be all that stood between them and murder by a troop of Iraqi soldiers.

The attitude of the *Observer* backbench when I filed the story the following Sunday showed how happy my sub-editing colleagues from the previous winter were with my feat. But, if they were happy, my superiors back at the *News* were incensed. Four months earlier I had clutched at a straw in the desert wind; now, the acting editor told me, this was the last straw. I was sacked.

This was not the only time I have been sacked, and serving out notice in such circumstances is always devastating. But, on those other occasions, there was time to pick up the threads and, frankly, money enough to go travelling and seek balm for the battered soul. Here and now, with so much turmoil around me, this quietly delivered order to remove myself had the effect of a bomb going off close to my troubled mind.

It provoked a terrible reaction in me which, nearly a decade and a half on, I can analyse with a wisdom denied me at the time. The tension between staying and going, which the invasion of Kuwait had generated, was suddenly heightened, as I had to serve out my time in a place where I was not wanted, where the choice of staying or going had been wrested from my hands and replaced with an ultimatum: stay, then go. Whether through my decision or others', it felt—just as my sense of physical cowardice had been tested and I was discovering a moral courage superior to it—that leaving just then was cowardly, nothing less than abandoning my colleagues in time of peril. They weren't there for me; but an old religion that I had formally abandoned but which still provided my ethical bearings told me I should not just wash my hands of their fate.

Now I look back on that combination of stressful events and say that, under the tension I then felt, it was probably a matter of time before I would have skedaddled anyway. But the decision only pulled one more tile of certainty from beneath my feet. I was discovering the weakness of a philosophy by which I had steered my life in the six years since leaving Australia, rooted in the conviction that by making a plan and following it you can always achieve what you set out to achieve, through sheer willpower.

Adherence to a plan will indeed bring success 99 times out of 100.

But the world is not entirely predictable and there comes a time when a plan, rather than being a life raft, is ballast that will drag you down to the depths unless you throw it overboard. As ever, I was learning the hard way.

Extreme anxiety triggered by the August invasion and its aftermath now combined with shame that I had been branded a professional failure, to produce a lethal psychological cocktail.

There was nothing for me to do but hang on grimly and see what would happen. By day, this meant going to the bank at al-Adliya and waiting an hour while other distressed expatriates jostled and shoved their way to the front before opening suitcases on the counter and angrily demanding their funds in cash. Tellers, frightened by their scowls, retreated into the manager's office under a barrage of threatening fists. The central bank, to prevent the loss of all its reserves, had ordered a freeze on foreign-currency transactions, and overnight the wealth of expatriates who had come to the Gulf to make their living was annihilated, worthless. They, too, were trapped.

I tried to humour myself, *Well, at least now I know what the Great Depression must have been like. I've seen what a 'run on the economy' really means.* Telling myself that this was some sort of privilege—that all experience must confer an advantage of some kind—was my way of reacting to the suffering of others, and nothing to be proud of, I can see now. But besides that I see from the perspective of distance that my struggle was to remain an observer, not a participant. If I thought all this loss were happening to me rather than about me, by God, what would I have left to cling to?

By night, unable to sleep more than a few hours while the mounting confusion of fears, dread and appalling news swirled through the tumble-dryer of my mind, a snatch of warning came back to me. In what I jocularly refer to as my Cambridge days, in late 1986, on the occasional Wednesday night after work I would relax with a colleague at a pool hall, a club where my colleague's father was a member. It must have been just before I went to Oman, my first sub-editing job in the Gulf. As a young professional with rising prospects expecting to hear nothing but words of warm cheer, especially when my colleague's father told me he had been to the region, I was taken aback when his face clouded over in a most uncharacteristic frown.

I can see him hunched over the table as, just before potting the black, he looked me in the eye and said, 'The Middle East will find out who you really are.' Now, adrift in a sea of unceasing thought, I wished to God I had asked that wise man to explain what he meant.

These apocalyptic days kept my mind's eye trained on multiple 'reality checks'. The first were the televised newscasts which told what was over the horizon, in more senses than one. They grew ever grimmer and more surreal. Having learnt in the morning that Iraq had taken Western aid workers hostage—the term 'human shields' entered the language around that time—I watched and listened at regular intervals for the rest of the day, and then weeks, as the sub-plot thickened, to learn their fate. News fixes as addictive as regular heroin injections proved every bit as dangerous to my sense of balance.

What the Germans call *Weltschmerz*—absorption in the woes of the world—kept upsetting that balance. On and on the news reports came, the airwaves of gloom swamping my boat and threatening to scuttle it altogether.

The other 'reality checks' occurred in the streets around me. They were deserted most of the day—with temperatures in the mid-forties this was not exactly surprising—but in the evening I found myself with too much time on my hands. Wandering the streets, I would be drawn again and again to a few ports of call: my favourite Syrian-run restaurant, where the talk was all of … well, guess what; and the English-run fish restaurant, whose owners were now thinking of getting out while there was yet time.

There was no escape from the strain: in the course of two weeks, excitement morphed into dread. Not knowing reduced me to a state of trepidation fuelled by rumours of the type that sound plausible only during an emergency. According to one which floated my way in office talk, the British SAS, convinced the Iraqis were about to launch an invasion of Bahrain from their Kuwaiti beachhead, planned to land paratroops at the southern end of the island (not far from the *News* office) under cover of darkness and evacuate us all in a meticulously timed operation.

Unlikely though it may sound, such rumours made perfect sense at that time. Why wouldn't the British look after their own? And, as Australia didn't have an embassy there, why wouldn't Britain include Australian nationals in the plan? I remember, when trying to fathom why no one had explicitly asked me to join such an action, oscillating in my mind between the explanation that, for it to succeed, secrecy was of the essence, so 'they' must be waiting for the right time to confide in me; and thinking that, as the paper had been willing to terminate my services, the silence from its ranks meant there was room for only a certain number on board the evacuation ships and I was not among those chosen.

Madness is cancer of the mind. It creeps, not cutting you off abruptly from an awareness of how absurd are the propositions it presents you with, but never giving you the peace of a settled thought, never yielding a settled conclusion. I know now that when you're going mad you do more thinking to less effect than at other times. Like a car in overdrive, the mind's gears rev to amazing speeds but the momentum cannot be summoned up to propel you forward.

So one day towards mid-August I found my steps leading me to the British Embassy compound, where—mindful of how ludicrous it must sound— I asked to speak to one of the overworked staff there who were indeed checking the names and addresses of British citizens resident in Bahrain. They noted down my name and contact details as well.

One night, perhaps that same day, I repaired to the Londoner pub, the one place where Westerners, in my few months' experience of the island, had gone to relax, to get away from their workaday cares. Propping up the bar, as he often did, was Les, the jaunty English news editor with whom I got on well, while the walls of mutual confidence between me and others were crumbling.

To look at him, you wouldn't know Bahrain was in the eye of a crisis. He seemed understanding, willing to explain what he knew—which wasn't much more than anyone else—and I see now that my gabbling rapid-fire speech must have been a sign to him then of the tensions that had me in their grip.

We drank, and talked exhaustively of the local, regional and global implications, as journos do, but at no point did Les tip me the wink as to what part of the island the boats would be waiting at, or when the SAS would be spiriting us to safety. Of course I couldn't ask straight out, because that would risk jeopardising the mission's success. When a 'phoney war' is on, all you've ever read about 'Loose lips sink ships' and how people are exhorted to react under pressure *becomes* your attitude; you play the role you think is expected of you. Already I was in the grip of a delusion, but no one else could see it—and that is the saddest thing of all about mental illness.

So I can be sure it wasn't from Les, but from a comment overheard by a stranger at the bar, that I became convinced that on the following weekend—on Sunday night 19 August—all the Westerners in Bahrain were meant to gather at the airport at a prearranged time (just when wasn't stated) for an orderly evacuation from the island state. It seemed to my logic-chopping mind that selecting the airport as the rendezvous must have been a ploy to divert attention from the fact that our evacuation was to be seaborne, and that transport would be arranged from there to wherever the ships would be waiting. Sunday it would be, then, and mum's the word.

We know now that the active phase of Desert Storm, the operation that drove the Iraqis from Kuwait, would create hundreds of cases of what was to become known as Gulf War syndrome. While never claiming to have been in a theatre of armed conflict as directly as those people were, but nevertheless as an early victim of the Kuwait invasion, I have an instinctive feeling for the casualties of that war: truth may have been the first but I wasn't far behind. Now there was nowhere to run, nowhere to hide. For the first time in six years abroad, I suddenly felt a very long way from home.

Chapter 4

THERE'S NO GOING BACK

You can never step into the same river twice, for fresh waters are ever flowing in upon you.

HERACLITUS of EPHESUS (540-480 BC) *COSMIC FRAGMENTS*

MAY 2001

Eleven years after some of the most dramatic and traumatic days of my life were played out there; and just seven months before the telephone call that didn't quite put me and my former colleagues in touch again; here was I making a two-hour stopover in Bahrain before setting out on the longest journey in all my allotted days.

I can recall the excitement as if it is happening this very minute. The dominant sensation is that all my birthdays are coming at once. The pitch of anticipation has triggered an adrenaline rush more familiar to adolescents than forty-somethings. For the first time in my mid-life, I can sit back and relax. Two years of online sub-editing for the Japanese have given me enough financial security to blow it all on a really ambitious journey my restless brain has been hatching for years: a crossing of the world's super-continent—Eurasia—from tropical southern coast to icy northern fringe.

Partly for financial reasons but mostly out of guilt at not keeping a daily travel diary, I have secured the interest of Gary Walsh, travel editor of my old newspaper the *Age*, in publishing my observations in an irregular column titled 'Emails from the Edge'. I have reached a similar arrangement with the *Sydney Morning Herald* foreign desk, telling myself that if nothing is published for the folks back home I'm off on a well-earned holiday, and the rest is all bonus—and maybe history, if anything remarkable ever happens in these places way off most people's mental maps.

But this is more than a holiday, it is a voyage of adventure through unknown lands and stunning cities: one that will encompass one fifth of the land surface of the globe, between 14° and 82° east of Greenwich and from 17° to 69° north of the Equator. The 41 countries to be explored divide almost exactly in half between Asia and Europe, and almost as neatly between those where the faith of the Prophet Mohammed and that of Christ dominate the landscape. For the first time in 6000 years of civilisation, more than half of humanity lives in cities, and some of the most distinctive are to be found like markers enticing me forward on my straggling route: Tashkent, Tehran, Damascus, Istanbul, Athens, Budapest and Prague.

Friends and casual acquaintances interpret many of these markers as danger signs. Aware that my 'dream journey' bears an uncanny resemblance to other people's nightmares, my thoughts fly faster than the jumbo whose port window I gaze out of this night in mid-2001, to the lands of Central Asia, the Middle East and even further to Eastern Europe. That is the direction I have chosen for this voyage, which should take two years to complete, and my return to Bahrain mentioned above will take place one quarter of the way through it.

No stranger to the road less travelled, I have already crossed Africa twice and left my footprints across vast tracts of East and South Asia, and in the course of all this wandering have trudged up mountain peaks in Borneo, China, Japan and Rwanda. Yet there is nothing aimless in the way I plan these journeys: an intricate plan, mapped out months ahead, provides a structure to be demolished only by the brick wall of reality or dumb bureaucracy—or, occasionally, by a willingness to heed local opinion. All I can foresee is that in the next two years I will be privileged to see the world as it is, not as the media or tour promoters portray it. I will meet real people in two score lands, and absorb something of the way they view the blue-green bauble we all share, most of the time in ignorance of one another's perspectives, beliefs, hopes and fears.

But even the adventurous traveller should observe the odd rule. Mine are as few as possible:

- Don't go to a country that is at war or slipping into it, or one under the sway of lawlessness.

• Try to visit all countries en route (except those to which the previous paragraph applies), taking to the air as little as possible. Since I travel to see how people live, not to meet other travellers, getting around at ground level and by public transport—trains, buses, minibuses, taxis, ferries and ships—is my preferred way to go.

• Stay in the most affordable hotels but, wherever possible, seek out lodgings with a difference. Monasteries, be they Buddhist or Christian, have a long tradition of offering hospitality to the unexpected visitor; and, as I will discover in lands as far removed as Kyrgyzstan and Montenegro, the best way to understand a country is to live among its people.

Of course, looking at the world from a metre or so above ground level, the height of my wheelchair, gives me a different view from other travellers—and this can be an unexpected asset.

As our plane begins its descent into Karachi, the intriguing vistas of Pakistan and Central Asia crowd upon my excited mind's eye. But from previous journeys I know it is not only the quirky individuals and breathtaking sights that will make this an unforgettable epic, but the self-same element of uncertainty that puts other, more placid souls off travelling at all. By definition, a journey longer than a single circumnavigation of the globe is bound to be jam-packed with surprises, not all of them pleasant. Nothing in my diary planner foretells a meeting with Osama bin Laden; my expulsion from Syria on suspicion of being a terrorist; a 'grandstand' view of the World Cup soccer final from a medieval monastery; or being dragged away from the Hungarian Parliament in handcuffs.

Of all that is unpredictable, however, one event will stand out above all others. September 11, 2001 will usher in the real 21st century and turn me into an eyewitness of the 'war on terror' from the other side of the frontline. Rolling around the Axis of Evil without a care in the world is the only way to see at close hand what 'they' really think of 'us'. And you may be surprised, too, to find that the image we have of the Mideast millions is a gross distortion of the realities on the ground, mirrored only by ... the grossly distorted view they have of us.

A blaze of city lights under a dipping wing announces Karachi at 3.30 am local time. After Indonesia, Pakistan is the world's most populous Muslim nation, with more than 150 million souls, and just over half the countries on my itinerary have Muslim majorities.

The tarmac is rushing up to meet us. Suddenly I'm here at the 'dangerous edge' of Asia—Graham Greene's phrase seems tailor-made for Karachi—and the apprehension that within hours I will be immersed in a sea of humanity, fighting for a foothold as a new arrival among the teeming millions, has driven all Bahrain-bred broodings clear out of my mind.

Chapter 5

HERETICS AND H-BOMBS

[The Pakistani bureaucracy was characterised by 1970s Prime Minister Zulfiqar Ali Bhutto as] a class of brahmins or mandarins unrivalled in its snobbery and arrogance, insulated from the life of the people and incapable of identifying with them.

CHRISTINA LAMB *WAITING FOR ALLAH*

MAY 2001

PAKISTAN: 3–27 MAY

After arriving in Karachi I soon found myself a room at the venerable Metropole Hotel in downtown Saddar district, where I knew I was in a city of 11 million because they all rattled past my room in an endless file. Though founded as recently as 1950, the Metropole—built as a five-star hotel, but now down to two and counting—has the grandeur of an establishment from the Raj.

I would have nothing against the place, really, if its habit of refilling plastic water bottles straight from the tap and passing them off as mineral water hadn't cost me a train ticket to the ruins of Mohenjodaro. Two hours before the train pulled out, my stomach and regions further south were devastated by a nuclear attack that laid them waste for a week. But it is the same hotel I have to thank for my recovery: for calling in a doctor who recognised that survival chances would be improved if I could be kept out of hospital; for propping up an industrial-strength fan next to my bed; and for cancelling all laundry workers' leave for the next 50 years.

Mohenjodaro, in the Indus Valley, is one of the cradles of civilisation. Had I not been struck down in Karachi, my fate on arrival—far from the nearest Western-style toilet, in all probability—does not bear thinking about. The Karachi daily *Dawn* newspaper mentioned that the maximum temperature around Mohenjodaro had been 52°C the day before.

I wrote in my notebook for May 2001, 'Every nation has to have a stereotype: Pakistanis are seen abroad as terrorist-cosseting, bomb-making, mullah-loving fanatics.' In Karachi a truer stereotype would be the *dhobi wallahs* (barefoot launderers who use riverbanks as their workplaces) who here prefer to call themselves *dhobi sahibs*. When I pointed out the satellite dish above one of their modest-looking houses, a *sahib* chided me, 'We're not so poor!'

Being a bit short of rivers, but notoriously resourceful, Karachi's dhobi sahibs use recycled water from local tanks. I was also amused to discover that they do takeaway laundry, drying in their lime kilns the clothes of even the most airconditioned guests from the plushest five-star hotels. As the sahib said, eyes gleaming, 'Who is to know?'

My Pakistan was a succession of cities, each with its own character: squalid, bustling Karachi; stately Lahore, home to the mighty Mogul fort and restful Shalimar Gardens; modern Islamabad, forever cemented in the memory by the sight of children playing impromptu cricket on the concourse of the majestic Saudi-built Shah Faisal Mosque; and Peshawar, where the world's freshest *naan* bread washed down with sweet green tea and enjoyed among curious onlookers in the depths of Qisa Khavani bazaar helped me ignore the gun-runners' stalls that give the neighbourhood a far less friendly reputation.

And then there was Chitral, a delightful town perched in the foothills of the Hindu Kush. The usual reason to visit Chitral is its proximity to the Rumbur Valley, hard up against the Afghanistan border and home to the gaudily dressed but also hard-up Kalash—village-dwelling, mulberry-wine-drinking and goat-herding folk who have resisted Islam more successfully than they have tourism. But equally memorable were a couple of individuals I met there: the first by—what should I call it?—predestination, and the other by prearrangement.

The predestined one was Imran Shah, 29 when we met, a one-eyed tour guide who taught in a Rumbur Valley primary school until the principal, a mullah, sacked him for telling pupils the Earth was round. 'He said this is against the teaching of the Koran, but that is not true,' protested Imran. When we stop at his old school, ex-pupils—who have not seen him for eighteen months—greet him more like a friend than a heretic.

My prearranged meeting was with an 83-year-old, gimlet-eyed retired army officer, Major General Geoffrey Langlands, who is the very model of an expatriate civilian. A lifelong bachelor, he arrived from England immediately after World War II and, finding himself on the Pakistani side of the border after Partition, stayed in Lahore where he felt at home. Although he would much rather be remembered as a classically trained teacher and one-time principal of Pakistan's closest equivalent to Eton (Lahore's Aitchison College), his more compelling claim to fame stems from having been kidnapped by sixteen Jamali tribesmen (bandits, if you prefer) fighting to bring self-government to North Waziristan (their patch of the North West Frontier Province) in 1988.

The Jamalis found their captive a tough old bird and released him six days later without receiving ransom money, after the authorities in Peshawar passed on an undisclosed threat.

I leave Pakistan in the most spectacular way possible: by overflying Afghanistan, looking down on the western Himalaya which appears to have been sprayed by the cosmic cake-icer especially for our benefit. Afghanistan, at war since the mid-1970s, is to be missed with regret, and no direct flights link Pakistan with my first Central Asian destination of Kazakhstan, so this flight is taking me to Tashkent, Uzbekistan, where a connection—not to mention a surprise—awaits me.

TASHKENT TRANSIT TERMINAL: 27 MAY

Too much of my time is spent worrying how to get around, now that my travelling days are spent in the seated posture, and perhaps not enough on thinking about how others will react. Now I can see humour in the fact that, not only at Tashkent but next day in Almaty, Kazakhstan, the airlines send a fully equipped ambulance on to the tarmac to meet their only wheelchair passenger. Now I laugh, and can see I should have gone along for the ride (200 metres to the airport terminal in each case). At the time, shame to say, I saw red and refused to accompany the kind medical staff, thus no doubt gaining a well-deserved reputation as a difficult customer and spoiling the prospects for anyone who follows in my tracks.

The point I believe I was trying to make was that, as just another passenger, albeit one who couldn't walk, I was not an invalid. However, in their *lingua franca*, Russian, that is exactly the term used for one in my position, and, as I would find throughout Central Asia, a wheelchair user in public is a target for unsolicited compassion and acts of Islamic charity.

In Tashkent they called in the military when I refused to get in the ambulance and, after a diplomatic sit-off, one bamboozled rookie was given permission to accompany me as I wheeled to the terminal, with him watching beady-eyed all the way lest I make one false move. Once safe inside the terminal, I was treated like any other passenger, and found I didn't like that much either. The terminal resembled a remand prison most of whose inmates appeared to be Indians suspected of trying to emigrate illegally to Britain—and the next flight to Kazakhstan wasn't due for 27 hours. Fortunately the washroom was navigable. Sometimes, toilets are at the back of impossibly narrow cubicles that require advanced acrobatic skills to reach, and I simply can't go there ...

Chapter 6

ONE STEPPE AT A TIME

[Thomas Carlyle] said he loved God but really worshipped Timurlane.

REBECCA WEST *BLACK LAMB AND GREY FALCON*

MAY-AUGUST 2001

In the West these days a wheelchair does not make you conspicuous, it's practically become part of the social furniture. New buildings are accommodating, and so for the most part are people on the street. No longer are you likely to attract unwanted attention of either the hostile or patronising kind. Not so once you find yourself in Central Asia, where the only 'wheelies' to be seen in public tend to sell cigarettes or play mouth organs. Begging is the price my fellow movers and shakers have to pay just to be allowed out of doors.

In time I came to see that the free-wheeler cruising down the streets of Almaty, Osh or Tashkent faced two types of problem in his interaction with the locals: one perceptual, the other conceptual. Put simply, the perceptual difficulty was that people unused to sharing the pavement with wheelchairs actually failed to see me bearing down. It being not only bad manners but counterproductive to barge through, the intuitive charioteer finds himself adapting to the city's pedestrian rhythms—in some societies pavement users tend to go in straight lines, in others they weave all over the place—and glides or slaloms along accordingly.

The conceptual difficulty is more intractable: the beholder sees you, all right, but thinks you must conform to his only previous experience of people in rolling chairs. (Think dogs: a society that had only ever known silky terriers would do a double take on seeing its first

Dobermann.) The odd taxidriver would refuse the fare until I hopped into the passenger seat and showed my bemused chauffeur how the wheelchair dismantled.

Both disregard and false regard have their amusing side. It was on 30 May that—for the first of many times during my crossing of Central Asia—someone approached me on the street and offered me money. Shocked, I handed it back. Every few days the same thing happened. Didn't these people know that I, a Western tourist, was hundreds of times richer than they? Apparently not. One time I was so annoyed at being mistaken for a beggar while minding my own business that I snapped in fractured Russian 'Nyet invalid—tourist!'

It took a kindly Kazakh to explain: 'You are in the Muslim world now. These people are practising zakat.'

One of the five sacred obligations of every good Muslim is to extend charity to those in need, and obviously someone who cannot walk is an object of abject dependence. But how blessed can it be to receive charity under false pretences?

From Bukhara in July I emailed a New Zealand friend for advice. Back came these truly wise words: 'Take the money and distribute it to the really needy.'

'Exotic' sums up Central Asia to a T. Even before I left Australia, the friend of a friend gave me a commission: send back a T-shirt, or any other article, with the word 'Uzbekistan' on it. There is something mysterious, perhaps other-worldly, in the very word. There is no vast tract of Planet Earth, I suppose, about which we in the lands of plenty know less. Even rural China or South America seems more familiar. Yet a mere 700 years ago the most far-reaching conquerors since Alexander the Great swept through in the fourth century BC—Genghis Khan and Timurlane, ancestor of India's Mogul dynasty—passed this way and put the very idea of Asia as we think of it today on the world map.

History brought Central Asia to world prominence on the hooves of vengeance, with a decisive loss by the Chinese to the Arabs in AD 751. The name of that battle, Talas, ought to be as familiar to us as Gettysburg or Stalingrad. But the past is another country to most of us now, so how can we go there except on the wings of imagination?

31

Certain things that everyone ought to know about Central Asia are buried under the sands of time. For everyone who has heard of Homer and the *Iliad*, how many know that—at 14 580 lines—the longest epic in world literature, the national epic of a nomadic people, *Manas*, comes from Kyrgyzstan?

At Merv, now in south-eastern Turkmenistan, up to 1.3 million civilians were massacred in a single week when Tuluy, a son of Genghis Khan, invaded in AD 1221. The sword was his chosen weapon of mass destruction. War on terror? Defence of civilisation? Excuse me. But the blade of creation, not just destruction, had plunged into the heart of the world's biggest continent 500 years before then, at Talas, when the defeated Chinese taught the victorious Arabs how to make paper and manufacture silk long before Marco Polo. Civilisation—in the form of those numerals the whole world uses today, algebra, medicine and civil order—was at its height here in the early centuries of the second Christian millennium and, while Europe groped its way through the Dark Ages, the triumph of Asian commerce—along the Silk Road—was its crowning glory. A sure token of advanced culture, the necessities of life coexisted alongside little luxuries. I have never forgotten once reading that Timurlane's capital, Samarkand, boasted lemonade fountains.

So what is it like today, more than a decade after the last (Soviet) empire ebbed away? Impressions, and odd encounters, are all the fleeting visitor has to relate, adding up, if he is lucky, to a sketch rather than a detailed panorama. Here is mine.

KAZAKHSTAN: 28 MAY–17 JUNE

DAY 34 (3 JUNE): ALMATY
My 47th birthday is spent in the well-shaded old capital of the world's ninth biggest country, whose mountainous backdrop is every bit as spectacular as Denver's or Tehran's. Spruced-up and reopened, Zenkov Cathedral sits in the centre of Panfilov Park, surrounded by balloon sellers, pony rides and refreshment stalls.

DAY 41 (10 JUNE): ASTANA
Today is the third birthday of the world's youngest capital. Formerly Akmola, this unprepossessing city of the steppes was chosen by

President Nursultan Nazarbayev who rechristened it with his customary inspiration. (Astana means 'Capital'.) At noon in the postmodern city square, a brass band strikes up something slightly non-Kazakh—a medley by Abba. A massed dance troupe in virginal white, accompanied by men dressed as harlequins, sways to those exotic Nordic rhythms. *Mamma mia!*

Nearby, a more authentically Kazakh spectacle is gearing up. Outside a yurt full of dignified elders in colourful costumes, highlighted by aquamarine caps and sky-blue vests, actors clad in the raiment of a medieval khan's court—warriors in chain mail, maidens in gold-studded jerkins—strut their stuff.

That night, in the stadium just 200 metres from my hotel, I sit among 60 000 citizens to sample fireworks, songs and humour from Russia's most famous entertainers, flown in from Moscow. Anita Su, a Korean singer, is the toast of the Federation while Efim Shefrin is a clown (in the complimentary sense). As they are staying in the same hotel as me I am honoured to meet them both, but the evening is spoilt by snivelling paeans of praise for Nazarbayev the demigod-president. After an hour of this, I turn to the stony-faced woman on my right and whisper in a sort of Franco-Russian, '*Stalinisme!*' She blanches.

DAY 46 (15 JUNE): HOURS SPENT IN A VAN FROM LAKE BALKASH TO THE BISHKEK TURN-OFF

Hitchhiking on Kazakhstan's outback roads reminds me of what private motorists hereabouts have to endure. Our van is pulled over at five roadside police checkpoints. At three of them, the coppers steal money from the driver before letting him pass: the most daring drives his police wagon onto the road and siphons off his petrol.

KYRGYZSTAN: 17–26 JUNE

DAY 48 (17 JUNE): BISHKEK

Unanswered emails have me wondering whether to visit Tajikistan (civil war ended in 1997; advisories say it's unsafe; I await local advice). A BBC news bulletin says 15 German aid workers, an American and a Tajik driver kidnapped in a remote corner of the country have all been released unharmed after pleas by the Tajik

President and his – get this – Minister for Emergency Situations.

DAYS 49–52 (18–21 JUNE): BISHKEK

I stay with a Kyrgyz family whose ground-floor room was adapted for a wheelchair-bound grandmother who has since, um, moved on. They're a friendly family but we have almost no language in common. The wife is a raspberry addict: the fridge is full of raspberry juice, desserts are made of raspberries or crimson jellies.

DAY 53 (22 JUNE): CHOLPON-ATA, LAKE ISSYK-KUL

My guidebook said that here, on the second highest lake in the world, an old Soviet Navy cutter regularly sailed up and down the waterway. Now that was rich: a naval vessel in a landlocked country. How were the enemy ships going to launch their attack? By being wheeled over the mountains from China?

My idea was to enjoy a pleasant lake cruise. Captain Victor let drop that a Chinese delegation was expected later in the day. Was this a war party, and could anyone gatecrash? Six hours' patience was rewarded with an invitation to join in.

I turned out to be in the midst of a high-powered meeting between Li Yenming, the Security Minister from China's troubled Xinjiang province, and the Speaker of the Kyrgyz Parliament, Esen Ismailov. Not for the first time, I had the distinct feeling my wheelchair got me into places where others would fear to tread.

As the evening wore on, Li became drunker and drunker—not, I noticed, on fiery Chinese *mao-tai*, but on vodka—and led us all in increasingly discordant attempts at compulsory group singing. Through his English-conversant translator, I coyly asked the minister while the combined effects of the vodka, his disco arrhythmia and the sea-swaying of the boat had him off guard, 'How does your government propose to deal in future with anti-Beijing dissent from the Uighur Muslims?' 'Peacefully!' he barked.

Diplomacy followed: 'China has fifty-six minorities and we are all members of one big family. One of the members cannot leave the family. We will not allow this.'

DAY 54 (23 JUNE): BISHKEK TO OSH BY AIR

At US$33, this flight is one worth breaking the surface-travel rule for. A 38-seater Yak-40 less than half full should make for a perfect trip. Certainly these small planes are a lot easier to board. I just position the chair next to the swing-out door ... and swing myself in.

But service standards are not world-class: this is the only flight I've ever been on where the stewardess keeps to her seat, spending most of the time munching her dinner. Asked in sign language when the passengers will be served, she makes it clear with a smug shake of the head that food on Kyrgyzstan Airlines is strictly for the crew.

DAY 55 (24 JUNE): OSH

I tour Jayma Bazaar. There's a twinge of referred pain when my guide, Zahid, explains that strange pipeline objects in the market are wooden catheters attached to a boy's penis before he goes to bed, to provide an effective antidote to bed-wetting. Great, I muse, so long as he doesn't turn in his sleep. Ouch!

There are red pepper, fennel and root remedies like those in a Chinese herbal-medicine shop. A table full of 'lucky charms'—the most popular line keeps evil spirits from harming babies—is a timely reminder that superstition lives happily enough alongside established religion here, as elsewhere.

DAY 56 (25 JUNE): OSH

Kickboxing at the *palvankhana* (hippodrome). The wheelchair gains me admittance inside the stadium perimeter just 15 metres from the 'ring', a steel octagon in which the fighters—combining kickboxing with Central Asian freestyle wrestling and gentlemanly fistfighting— pummel each other until one submits or is dragged out by white-coated medicos. I ask a fellow spectator why there are so many soldiers around the stadium. He says calmly, 'Their big fear is a bomb going off.' Great. Instead they find their hands full putting down violence – not in the octagon but in the grandstands, between overenthusiastic fans.

UZBEKISTAN: 26 JUNE–3 JULY

DAY 58 (27 JUNE): ANDIJAN

From my taxi I see a building with the 'Sydney 2000' logo and ask the driver to make a detour. It turns out this is the national Olympic squad's training camp and not only are the Olympians all present, but one—a Sydney boxing gold medallist—agrees to be photographed with me. Mindful that Uzbek President Islom Karimov had promised a US$100 000 prize to any gold-garnering compatriot, I ask Mohammad Kodir Abdullaev whether he is looking forward to Athens. 'No,' he says in halting English, 'I am gone professional. Las Vegas.'

DAY 60 (29 JUNE): TASHKENT

Hotel Torun wins the prize for world's worst hotel hands down. Why should it take 45 minutes to descend nine floors in the lift? Why should a request for mineral water, made to the Russian-style 'floor lady' parked in the foyer, be turned down? Why should the same *babushka*, when eventually given money to make the purchase, just pocket it after pretending to fetch the supposedly non-existent bottle? Why doesn't reception care about any of this? Why am I dying from dehydration and diarrhoea? At least the last question has an answer: because I trusted the Uzbek barbecue skills of the *shashlik* vendors outside the Torun. A meaty obituary headline floats through my delirium: 'Underdone to Death'. By morning, the food poisoning has passed through me, so to speak, and I move to a friendly private hotel in the suburbs.

DAY 63 (2 JULY): TASHKENT

Before September 11 there were three types of tourist destination in the world: countries any holidaymaker would visit without a second thought; countries whose main interest was their 'edge'; and no-go areas. Officially, Tajikistan was in the third category but, from what people in neighbouring Uzbekistan told me, I thought it probably qualified for an upgrade. Today my residual doubts are dispelled by a most reassuring document: a personal security guarantee faxed to me from the Tourism Minister. This year the country is getting about two tourists a day. I feel privileged. After this, how could I not go?

TAJIKISTAN: 3–8 JULY

DAY 65 (4 JULY): KHOJAND

Once the easternmost outpost of Alexander the Great's military empire, nowadays this city of 160 000 publicly venerates Lenin (a huge bronze statue still commands the approach to the Syr-Darya River).

Tonight a restaurateur repeatedly refuses payment for a thoroughly satisfying meal. There must be a first time for everything.

DAY 66 (5 JULY): KHOJAND TO DUSHANBE

I travel from north to south, 350 kilometres across 3000-metre-high mountain passes in a shared taxi, a sturdy Volga limousine. This is the type of perfect day travellers will go thousands of kilometres for. At a morning roadside stop we buy fresh bread and honey, enjoyed in the shade of huge upside-down umbrellas.

One hundred kilometres from Dushanbe, a Kalashnikov-toting fifteen-year-old stops the taxi. After a few nervous moments, he lets us go for the price of a watermelon. Fifty kilometres on, entrepreneurs have turned a gushing rock waterfall into a profitable car wash.

DAY 67 (6 JULY): DUSHANBE

Broad leafy boulevards make this capital an unexpected joy. There's one fall from grace: as I co-opt a young Tajik to help my chair down from a high kerb, he distractedly asks, 'Are you American?' At the same moment he lets go of the back rest and leaves me sprawled on the asphalt, unhurt, but angry and disinclined to discuss my nationality. He runs off: a passer-by helps me back into the chair.

UZBEKISTAN REVISITED: 8 JULY–4 AUGUST

DAY 72 (11 JULY): TASHKENT

Two months before a date no one in the West will easily forget, I meet a brutalised man whose anger could in time turn him into a terrorist. So far as I can tell, he is not one yet, more's the wonder.

In whispers they call Karimov, ex-Communist and founding president, 'the Pharaoh'. Nine days ago, plainclothes members of the SNB, the Uzbek security police, broke up a peaceful protest by a hundred women in Amir Timur Square, the symbolic heart of this Central Asian capital. A witness says that SNB operatives used truncheons on the women, many of them with babes in arms, before herding them into buses and driving them away.

The women had gathered to make a terribly revolutionary demand: the opening of more mosques in Tashkent. The Western media portray a goodies-versus-baddies vision of Islam. But the Pharaoh will have no God before him, not even Allah. Mosques here are prohibited from broadcasting the call to prayer. Faith-based political parties are banned.

I meet Juma Bahadur (not his real name), a 20-year-old working at a Tashkent Internet club, when I go there to send an email from the edge. He introduces himself simply as 'a Muslim' and asks if we can take a walk. Wheels and heels, we amble around the block. What can be so important that he prefers half an hour in the blistering summer sun to the fan-cooled interior of a cybershop?

Bahadur doesn't keep me in suspense for long. The story he tells dates back to last January. An SNB officer approached him and asked why he had just spoken to a woman on the pavement. When he replied that she had stopped him to ask directions, the officer in plain clothes told him to come along quietly. As Bahadur tells it, he was taken to a police cell—a wooden stool its only furniture—handcuffed and left alone for several hours. After an indefinite period, four policemen entered the cell, covered his chest with a pillow, and pummelled him incessantly on the torso and limbs until he lost consciousness.

He was kept in detention along with 50 other men for four days, until the agent who had stopped him on the street 'called my parents, and my brother came and took me home'.

When Bahadur asked why the police had treated him like this, they told him 'because I went to the mosque'.

Every minute or so, Bahadur looks furtively round, as if the trees have ears. He is convinced he understands what motivates Karimov's police state: 'Islam, our religion, teaches every person to own his property. When a person knows his power—that I am a man—and everyone wants to own his property, control is difficult. When people are (treated) like pigs, control is easy.'

Only the day before the SNB suppressed the Muslim women's protest, the Uzbeks suddenly announced they were closing the

Kyrgyzstan border to all road traffic between Osh and Andijan, the border I crossed in peace a month beforehand.

I make a wry mental note: at the end of next month, Uzbekistan will officially celebrate ten years as a post-communist state. Ah, but old habits die hard.

DAY 74 (13 JULY): TASHKENT TO SAMARKAND

Have developed a good technique for boarding minibuses. I offer to buy two tickets—one for me, one for the chair. This way it doesn't get squashed under a mountain of luggage (or chicken shit on rural routes) and the drivers, who leave only when their vehicles are full, manage an early departure. Not only does this tactic transform initial scepticism, even hostility, towards the idea of someone in a wheelchair coming along for the ride, I invariably get to sit up front. Call me elitist but I do like the unhindered views. After all, there is a practical angle to consider: these people will probably pass this way again; I almost certainly never will.

DAY 76 (15 JULY): SAMARKAND

Some place names make you want to drop everything and rush off at once. Zanzibar is one, Samarkand another. Here, in what was once his fabulous desert capital, lies the tomb of Timurlane, that all-conquering warrior-king who stopped the Ottoman Turks in their camel tracks. Having found a welcoming guesthouse in the town's backblocks, and partaken of a generous breakfast under a trellis covered in purple grapes, I (st)roll down the lane past curious urchins, and there on the left—towering over me—is the great man's mausoleum.

A nondescript official tells an English-speaker to inform me I cannot go inside with a wheelchair. I adopt a suitably noble mien and inform him that, as I rely on the goodness of helpers (miraculously two step forward from the growing throng at this very moment to offer strong arms) and, more important, as Timurlane was short for 'Timur the Lame', nothing is going to stop me paying my respects.

The gamble pays off; I enter the dark hall. Later, my little triumph loses some of its savour when a local resident tells me that the tomb everyone takes for Timur's is actually a replica: the original lies directly beneath it in a crypt (discovered, intriguingly enough, only in 1959 when a girl playing ball fell downstairs).

Perhaps, I reflect, the official was only telling the simple truth.

DAY 80 (19 JULY): BUKHARA

If Samarkand has been tarted up for tourist groups, Bukhara is the first place I have ever been where people live comfortably in the 15th century. You feel absolutely certain looking around you at bazaars, caravanserais, towering minarets and crumbling medieval mosques that others must have seen and absorbed this same reality more than 500 years ago.

The daytime maximum temperature now regularly exceeds 40°C, giving new meaning to the city's proudest boast, 'Elsewhere light radiates from Heaven onto the land; in holy Bukhara, it radiates upward to illuminate Heaven.'

But the brighter the light, the darker the shadows—and nowhere are they more tenebrous than in the Bug Pit (*karakhona* to the Uzbeks), into which I peer today. Dating from the days when Bukhara was a feudal state ruled by its own emir from the Ark—an awesome citadel with ramparts that still dominate today's city—the Bug Pit is the fourth cell you come to in Zindon jail. It is a black hole, 6.5 metres deep and covered by an iron grille. Lowered in by rope, the prisoners—five or six in a space no bigger than a well—shared their lives with lice, scorpions and other vermin. Here two English emissaries, Colonel Charles Stoddart and Captain Arthur Conolly, spent their last years before being executed in June 1842. The story goes that they were marched out before a huge crowd just in front of the Ark, forced to dig their own graves 'and, to the sound of drums and reed pipes from atop the fortress walls, beheaded'.

Through an interpreter, the ticket-seller tells me that in Victorian times the pit was twice as deep as it is now. I believe her implicitly: a grim-faced crone, her voice conveys the authority of someone speaking from personal recollection.

DAY 81 (20 JULY): BUKHARA

Deep in the Old City lies a minor miracle, and a lesson for the 21st century. Here, for thirteen turbulent centuries, ever since the Arab conquest, a Jewish community has survived. How is it done in Central Asia, I wonder, when in far-west Asia enmity has blasted the so-called peace process apart? The first difference I note, listening to Rabbi Gavriel Matatov, 65, is that, unlike the dogmatism spewing out of the Holy Land, the predominant tone is *not* one of absolute certainty that the promised land won't be taken over or taken back from time to time.

Ask Matatov about the future of Bukhara's Jews, and he replies, 'Only God knows.' Would that Sharon or Arafat—and all of their successors—had such humility.

Chapter 7

TURKMANIA

'Bahram Khan,' I said, 'suppose you get what you want. When you have built your asphalt roads and forts, and when you have sent the worst servants to the most modern schools—what will become of the soul of Asia?'

KURBAN SAID Ali & Nino

AUGUST 2001

TURKMENISTAN: 4–20 AUGUST

DAY 96 (4 AUGUST): TURKMENABAT TO BAIRAM ALI

My guidebook had given me fair warning – 'Turkmenistan is no fun in the summer.'—and this was the hottest time of year. However, if I could survive a Central Asian summer I could look forward to the bliss of an Arabian winter. Swings and roundabouts. But right now I was not feeling so philosophical: I'd travelled in Africa and never experienced such a hot day. Searingly, suffocatingly hot. From what those who live here told me, it had to be between 50° and 52°C. In the shade? You must be joking: there's no such thing in the Kara Kum Desert. Even camels were hot-footing it across the dunes.

DAY 97 (5 AUGUST): MERV

We are in the homeland of the biggest megalomaniac of our time. Suparmurat Niyazov, better known as Turkmenbashi (Head of All Turkmen), makes North Korea's Kim Jong Il look like a shrinking violet. So let us give thanks that Turkmenbashi doesn't have Mao's or Hitler's tens of millions at his command. Today an embarrassed-looking Turkmen recites for me in English the vow of fidelity every Turkmen schoolchild must learn by heart:

At the slightest evil against you,

May my hand be lost.

At the slightest word against you,

May my tongue be lost.

At the slightest betrayal to the Superior Turkmen …

… and so on, *ad*-solutely *nauseam*.

Turkmenbashi is everywhere. His larger-than-life photo—that of a pudgy-faced tinpot dictator going to seed—hangs on walls from one renamed extremity of this vast flat land (Turkmenabad, city of the Turkmen) to the other (modestly titled Turkmenbashi).

Here, a half hour's drive from Mary and Bairam Ali, we are in another seat of power, known to the Persians as Margush, the Greeks as Margiana and the Arabs as Merv.

From Alexander to the Mongol hordes of the fearsome Khans, this place—in what was known variously as Turkestan or Turkmenia—has been overrun by world conquerors, lords of terror who would have argued to a man that they were on a mission to bring civilisation to the barbarians.

Eight centuries ago, with Europe still in the Dark Ages, the mighty city that stood here was Baghdad's only rival as the centre of the civilised world. Like a candle flaring brightest just before it is snuffed out, Merv was known far and wide as Queen of the World until Genghis Khan's envoys arrived demanding a tribute—in grain and sex slaves—that the local Seljuks were unwilling to pay. In AD 1221, the Mongols returned, slaying upwards of one million citizens in a single week. However, even a massacre on that scale did not put paid to Merv's days of greatness: a Timurid dynasty (yes, our old friend Timur the Lame) would revive some of that.

But, today, all you can do is wander among the crumbled ruins of mosques and citadels, pick up the odd shard of 2000-year-old pottery, and marvel at the vanity of Man's pretensions to power.

DAY 101 (9 AUGUST): ASHGABAT
Ever on the lookout for lodgings with a difference, I had marked it down in my diary to check out a guesthouse in the suburbs that the

Lonely Planet author said was actually an asylum. That should be an interesting experience for one night, I thought. On arriving at the place in question I was greeted by an hospitable couple whose only eccentricity was the husband's total obsession with pigeons. Dovecotes abounded and he spent half the day banding his beloved birds. As I accepted a mug of tea and tried to make small talk, a tall ponytailed Englishman in his late twenties sat down opposite me. Introducing himself as Richard, a guest at this out-of-the-way guesthouse, he looked like just another adventurous soul until he mentioned that he had just come back from Afghanistan—one of the few places I had excluded from my itinerary. This hadn't been his first visit there, he said, and although it was true about the hard line the Taliban rulers took on many issues he had got to know and respect them, and they did some good things too (eliminating opium crops, for one). And then he said the most curious thing: 'I got to know them really well and we got to trust each other … Watch out, something big is going to happen soon.' Naturally, I asked him what, but he kept changing the subject, as if he had said too much. My curiosity was so piqued that I returned the next day, but Richard had gone. A month later, when the news came in from New York and Washington, I couldn't help wondering how much he had known.

DAY 103 (11 AUGUST): ASHGABAT

As Oriental despots go (and they eventually do), Niyazov/Turkmenbashi is nothing out of the ordinary; but long-time observers collect his wackier ideas like precious stones. His Edifice Complex has already given the nation a solid smattering of distinctive landmarks. This capital of his is a postmodern tribute to the sheen of marble, not to mention the glint of gold. Centre stage is occupied by the Arch of Neutrality, colloquially known as the Tower of Power, a skyscraping tripod topped by a scintillating statue of guess who, pointing towards the rising sun at dawn and rotating all day until his all-powerful finger commands it to set in the evening. This being Turkmenistan, the sun does what it's told.

A more poignant monument lies out of town: the Palace of Orphans. Like vast swaths of his mint-fresh capital, the Palace reflects Turkmenbashi's love of shiny surfaces, and—so the tourist guide is heard to say—his love of children (which I suppose is just as well for the children's sake). The chief of the five great Turkmen clans claims his father was killed in World War II and his mother died in the 1948 earthquake catastrophe that killed 160 000 Ashgabat residents in ten seconds flat.

That memory spurred him to father the Palace, which is actually a prestige school financed by a US$20 million donation from the UAE. Credit where it's due: 250 orphans receive an education fit for a future elite (the world's only orphanocracy?) in the impressively equipped rooms and playgrounds of this Eton in the desert.

DAY 107 (15 AUGUST): TURKMENBASHI

After an orange sunrise afforded me a glimpse of the Caspian Sea from my second-class Turkmenistan Railways carriage, I thought I had arrived in Turkmenbashi, on the Caspian shore, just after 9 am on a torrid summer's morning. The conductor must have been so glad to reach the end of the line that he simply forgot me. Anyway, it took some vociferous shouting to get anyone to come and help me and the chair down from the carriage, and then the total folly of having bought a ticket in Wagon 21 set in.

I was at the back of the train, about 800 metres from the station, stuck fast in a sea of sharp stones of the type mysteriously beloved of railway station designers the world over. After half an hour sweating it out, a couple of Turkmen motorists appeared out of nowhere, drove their car the length of the train, and gave me a lift into town. Now I had arrived.

DAY 111 (19 AUGUST): ON THE CASPIAN SEA

Ships are not made for wheelchairs. High cabin thresholds and cramped bathrooms are well-known foes but, ultimately, conquerable.

A smooth ride to Transcaucasia: that was the theory. But post-Soviet reality had a lesson in store for me. The Thursday before sailing, Sirdar the ticket-seller was roused from his pallet in the bedroom-cum-office he occupied down by the wharf and sold me a US$45 ticket for deck space on the passenger ship *Dagestan*, due out on Saturday evening.

Following his directions to be there hours early, I was wheeling along the esplanade at 10 am on Saturday when my heart sank at the sight of a large vessel heading out to sea. Surely that couldn't be the *Dagestan*? It was, Sirdar sighed. But I was in luck: another ship would be leaving port that night. It was already 40°C, and I was in no position to argue. I bought a second ticket, ignored the demand for a new 'service fee', and returned to the Customs Hall for a long day's wait. (Much too late I learnt that to obtain a space on a cargo vessel— my replacement ship—the going rate was US$15.)

Officially 'stamped out' of Turkmenistan at 11 pm on Saturday, the ensuing hours of stifling heat in a poky cabin (kindly vacated by a Russian-literate Azeri crewman who on scanning my ticket told me 'Those Turkmen no good, they lie to you') were spent dozing listlessly and waiting for the barren cliffs that dominated my porthole view to move.

When I found that the cabin ensuite was accessible and therefore depriving myself of food and drink during the journey would be unnecessary, there was no food to be had. At long last a crew member who must have remembered the presence of this unusual human cargo turned up with a plate of pancakes which I wolfed down.

Afloat with uncertainty I might be, but sailing blithely into the unknown is what all of us do every day of our lives. The troika of waiting, the heat and the stillness steered my thoughts round to other times. Perhaps it was because my journey was now closing in on West Asia, which once closed in on me.

The outward impression that the world can be relied on, as witnessed in a clear sky and a low tide, would never deceive the boy who had learnt his lesson, still my scroll map lay on the cabin table unfurled and duly weighted.

I spent those hours of enforced idleness reviewing my plans for September 2001, little thinking that others might have others. Bahrain had taught me the folly of believing that, even when everything you can think of is charted, you can be certain what lies over the horizon. Even yet, I'm enthralled by maps.

The clock was creeping towards four on the Sunday afternoon when those eternal cliffs finally exited porthole right. As evening drew in, I left hardships, imaginary ships and the baked terrain of Central Asia astern. Hoisted up on deck with the help of grimy but willing hands, I felt the time was ripe for a spot of self-congratulation. It had taken me almost four months, at the hottest time of year, to cross one of the most enticing yet challenging and unfamiliar regions of the globe. As a tangerine sun bobbled over the waves before losing its balance and slipping under, a beaming captain slipped a cold can of beer into my unsuspecting hands. Silently I toasted Sirdar.

Chapter 8

NIGHT VISION

Observe, in short, how transient and trivial is all mortal life; yesterday a drop of semen, tomorrow a handful of spice or ashes.

THE ANCIENT GREEK PHILOSOPHER ZENO, QUOTED
BY COLIN THUBRON IN *JOURNEY INTO CYPRUS*

AUGUST 1990

Going mad isn't easy to describe. It is a journey of a unique kind, to a territory where most guidebooks don't venture. Going mad is like visiting another world where all the signs are written in a mysterious alphabet that nothing back home prepares you to decipher. If you travel far enough from your starting point without reliable companions, you will arrive at madness too—but I didn't know that then.

Unreliable companions in the form of voices accompany some of us down that sloping road. Although this account of my crisis is spiced with the doubts that assailed me, it would be wrong to infer that I had actual aural delusions. My descent was deep into myself, not into the realm of ghosts.

Towards sunset on that sultry Sunday 19 August, which that hint in the bar had primed me to expect would be so fateful, my plan of action became clear. As someone brought up to believe in God, I reflexively sought out a church I had seen a couple of kilometres from my home in Manama's inner suburbs. In Muslim Bahrain, churches are the virtually exclusive preserve of foreigners. My watch showing 7.30 pm on this day of no rest, to find the church locked fast seemed inexplicable from a rational point of view. But by then I was no longer on good terms with rational thought, sensing it had let me down of late.

Creeping paranoia had usurped the throne of thought: wasn't this suspicious, the thought occurred to me, that there wasn't even an explanatory note on this of all evenings? After all, wouldn't Westerners hide or even go to pray there if the Iraqi troops were about to invade?

Had I been thinking logically, even within the realm of cloak-and-dagger hints that I believed were being dropped at the Londoner, I should have been at the airport. But it was symptomatic of my mental agitation that I couldn't join up the dots between theory (belief) and practice (action). *If* expatriates were expected at the airport this evening, *then* I should have hopped into a passing taxi and damned the cost ... but dread had washed away the road linking *if* to *then*.

Here I was, trapped in a real-life version of Zeno's paradox, which we had studied at high school. Zeno taught that before you can go from here to there you first have to go half the distance; and before you can go from here to half the distance you have to go half *that* distance; and so on, *ad infinitum*. But because you can never go half the distance (because first you'd have to go half ...) all attempts to get from A to B are bound to fail. Well, you can never get anywhere with a philosophy like that. If you're stuck fast, you'll never be able to move.

'Know thyself' is asking a lot: the self remains the great unknowable. All we can do is construct a more or less useful map of who and where we think we are. My map was out of date: the reference markers provided by purpose (work) and friends were absent; and unnerving danger signals now flashed red.

A tintinnabulation of alarms streamed through my consciousness as I left the churchyard and headed south towards my apartment. *If this is evacuation night, everyone else will be at the airport and I will be the only Westerner left in Bahrain. When the Iraqis land I will have nowhere to hide. If I do find somewhere I won't be able to go out and get food. If I have to starve to death it will be a long, slow and torturous process. If they find me I will be tortured too, perhaps just as slowly.*

These fears, and many more—presenting extremely remote hypotheticals as impending threats—reduced me to a state of near terror. I was experiencing the onset of a panic attack. The strings were snapping. Nervous exhaustion was exacerbated by sheer physical fatigue brought on by two hours of non-stop and increasingly directionless walking in the 35°C heat of an August night.

Even more unlikely scenarios shuffled like cards to the front of the deck. The fear—or thought—struck me that maybe the arrangement for Westerners to assemble at the airport was an Iraqi ploy, disinformation, and that the planned airlift (surely sea evacuation? My mind was a blur) presaged a massacre.

Sane or mad, the mind controls the body. As I neared my apartment, my breathing was laboured and I could hear my heart pounding furiously. Others have since explained that I would have been hyperventilating; all I knew was that everything in my field of vision was swaying and swimming in and out of view. It was as if the physical laws of the universe had been suspended, gravity first.

For several minutes, it must have been, I paced the pavement in front of the tower block where my apartment was, in quest of a balance that had deserted me. I have a hazy recollection of taking the lift to my floor, fumbling for the right key, going into the living room and scrawling a hasty farewell note to my parents (while struggling to believe it would ever reach them in the event of an invasion, which now seemed to me a much greater certainty than tomorrow's sunrise). Whatever else I did is lost to memory.

It must have been mid-evening now, but time becomes fluid, neither measurable nor of the slightest importance, when the world appears to be breaking up. To unbuckle my watch and fling it away, heedless of where it landed, seemed the most sensible thing in the world to do. This was the end time, whether the Iraqis were poised to invade or the Second Coming was in the wings. *End time.*

It must have been the mixture of religious and military signals that suggested it. The word 'Armageddon' blitzed my mind and the burden that had borne down on my struggling sanity for the seventeen days since the outer world had lost its stability now crushed it utterly, breaking through my last reserves of self-control. I ran down the road, hands outstretched in front of me, screaming, 'The world is ending! This is the end of the world!'

As tends to be the case with such declarations, I was wrong, or maybe just premature. But no one told me that at the time. If anyone had been in the vicinity, no doubt they would have shrunk from the crazy apparition hurtling down the boulevard. But, after what must have been a few hundred metres, I did attract someone's attention: behind me, from out of nowhere, I heard the wailing of a police siren.

The van stopped, officers got out, a couple of them came over, pinned my arms behind my back and dragged me inside, forcing me to lie face down on the flatbed behind the sealed-off cabin. The driver, after furtively looking around and grinning, or grimacing (I was in no position to tell which), gunned the engine and sped away.

In the back of the van, my police escort—between trying to keep me prone, with wrists pinned over the small of my back—were discussing me in Arabic. How easy it is to make sense of a conversation by tone alone, it occurred to me, even when spoken by people whose language you don't know. These tones spoke to me of hostility and uncertainty combined. Yet at no time did I feel threatened by them. 'Fatalism' is too weak a word for what I felt; it was not so much 'what will be will be' as 'what must be has begun'. The unknown held no fears for me, perhaps because it was infinitely preferable to the terror of waiting for what my fevered imagination, fed by other people's fears and speculations, could apprehend.

I was passive and powerless, unable to see where we were going. I couldn't be sure which police station the van delivered me to, while sensing it must be on the edge of the built-up area. But, for once in my life, curiosity had outrun its course. They could do what they wanted with me; careless was I now, in the grasp of Fate.

Once inside the police station—a shabby block of concrete with mustard-coloured walls—my passivity reached the end of its tether. The tension was palpable as my guardians, taking no chances, forced me to sit on the floor while the formalities that govern police procedures the world over were carried out. Asked my name and address, I gave nothing away.

This was valuable time, and I used it to survey my surroundings. What had been an increasingly insistent headache now made concentration difficult, and as I looked at the three photos above the desk officer's head—which would usually have been of the Emir of Bahrain and two princes—staring back at me were the faces of Saddam Hussein, Gamel Abdel Nasser and the Ayatollah Khomeini. I have never been able to make sense of this and seldom think about it, but daresay a psychologist would conclude that to focus on the fiercer face of nationalism in the Middle East was an understandable illusion, flowing directly from recent harsh realities. My perceptions were like a door blown open, unhinged but not yet entirely detached.

Of course I didn't think at the time *I am hallucinating*. The appearance of dreamlike reality, albeit of the nightmarish kind, only confirmed the idea that this was exactly the sort of sliver of consciousness you might retain if your brain had been blown apart. Cut loose from my mental moorings, I became obsessed with the idea that this was Hell and that, to get out of it, I had to fight back against those from the Dark Side holding me captive. So, acting on the principle that action begets reaction, I lunged at the nearest officer with my fists—clearly the act of a crazy man, since he was armed with a truncheon.

He raised it above his head, and his fellow officers shouted sharply at him, but something told me he wouldn't bring it down. I growled at him, like a wild dog, trying to provoke him, just so that we could reach the next stage of the ordeal. That came quickly, in the form of officers' hands gripping my arms, the cold clasp of handcuffs being fitted over my wrists, and a small posse of police herding me into a corridor that ran off at a right angle from the front desk. With an almighty shove in the back, they pushed me onto the concrete floor of a cell and locked me in.

The cell was surprisingly large for just one person, although maybe it had been built to hold several. A strange inhuman caterwauling in the corridor, which broke out intermittently most of the night, had me wondering whether other inmates had been turfed out because a Western prisoner here would be so exceptional that any harm befalling him would incur consequences for the guards. The cell must have been occupied not long before because the only item in it was a urine-soaked mattress. Its walls enclosed ten metres by four, with standard-issue iron bars high up admitting shafts of harsh electric light.

Avoiding the mattress at first, I sat hunched over, back to a side wall, holding my head in my hands. The front of my brain felt as though lasers were boring into it, zapping the cells and melting them down. The mugginess of the night—of course there was no airconditioning— and the absence of any water aggravated everything. Misery and suffering are beyond words: anyway, in my psychotic state, it appeared quite conceivable I was dying but more likely that I had already done so. Visions of my parents calling out to me, unaware that I could see but not communicate with them, made this irrational thought highly believable. A flood of self-pity rolled over me, extracting a few salty tears that blended with the perspiration streaming down my cheeks.

The only measure of time now was the watch: not my discarded wrist ornament but the warder pacing past the cell at what I judged to be quarter-hour intervals. In the deepest part of the night, a scream from one of the other cells further along the dim corridor rent the stillness. A policeman's lot need not be an unhappy one; a torturer's work is never done. All at once, I felt that being in solitary meant someone was looking after me.

Sometime just before dawn, the sense of my own miserable state reduced me to lying down on the piss-soaked mattress. My nervous exhaustion induced a state of slumber (I hesitate to call it sleep) that was somehow hyper-aware of my physical surroundings; and the fire in my brain crackled on.

With morning came a change of shift. Gabbled Arabic, excited talk between arriving and departing cops. The officers' talk woke me up. *A Westerner must have novelty value here*, I told myself. Two of the policemen came to the iron door. One joggled a key in the lock while the other kept his eyes fixed on me. I remember thinking, *Don't worry, I'm not going to make a false move. I made all those last night.*

They motioned me further along the corridor, away from 'public' view, towards the cell where I'd heard screaming in the small hours. One of the jailers pointed to an overhead shower rose, and blinked an order, as if to say, 'You know how to use it. Do it.'

Privacy wasn't an issue, and in my weakened state shame wasn't either. I undressed, piled my clothes out of spray's way, and turned on the tap. The rusty waterworks shuddered and snorted, a sand-coloured squirt of liquid shot me in the head, and I applied the wafer of soap I'd been given to the steadier flow that followed. It was cold, but coming after my night in the furnace that was a relief.

Upon dressing I was led back down the corridor, past 'my cell', to the duty desk where an officer I didn't recognise—but at least one who spoke English, unlike his colleagues of the night—barked instructions at his juniors before training his gaze on me and saying in the neutral manner of a cyborg, 'We will take you soon.'

I still had no handle on reality. Had the Iraqis arrived during the night? Was this new officer one of the occupiers? Where were they going to take me? Questions dripped like beads of sweat through what was left of my mind. The future would reveal itself in due course, I could make no sense of the present, and instinct was the only survival tool left to me. It told me that to ask where I was going would be construed as a sign of weakness. *The future is coming*, I told myself. *Patience.*

The morning shift must have been told all about the gibbering idiot brought in overnight, but now a self-absorbed silence was all I could manage. Vacantly I stared at the floor, looking up only once to the rulers' portraits above the duty officer. Yesterday's tyrants had vanished; occupying pride of place were the Bahraini ruling family, but instead of the accustomed regal pose their eyes exuded fear. *Nothing makes sense any more*, I told myself but, in the view of those ever-attentive officers, not a word passed my lips.

I can't recall exactly when the new transportation arrived, perhaps between 9 and 10 am, but this was no police van. The tones had changed too. Last night the voice of officialdom rasped; this morning it cooed. Like a child at the dentist's, I was assured that everything would be all right (and, like a child at the dentist's, I knew they were lying). Hemmed in either side by officers, I clambered into the back of the van, and sat myself down in the middle of a bench. A lozenge-shaped pane of glass afforded a view, but my vision was still unsteady so the townscape held no charms for me.

By this time, not only were purposes hidden but our whereabouts and direction were utter mysteries as well. The driver seemed to be swerving all over the place—mosques, schools, shops swam across my field of vision, my hands clutched the bench to keep balance—as if he were in a movie trying to shake off a pursuer.

Eventually, my sole surviving rational brain cell concluded that we were somewhere not far from the Old Town but in a suburb seldom if ever visited by me before. Like a slingshot in slow motion, we came off a roundabout that looked familiar (but Manama has more roundabouts than a centipede has legs) and the driver made a wide-arcing left turn across a driveway and into neatly kept grounds dominated by a long, low, palm-fringed building set back from a high wall topped by razor-wire.

As the remorseless August sun glared down, the officers walked me into the building, a hand under each elbow as if I were going to run away. Only one question remained in my crumbling mind: *Where in Hell am I?*

I didn't have to wait long for an answer. It was in the writing on the wall, a sign in Arabic and English. We were passing through the foyer now, past Indian guards, going up in the lift. Ignoring me, a matronly woman in nursing-issue white and grey addressed the police in practised no-nonsense tones. My vision stopped swimming. I saw her, and my new home, with clinical clarity. My future, so agonising in its approach, was now here, in the Bahrain Psychiatric Hospital—the insane asylum—and there was no telling when or where the nightmare would end.

Chapter 9

WHISTLING IN THE DARK

But darkness opens like a knife for you

and you are marked

down by your pulsing brain

and isolated

and breathing

your breathing is the blast, the bullet, and the final sky.

LAURIE LEE A MOMENT OF WAR (MONTPELLIER, OCTOBER 1937)

AUGUST 1990

Arabia's burning daylight had closed down the night like the flick of a switchblade. But the knife in my pulsing brain was still there, driven up to the hilt. The shearing of my consciousness sent past, present and future possibilities colliding and crashing together, shooting sparks through my unsleeping brain: thousands upon thousands of glimpses of what was, is and might yet be, most of them dire and many pointed straight at the final sky.

If my mood was manic, my basic curiosity had returned. Knowing I was in a madhouse—in the Middle East, of all places—certainly wasn't a jolly adventure but what I call my rational sense (or the observer within) received enough stimulus from the new situation to ignite a host of inquiries: *Am I safer here? Isn't this still Bahrain? If Iraqi troops are going to land soon and Westerners are to be evacuated I will still be here when they arrive. With all the other Westerners gone, will I be (a) slaughtered in my hospital bed; or (b) missed altogether because nobody would expect to find a Westerner in a Bahraini asylum?*

Every question led to a split choice; every mental road forked—and yet the questions bombarded my mind without let-up. *Does anyone else know I'm here? Will they have phoned my family in Australia, spreading alarm? Won't that mean that when I get out of here (when will that be?) I will be forced to go home, thus burying my six years of travel and word-work with the shame of returning with my tail between my legs?*

The contrast between my racing, overheated mind and the loss of my physical freedom imposed an immense, almost unbearable strain.

Will I be strapped to a bed and given electroconvulsive shock therapy? Does anyone here speak English?

Anything could happen and there was nothing I could do about it. Again I felt panic rising, my breaths were gulps for air.

Putting its purpose to one side, it could have been any hospital room. The deadlocked doors contained small square windows covered in chicken-wire gauze, which rendered them a tad less opaque than the face of the security guard who sat just inside the door.

The first room I was shepherded into was a games-cum-lounge space converted to a meal room three times a day. When the plates were cleared away, table-tennis trestles went up, and most of the day a large TV screen played, with the sound turned down, though none of the other inmates seemed aware of its presence.

From the meal room I walked down a wide corridor, with the doctors' and nurses' rooms on the left and, a few metres on, the wards themselves. Sterile hospital beds with plastic coverings to guard against bedwetting were my first impression. At the far end of the room were a couple of beds with leather restraints to prevent the uncontrollable patients from falling out. *Oh God, don't let them put me in one of those.*

Now I was in the matron's charge. Grimness of face, seriousness of purpose epitomised her every gesture. Until I met her, I noticed that one of my more obvious traits—a sense of humour, however warped—had vanished without trace. Matron brought it back. Once she had established that I knew my name, she asked, 'Do you know why you're here?'

'Because the police brought me here,' I said, deadpan. She reminded me that I had been running down the road in the middle of the night, screaming. I didn't deny it, but tried to pass it off as a natural occurrence, a routine event like stocking up on groceries.

Most of her first day's efforts were spent calming me down. To this end, she prescribed regular doses of lithium and plenty of bed rest. I was assigned the bed nearest her office, and it was only with the greatest difficulty that I could stay on it. Later in the afternoon, Matron must have added Valium to my light pharmaceutical diet, and this—combined with the debilitating impact of nervous exhaustion—plunged me into dreamless unconsciousness, from which I awoke sometime after sundown. The distant blue light of the TV in the meal room, and the murmur of its canned voices, punctuated by the evening call of the muezzin, reminded me of where I was, resolving a puzzle that had given me a startled half minute or so.

Occasionally, a low moan would issue from the other end of the ward—ominously from one of the beds with leather straps—and this would send a new shiver of fear down my spine, but my mind was still too seized with its own torments to dwell on other people's pain.

At six in the morning, lying on my right-hand side, I opened my eyes and saw—as one sees a picture hung askew—two Filipino male orderlies, in starched white coats, seated opposite each other at a table, reading the morning paper. This was the paper I was supposed to be still working on. One orderly turned to an inside page, so that the old newspaperman in me (able to read type upside down and now, I found, sideways) could not miss the front-page banner headline: HUMAN SHIELDS, which set a new train roaring out of control down my mental track.

If the Iraqis come, they will take me hostage. The terror will increase, the agony will drag out. Will it become so insupportable I lash out, am punished, tortured, or shot, or will I go insane?

The already insane constantly ask themselves that last question, I discovered: it's the most logical thought they have. *I don't belong here*, I told myself. But then I could also see that, the way my world had dissolved, perhaps others would be better judges of that.

58

Breakfast meals were brought in on a trolley with the main course on hotplates. In this respect, you get better service in an asylum than at most hotels these days, if only because hospital managements don't consider self-service to be a safe option. If I had one complaint, it would be that plastic cutlery tends to be inadequate in any given encounter with chargrilled sausage.

The meals were wrapped in cellophane, their destination written in marker pen: 'EUROPEAN MEAL' or 'ASIAN MEAL'. Quite a few of the residents were Indians, perhaps not surprisingly in a society where people from the subcontinent are often treated little better than slaves. At the time I thought it reflected an odd strain of racism that the meals should be segregated thus, but it was probably an attempt to cater for the cultural preferences and religiously prescribed dietary imperatives of one and all. Not that this mattered much: the psychological upheaval of my life had left me with little appetite.

That morning I was invited into one of the administrative offices. Ranged on seats, from left to right in front of me, were four medicos—three men and a woman—in white coats, each with biro poised over clipboard.

'Do you know what has happened to you?' the woman asked in a clipped professional manner.

I wanted to say, 'I went mad.' (That says it so much quicker.) Instead I said, 'I was running down the road last night screaming it was the end of the world.'

The tallest man, on my left, asked, 'Why did you think it was the end of the world?'

To tell the truth I can't remember what my answer to this was, but clearly this was no time to discuss theology.

'Do you remember attacking the police?' came another verbal arrow, this time out of right field. I did. This had a psychological, fear-based cause but to put that into words was beyond me: I felt as if this were a 'job interview' where certain answers would win more favour but one could never know what answers those were.

While the chorus line of pens jigged its way across the massed clipboards, trying to make sense of my stuttering response to the previous question, I turned to the woman—the matron who had greeted me upon my arrival—and put a couple of queries of my own.

59

'How long will I be here?'

'A few days, until you are better.'

'Where will I go then?' (Clearly, the question presupposed I wouldn't have any choice in the matter.)

'That is yet to be decided.'

'Where are you all from?'

'We are Egyptian psychiatrists,' Matron replied archly. It occurred to me that the diagnosis of the best Egyptian psychiatrists living in Bahrain mightn't take account of my odd Western, even Antipodean, character.

Back to bed I went, none the wiser about their assessment of my mental state. What struck home was that, if my inquisitors could deduce that state only from my behaviour and words, they could not know my background, fears, loves, dreams and hopes, and so whatever they concluded was likely to be wrong. The idea that 'You can't know me so you can't help me' first took root there. It was to prove a dangerous one.

The lithium continued. That afternoon, when I asked Matron about my diagnosis, the cement in her face set so hard I thought it would crack: 'You are not entitled to know that.' I disagreed emphatically but then withdrew into my shell, biding my time. Some 24 hours later my vigilance paid off. Matron was called away and, after briefly checking the coast was clear, I ducked into her office and riffled through the notes on her desk. I was in luck: the second page was headed 'James, Haley Ken (I thought *Western name order mustn't be a subject in Egyptian medical universities*). 'Diagnosis: Borderline manic depressive. Post-traumatic stress syndrome.' I darted out again: no one had spotted me.

Back on the bed, a corner of my pulsing brain seethed with anger. None of this would have happened if my immediate boss hadn't bad-mouthed me to the deputy editor and played on the insecurities of an office newcomer to bolster his own self-regard. In a perverse way, my being here seemed like karmic retribution: *This'll make him ashamed he treated me so badly.* It was a couple of days before an alchemy of the heart transmuted such crazed thoughts of pure vengeance into something nobler: *I wouldn't want anyone to go through what I'm going through. So if he is shamed by this turn of events it will make him better; and if he isn't, or cannot be, his reaction is not worth adding to my worries.*

I don't mind saying now that such meditations were so intense, and cut so deep, they amounted to a prayer.

Compassion didn't come from any expected quarter or in any expected form. None of the news executives visited, a disappointment that spun off a cycle of emotions, from contempt to eventual acceptance that there must always be an explanatory factor we cannot know but that, if we did know, would enable us to forgive all. In my plight, the factor I *could* grasp was the need for a newspaper's top management, in days of uncertainty, to be on deck, attending to a hundred more important matters.

Just then, a wrapped parcel arrived from the editor himself. It contained a new set of clothes and a couple of books: one Agatha Christie, and John Le Carré's *The Russia House*. (Thankful though I was not to have been forgotten, I wondered about the choices, although now that sounds churlish.)

I received my first visit—and it wasn't from the preoccupied managers but from one of my colleagues: an Indian named Sunil who, I knew, in these extraordinarily unsettling times had lost virtually his entire video sideline. He and his family were doing it hard, and I would have guessed the names of a dozen other people before imagining he would walk through that doorway. My eyes brimmed with tears; he and his wife had brought me a cake. That simple gesture in my hour of adversity taught me that, while the gifts we usually choose are infinitely replaceable, the one thing we treat as infinite—time—is finite. Which is why the freewill offering of our time is the most valuable of all gifts.

Sunil and his wife visited three times during the ten days I was kept in the hospital. Without that repeated signal of caring, I feel sure my inner turmoil would have resulted in some drastic explosion. As it is, I distinctly remember growling at another inmate one afternoon (as I had at the policeman) and pushing him provocatively, even though he had done me no harm. Only the remembrance of a connecting thread with the outside, and the steadying hope that this surreal existence would end at some point, prevented me from boiling over altogether.

My only other link to that larger drama going on outside—the geopolitical one that triggered my mental collapse—was via the media. Seeing those newspapers with their HUMAN SHIELDS banners had piqued my journalistic curiosity.

As mentioned, the TV volume was down low but no attempt was made to keep the daily newscast from us. At one point I was sure the Iraqis had invaded Bahrain and taken over the television studio because the evening prayers, which came on just before the 7 pm bulletin, were chanted against the backdrop of a Shia mosque in Baghdad.

And so the days passed, without any hint how long the doctors would keep me there. No one suggested my parents or other relatives back home had been notified: the shiver of humiliation that ran down my spine at the very thought made me hope against hope that they hadn't. (They hadn't.)

It must have been a week into my stay that Matron called me into her office and told me I wouldn't be going back to the paper (I suppressed a wry smile) but that the paper had agreed to pay for my air ticket out of the country. The term 'shipped home' sprang to my beleaguered mind. Then I realised that, the Gulf being on the England–Australia flight path, I could choose either destination.

The chance to 'right myself' and pick up the threads of my life—composed for the previous six years of one part journalism, one part what a perceptive friend once called being an 'international vagrant'—appealed strongly.

That argued for a flight to England, where nearly five months ago I had clearly made a wrong turning. Adding more weight to that side of the scales, the prospect of going home the way I felt appalled me.

But the cataclysm that had turned my world upside down had drained me of so much energy that setting myself up again in England, and searching for freelance sub-editing opportunities while scouting out accommodation, loomed as a mountain too high for the climbing. I took the ticket home.

At least that is what I told Matron I was doing on the afternoon of the day I was to depart, accompanied to the airport by only a driver and one staff member from the newspaper (curiously, I cannot to this day recall whom). Matron sternly instructed me that, whatever else happened, I must keep taking the lithium.

Quietly I assented, but it was a lie intended to assuage her concern. Why would I need any more drugs? If I was travelling, it was because the psychiatrists thought I had recovered my mental balance. I felt well enough to travel, and—most important of all—I was about to escape the danger zone, the hovering threat of invasion. Once safely beyond the reach of Scuds or tanks or 'supergun' missiles, not to mention a landborne invasion force, wouldn't my jubilation at having escaped the danger replace my terrors with a rational calm?

Convinced after phoning home that no one in Australia even knew anything had gone wrong in my life, I made a mental note to turn the Hong Kong stopover into a weeklong break. This would give me plenty of time to decide whether to fly on home or change direction. From a previous visit, in 1984, I knew of a wonderful getaway in Hong Kong, a guesthouse-cum-restaurant on the outer island of Lantau. That would be my refuge, I thought, my personal sanatorium.

As the plane lifted off from Bahrain under a starlit summer sky, my mood was buoyant, even a little smug. *I've escaped the worst*, I recall telling myself.

I could not have been more mistaken ...

Chapter 10

CAUCASIAN FEATURES

I always go more boldly forward when I know nothing of what lies ahead. After all, the worst you can do is die, and you've got to die some time.

MIKHAIL LERMONTOV A Hero of Our Time

AUGUST-SEPTEMBER 2001

In the ruff of earth bunched between the Black and Caspian seas lie three countries more striking for their differences than their similarities. The Caucasus is home to peoples of sharply conflicting outlook, sitting side by side but never in harmony, jostling not nestling. Above all, it is a place of instability, with an extreme liability to sudden upheaval, and has ever been thus: it was in the Caucasus that Prometheus, the bringer of fire, ended his days, vultures pecking at his vitals.

There are excellent reasons for things here being so unstable, so temporary, so edgy. Here, for centuries, empires have crossed, clashed, or been thwarted in their headlong rush. Today none of the three countries is officially at war, but Armenia enjoys the spoils of a vicious and little-reported conflict with Azerbaijan that raged for much of the early 1990s. To seek evidence of more recent instability, you have only to recall the bloody pictures of members of parliament being massacred inside Armenia's legislature in November 1999 or gaze in disbelief as Georgian businessmen walk down the pavements of their stylish capital with pistols on their hips.

Religious differences offer a clue: after all, this is where the Muslim world meets some of the earliest Christian lands. Georgia and Armenia vie for the title of oldest Christian country in the world: my visit coincided with the 1700th anniversary of Armenia's declaration as a Christian state. A generation later, in AD 337, Georgia began its conversion to Jesus-worship.

However, 'watching your back' seems to explain the divisions between these countries better than anything else. For these three small nations occupy precariously small spaces with, at their back, powerful and numerous populations: Russia's 150 millions, Iran's 70 millions and Turkey's 70 millions. At their backs lies one big menace apiece, a threat to their very survival (Iran at Azerbaijan's; Russia at Georgia's; Turkey at Armenia's).

All three now want to link themselves with Europe—they woo NATO and eye off the European Union—but Europe is inevitably more important to them than vice versa. Geographically, they are not even part of Europe, just eternal wannabes, and all the technical assistance and commercial interest in the world (the Caspian's oil reserves are mighty indeed) are never going to change that.

Finally, 'Caucasus' reminds a Westerner of 'Caucasian', the predominant racial grouping that conquered the West and, through imperialism, the Old and New Worlds: the Americas and Australasia. When looking from afar at the region's brutality and even genocide, we really cannot afford any conceit.

AZERBAIJAN: 20 AUGUST–3 SEPTEMBER

DAY 112 (20 AUGUST): BAKU

'Khosh gyalmisinis' means 'Welcome' in Azeri—and they do mean it. After four months on 'the road', this is the first destination where I have been met on arrival. Ismail, an employee of the Deugro freight-forwarding company—whose factor in Turkmenbashi ran into me before I boarded—is on the other side of the Customs barrier. This is a doubly pleasant surprise because, for once, the sight of my wheelchair doesn't soften an official's heart but has quite the opposite effect and, before Ismail pipes up, I have been sent to the back of the queue for an exhausting game of bureaucratic patience. Ismail's presence and quiet but firm manner convince these bombastic types that somehow I'm connected to the regional transport leviathan, and

I'm not saying anything to 'unconvince' them.

Within minutes, Ismail has driven me into the centre of Baku and waits while I complete the formalities at the imposing Hotel Absheron and secure a room with a magnificent view of the city square and the sun-spangled expanse of the world's largest lake. From here it is off to meet his boss, Katya, who insisted on this totally unexpected welcome simply because the idea of someone travelling across these lands by public transport struck her as so exceptional it called for a celebration.

An hour later I have negotiated the cobblestone lanes of the Old City and we are dining in the Caravanserai Restaurant, a place where cameleers and other transients have been putting up, feasting, or both, since the 15th century. On this simmering summer's afternoon we sit like old friends at a table in a shaded courtyard surrounded by eighteen pointed arches, formerly the entrances to the inns, the cool flagstone-floored cells where the caravans used to stop a night or two before moving on. Of course I offer to pay; of course they refuse.

Later in the afternoon comes one of those time-out-of-joint experiences. Turning the TV on in my hotel room I hear Australian actor Bill Hunter's gruff voice dubbed into Azeri: they're screening *Muriel's Wedding*. I collapse onto the bed and lapse into a reverie in which I endlessly haul myself up a ship's gangway, *a posteriori*, while Captain Turkmenbashi hand-cranks a gramophone that sends Abba tunes wafting over the Caspian.

DAY 116 (24 AUGUST): BAKU

I'm up ISR Plaza Tower, Baku's only skyscraper (well, at five storeys, skypointer might be a better word). The idea was to get an overview of the New Town: instead, it's not only the building pointing skyward but our eyes as a formation of Turkish NATO jet fighters soars overhead. This is sabre-rattling or gunship diplomacy, modern-style. The Iranians sank an Azeri fishing boat in the disputed southern Caspian last month. The Azeris are a Turkic-speaking people and there is great official friendship between Turkey and Azerbaijan. Tension, and sonic booms, are in the air ... now you can feel the instability.

DAY 119 (27 AUGUST): BAKU

This afternoon I hook up with Fuad Axundhov, the best city tour guide it's ever been my luck to encounter. He takes one look at the wheelchair and sees the hilarity in my wanting to join his 'Walking Tour'. Allowances are made, he goes at my pace (faster than he would like downhill), but in terms of understanding I'm puffing to keep up with him. What Fuad doesn't know about his beloved hometown probably isn't knowable.

Although a specialist on Boom Town, the first city anywhere to be built on oil wealth, he is equally expert on the Soviet era or the works of Azerbaijan's great literary hero, the 12th-century Nizami. He has a literary turn of phrase himself, does Fuad. 'Stalin's chessboard' suddenly sounds too tame a way to describe how the Georgian-born Soviet dictator created countries and 'internally deported' whole races: my guide, more pointedly, calls these new republics 'Stalin's time bombs'.

DAY 126 (3 SEPTEMBER): SEKI

I'm in luck. Staying at this 17th-century caravanserai, I meet an American couple who have been taking a break from their work in Georgia. They are driving back to Tbilisi and are happy to cram me, chair and baggage, into their car.

GEORGIA: 3 SEPTEMBER–3 OCTOBER

DAY 126 (3 SEPTEMBER): TBILISI

Just before dusk we arrive in this hilly, elegant capital. The muddy Mtkvari, coursing past the longest-settled districts of this 1500-year-old city, is about the same width and texture as the Yarra, so—startlingly—I feel at home.

Finding somewhere affordable to stay 'at home' is even more startling. The Americans introduce me to a Georgian woman of their acquaintance who asks US$90 a night for her barely furnished studio, above a street as steep as a ski jump. Spoilt by Asian prices, I plead an upper limit less than half that. She lets me stay one night on my terms. The next day I move out to Nika's Guesthouse, a charming *pension* in Saburtalo, 5 kilometres out of town, run by a widow of 60 and her niece.

After four months of travel, perhaps it shouldn't surprise me that one of my chair brakes has chosen this moment to lose its grip. Twice in the past week it has actually fallen off, astounding passers-by just as much as me. Not being mechanically minded, I have had to study the ingenious complexity of this model, even though it takes the worse part of an hour to reattach it.

DAY 127 (4 SEPTEMBER): TBILISI

After a generous breakfast I'm off to the central post office to phone my wheelchair-parts supplier in Melbourne, then to DHL to notify them that new brakes are on their way: should be five or six days away.

Rolling down the pavements of the city's central boulevard, Rustavelis Gamziri, is enough to impress me with what a cultured and appealing place I am in. By contrast with the often European-style architecture, all street and commercial signs are in the straggling, Tolkienesque script that looks to my untrained eye like no other alphabet on Earth.

Halfway along Rustavelis, I pop into Laghidze Café, a local landmark, and discover a highlight of Georgia's unique cuisine: *khachapuri*. Picture a platter of golden-crusted bread, shaped like a clam shell as wide as a computer keyboard and fresh from the oven, with the base covered in melting cheese and, in the centre, soft, fresh egg yolks, slightly runny. 'Scrumptious' doesn't begin to do it justice. Georgian cooking is richly original but to my ravenous taste nothing could match the discovery of *khachapuri*: this is what we would order from a million home-delivery outlets if Georgians had beaten the Italians to New York.

DAY 130 (7 SEPTEMBER): TBILISI

I locate the tourist agency that has obligingly agreed to hold mail sent from home. One of the great joys of long-distance travel is receiving a satchel full of mail and absorbing all the personal news of three or more months at a sitting, preferably over coffee.

This post brings a letter from my parents informing me that sometime in June my bank balance fell to $7.67 but that newspaper payments for some of my 'Emails from the Edge' articles have since retrieved the situation. This is why I like to get the mail only periodically.

This afternoon, my humble taxi is cut off by an arrogant silver Merc and, unwisely, I poke my head out the window and shout, 'Mafia!' Three minutes later, our modest vehicle emerges from an underpass and is again cut off—forced off the road, with no way out—by the same car.

The driver and his henchman both step out and stride towards our jalopy. The offended man, who looks like a cross between Schwarzenegger and the Incredible Hulk, could pick up the car and throw it away, or eat it, but clearly intends something more specific, balling his fist and rapping on my passenger-side window (which I've hastily wound up). The driver pleads that I'm a foreigner, tourist, idiot (I think the Georgian word may be the same for all three) while I nod like an idiotic foreign tourist. His anger unassuaged, the Georginator demands I wind the window down, but then, in a moment of inspiration, the driver points to my wheelchair stowed on the back seat.

Mafia man utters a kind of grunt and follows his minder, who is now grinning, back to the parked Merc. Halfway there, the *mafioso* turns round and cups his hands around his groin, giving an emphatic thrust to the gesture I would have associated with an Italian rather than a Georgian. The message is unmistakable but it doesn't require a reply.

DAY 131 (8 SEPTEMBER): TBILISI

This early Saturday afternoon I enjoy a meal at the Borani floating pontoon restaurant moored on the Mtkvari. Between the soup and the *khachapuri*, unusually dark clouds build behind the hilly city's spires, and raindrops begin spattering with increasing vehemence on the previously placid waterway. The smell of summer meeting autumn is intoxicating. Change is in the air.

Tonight I satisfy the curiosity spawned by my discovery that the capital of this country, better known for its monasteries and urban mafia, is also home to the Beatles Club. Impresario Murtaz Khudoev has re-created the best of the Sixties in a replica of the Liverpudlians' favourite haunt, the Cavern. The club occupies a superb location, astride two avenues on the city's edge just where they funnel into Rustavelis.

I descend the stairs to the basement, after pausing at the entrance to note the words: 'This club is dedicated to the memory of Sir John Whinston [sic] Lennon.' At the foot of the staircase are strobes of various hues, mostly blues. By now my eyes, gradually acquiring their night sights, gaze in disbelief towards the far end of the … well, 'room' hardly describes it; we're in a barrel-vaulted brick-walled carbon copy of the famous Merseyside dance hall.

I gasp in admiration. They've resurrected the music, the architecture and an entire era. Have they also resurrected the Beatles? Well, there are limits, but the illusion is convincing enough. The 'Bleats' are technically flawless Georgian Beatles, dressed in Epstein suits à la 1964. During a break, I'm not surprised to hear from Khudoev that this Fab Four—who have been together now for fifteen years, longer than the originals themselves were—recently won first prize in a contest for Beatles impersonators held in Liverpool.

Chapter 11

SEPTEMBER 11, 2001

Even they [Americans] may one day know fire and ... the sword ...
for it is hard to believe that when one half of the world is living
through terrible disasters the other half can continue ... learning
about the distress of its distant fellow-men only from movies and
newspapers. If something exists in one place, it will exist everywhere.

CZESLAW MILOSZ THE CAPTIVE MIND (1950)

SEPTEMBER-OCTOBER 2001

DAY 134 (11 SEPTEMBER): TBILISI

On this beautiful autumnal afternoon I wander through the picturesque quarter of Zemo Kala. In a sun-dappled park, two old men play chess under a tree while others watch on intently. The world is at peace.

At seven o'clock this balmy evening I take my seat to the back of a private box at the glittering Paliashvili Opera House. The curtain is about to rise on a performance of *Turandot* by (drum roll please, maestro) the Batumi Children's Opera and Ballet Company. Billed as the world's only juvenile troupe presenting works from the standard repertoire, the Batumi is an ensemble whose accomplishments I await with a dull dread. 'Puccini by six-year-olds?' I wonder condescendingly as the recorded orchestra strikes up.

I need not have feared. The singing is pitch-perfect, the costumes are resplendent. Who cares if *Summertime* and *I Could Have Danced All Night* do not seem entirely of a piece with Italian tradition? American themes divert our attention, but inclusion is not the same thing as intrusion. 'If something exists in one place, it will exist everywhere.'

Batumi, on the Black Sea coast, is the capital of Adzharia, virtually a

71

breakaway province of Georgia. Whatever their motives, the Adzharian government and other sponsors of the company, comprising 250 performers between the ages of six and sixteen, invested A$150,000 in the dream of a children's opera.

If a dream can become reality, the reverse also holds true. The odd aria still coursing through my mind shields me from all thought of the real world as the taxi drops me back at Nika's pension. On the stroke of midnight I press the buzzer, the gate swings open and Nika's niece, looking more pallid than usual, whispers, 'Have you heard what has happened in America?'

DAY 135 (12 SEPTEMBER): TBILISI

Nika appears on the balcony, her grey hair Electra-wild. 'This is the end of the world!' she exclaims, hands flailing. I tune into the BBC on shortwave while her niece fetches a black-and-white TV from the first floor. An incredulous onlooker is describing the fall of someone from the 104th storey of the World Trade Center, but already the 'live' report is taped history. The images I see, when the old set sparks into life—including the one of that airliner banking round to register its fatal impact on the temporarily spared twin tower—are spectral, like those long-ago images of Neil Armstrong planting white boots in moondust. These images, too, appear to come from another world: certainly not the one we have lived in until now. The times have lurched us forward, or maybe backwards, and it occurs to me that— even if Nika was being more hysterical than historical—the crevasse between yesterday and today is so jagged that those seven words she uttered may prove to be right.

This is the day my distant fellow-men have come to know fire, and the 'sword', at least in the form of the box-cutter. My heart goes out to the victims, and not just the dead. Being caught in the crosshairs of history is something I can identify with – even if the analogy is imperfect (I, at least, am alive to tell the tale). Their lives were cut short in an apocalyptic second; my own trauma extended over months.

The acute and eternal pain inflicted on those hundreds of thousands of Americans related to those who perished, or who knew them as workmates, church-goers—mosque-goers, come to that—reminds me that behind the gruesome pictures and war-size banner headlines lies a deeply disturbing fact: for these people, the world has gone mad.

Weltschmerz engulfs us all today but, while others gaze on scenes from Dante's Inferno for hours on end, I spy the madness through a keyhole. A world gone mad is something I have comprehended since 1990, because that's when mine did. Madness is being disconnected from everything you expect. One thing in my life—but nothing in my lifetime—was as unexpected and horrible as this. I sleep, but fitfully.

Pre-dawn TV, BBC for breakfast, more Fukuyama pronouncements from Nika. The need to travel—to escape the 21st century, to grasp something permanent in a river swollen with flotsam—bears down on me. By a quirk of historical timing, my original plan to visit the town of Mtskheta, Georgia's spiritual centre, now seems far-sighted.

Only the religious trinket-sellers outside the cathedral compound detract from the timeless peace of Georgia's Westminster Abbey. Past the sadly solitary bronze bell lying on the ground, I enter the vast dark interior of the church between age-weathered sandstone pillars. If Catholic rites seem dramatic to one raised amid bare-bones Protestantism, Orthodox churches can only be described as melodramatic. Priests clad in all-black soutanes glide noiselessly to and fro, lighting candles which glow mesmerically in the gloom but do nothing to lessen the sepulchral atmosphere of the great vault.

Even with the silent tread of a wheelchair tyre, I alter course to avoid trampling on the grave of an elder of the church, or the tombstone of a king.

A stocky woman wearing a coloured headscarf rhythmically sweeps the slate floors and marble-topped resting places of the great and glorious. At the far end of the nave I can make out the fresco of a haloed Christ. A single speck of sunlight strikes the open palm, for all the world like his own votive candle held out as a timely peace offering to the 'real world'.

In the afternoon I am back in Tbilisi, wading through a deluge of shell-shocked emails at a suburban Internet café, when I turn to the cubicle behind me and see a big strong man blubbering like a baby. 'Are you all right?' I ask, foolishly in the circumstances. He is an American, a law student on an exchange of some type. The details escape me; his shock is with me still.

DAY 137 (14 SEPTEMBER): TBILISI

This evening is spent in a bar frequented by expatriates, a rendezvous arranged before September 11 with the couple who gave me the lift from Azerbaijan. Now, with quite a knot of Americans among the clientele, the Friday-night get-together has the air of a wake. The TVs, which would normally be screening sports matches, are tuned to the memorial service from Washington. The sound is off, but pictures convey all the essential information: Bush speaking to the mortified crowd, the flag at half mast, Billy Graham at public prayer. To break up the sombreness, we get—instead of ad breaks—incessant replays of those grisly, now eternal, moments of impact.

DAY 138 (15 SEPTEMBER): TBILISI

For the first time I consider the impact on my own plans. Do I carry on regardless? Should I wait and see how things develop? An email arrives from a Canadian friend living in the Philippines. 'GO HOME, KEN!' it screams. That's one option I dismiss out of hand. As my travel plans don't include New York, where's the danger? Reason counsels me to note down the trend of events, and take my cue from that. Intuition isn't so sure.

DAY 139 (16 SEPTEMBER): GORI

After 70 rollicking kilometres, the morning train from Tbilisi judders to a stop in front of the station entrance in this ancient town, now best known as the birthplace of one of the biggest mass murderers of the 20th century, Josef Stalin. A large oil portrait of the original Man of Steel keeps guard over the entrance.

Well over half those of working age in Gori today are unemployed. A group of louche youths with swastikas tattooed on their forearms hang about outside the museum dedicated to Josef Vissarionovich Dzhugashvili, workers' hero. His childhood home is a humble log cabin. The clear impression is that young Joe learnt early on how to get by without the necessities of life, an attitude he would strive diligently to pass on to the masses in later years.

This man, or monster, arguably influenced more lives in the 20th century than any other, keeping in mind his mass deportations of whole nationalities as much as his purges and diabolical pact with

Hitler. So it is fitting that the Stalin Museum, erected in 1957, is a 'palace' on a grandiose scale. Today the museum is officially closed but a security guard opens it up in return for a vodka-money bribe and somehow summons Larissa, the English-speaking guide, from only he knows where.

I take five minutes to haul myself up the grand marble staircase while the guard carries my empty chair to the first floor with cavalier inexpertise. Here, restored to my perch, I see the life of Stalin unfold through several memorial halls. The most remarkable exhibit of all is Larissa's unshakable belief in her hero as 'the most popular figure of the 20th century'.

'But what,' I confront her, 'about the 60 million people who met a violent end during his quarter century in power?'

Larissa will have none of it: 'He is pictured as a very cruel man in films but he was not a harsh man. He was a very plain, ordinary and modest person, and used to listen to people.'

DAY 141 (18 SEPTEMBER): KOBULETI

I have taken a bus to the Black Sea, which means I have now crossed the Caucasus from sea to shining sea in just under a month.

Here at Kobuleti I have planned a two-week halt to work out the following five months' itinerary. For the next fortnight I will map out the route ahead, country by country, choosing in what order to visit them, where I will need to seek visas, where not. But now there is no way to know what lies around the corner: pleasant and stimulating times, a jihad or a fifth Crusade that will imperil the life of any Westerner who sets foot—or wheel—on the Arabian Peninsula.

On calmer reflection, the best course becomes clear: wait to see where the Americans, or their enemies, strike. If the Middle East is too dangerous to contemplate, switch the original order and go to Eastern Europe first. Perhaps after a few months the Middle East will have stabilised and the way will be open to make it the last leg of the voyage.

DAY 142 (19 SEPTEMBER): KOBULETI

Dining tonight at a corner table on a pavement outside a local restaurant, the soup course is interrupted by a car ramming the pillar a metre in front of me and threatening either to come crashing into the table or explode. The driver keeps revving the engine until smoke pours out of the cabin, forcing him to eject while there is time to do so. Waiters hover, warily, but before they can usher me away to a less exposed table the driver—a wild-eyed man in a ragged wine-drenched shirt—rushes into the restaurant and starts yelling incoherently. The waiters disappear, replaced by the apologetic owner offering a word of explanation: '*Morphinisti*', which I assume means 'drug addict': Kobuleti is clearly not quite the backwater I'd imagined it to be.

ARMENIA: 3–23 OCTOBER

DAY 156 (3 OCTOBER): VANADZOR

At the Armenian border a Georgian immigration officer, spotting that I had spent exactly one month in his country on a 30-day visa, muttered something about 'overstay'. His mental calculator could almost be heard clicking over and dollar signs gleamed in the reflection of his stare. But, after ten seconds of suspense even he had to concede the truth in the old rhyme: 'Thirty days hath September …' I will say this for him: he managed a gracious chuckle while bestowing my exit stamp.

The most gripping thing about Vanadzor is that everyone, it seems, wants to leave it. On the main street a large crowd of grim faces mills outside the police station day after day. I am told they are there to pay bribery money for the next step in the emigration process that will take them, they all hope, to one of the promised lands: France, the US, and I suppose Australia.

The only guesthouse that can accommodate me is a real find: family-run, its elderly owners ply me with tea and homemade cake. This is my introduction to Armenian hospitality, and after a whole night of undisturbed sleep I am in for a hearty breakfast and a welcome surprise: the grandparents run a bakery out the back that makes my first morning in Armenia the sweetest-smelling of the entire journey. I head for the bus station laden with fresh gifts.

DAY 157 (4 OCTOBER): VANADZOR TO DILIJAN

A fellow passenger on the bus strikes up a conversation. His English is of the barest minimum but persistent, and eventually I make out that he is asking where I will be staying in Dilijan.

As I can never be 100 per cent sure in advance, my vagueness encourages him. Pointing to his chest, and then to me, he says, 'Home!'

How can I say no? While it will be very embarrassing all round if it turns out I cannot use the toilet—we are in the sticks of western Asia so I don't even know if it is a Western-style fixture—neither of us has enough language in common for me to broach the matter diplomatically. So, I accept.

My new friend Samuel, it emerges, is one of the bus drivers on this line, but today he is returning home as a passenger. I needn't have worried about creature comforts, as I discover soon after our arrival in the ex-mountain resort of Dilijan. Samuel, Susan, Fruzik, Alva, Mane, Marie and Samson are an extended family. From the first hour when I am respectfully left to rest in the hammock on their porch to the moment four days later when I catch a Yerevan-bound *marshrutka* (minibus) at Tsakhadzor, these are days that travellers live for, to write home about and recollect years later.

Four days is long enough to meet the cousin who teaches English and comes for what I would call dinner, if the richest banquet ever laid before a non-head of state can merit such a mundane description. It is also long enough to discover that the Saruhanyan family own four cows (one of them kept in the garage, exposing Samuel's car to the elements) and that, from their bountiful milk supply, the grandmother of this extended family, Alva, makes the world's best, tangiest cheese. Scoured into tongue-tempting kiss-curls, it goes with the creamiest of butter on the most enticing of bread rolls.

The Saruhanyans may live a long way from the big smoke but they are as clued up as anyone in New York or Sydney. The TV is tuned into Moscow these nights and they glance at it sidelong from the dinner table, as if Frankenstein's monster has taken up residence in the living room. Once their thoughts are translated, I know they await the outbreak of hostilities in Afghanistan any day now. They are quiet Christians, and the invasion of their land by Muslims—Arabs and later Persians—is unforgettable folk memory.

DAY 158 (5 OCTOBER): LAKE SEVAN

Samuel drives me an hour across verdant valleys—we're still following the Silk Road thousands of kilometres west of Uzbekistan—when suddenly, as if viewed over the rim of a silver goblet, the blue-green waters of one of the world's highest lakes take the breath away.

We skirt the shore south-east to Noraduz, a stunning lakeside cemetery of ancient, medieval and modern stone crosses. Known as *kachkars*, these highly decorated crucifixes are uniquely Armenian works of art. In one instance, several *kachkars* line the walls of a tomb vault reminiscent of a small house, complete with its own doorway. Writing with a stick in the sand, Samuel indicates it is a thousand years old.

DAY 160 (7 OCTOBER): YEREVAN

Down a winding mountain our marshrutka snakes its way towards Yerevan, Armenia's ancient and modern capital.

I'm in luck finding a room at the Hotel Erebuni, smack in the centre of town. The hotel faces onto Republic Square; and backs onto a car park that doubles as the pick-up point for buses to what may still be my next destination, Iran. The manager interrupts a meeting to greet me personally and offers me a complimentary bottle (not a glass, mind you) of cognac, the country's most famous product (not counting emigrants). The message is coming through loud and clear: Armenian hospitality never fails.

I remember to ask for a room with a view of Mount Ararat and, once inside, lie down on the bed for a quick rest. Two hours later I lift my head from the pillow and begin unpacking my bags. After a modest drop of the smooth liqueur, I tune in to cable TV. 'This is CNN.' The 'war on terror' has entered a new phase. Bombs are dropping on Kabul. The campaign to oust the Taliban, and hunt down Osama bin Laden, has begun. Propped up by pillows, I sit transfixed till midnight.

DAY 166 (13 OCTOBER): YEREVAN

This must be the Year of Big Numbers. Two weeks ago the Pope was here (even though this is not a Catholic country) to celebrate the 1700th anniversary of Christianity in Armenia, and today is Yerevan's 2783rd birthday. This makes it (as everyone here is proud to tell you) the world's oldest capital city, beating Rome by 29 years.

I join the party, as mass dancers in Republic Square go through a sort of mazurka that should serve Yerevan well if it ever hosts the Olympics. Women in coloured fezzes trailing silver veils either side of their face step out opposite men in gaudy vests and matching pants who resemble nothing so much as a mass meeting of toreadors. Bagpipes supply a sinuous quasi-Oriental accompaniment. Did the Armenians invent bagpipes? Quite possibly. Nearly every other country in the world seems to have done so.

DAY 167 (14 OCTOBER): YEREVAN
I hate to bring up personal details but I woke up this morning with a red-raw patch on my right buttock. I hope the salve from my medical kit will be enough to remove the welt along with the discomfort.

DAY 169 (16 OCTOBER): YEREVAN
Having paid more than the usual attention to my posterior, I am sure that the rawness and soreness result from long hours sitting in minibuses and trains where the constant movement abrades the skin. I've always shied away from fancy and expensive cushions, preferring a simple square of foam rubber, but now that's worn down and I'm going the same way.

DAY 170 (17 OCTOBER): YEREVAN
With the Afghanistan campaign continuing, little time is left to put off the decision where to go from here. To Europe via Turkey is not quite as straightforward as it looks on a map, since eastern Turkey is still considered a no-go zone for travellers because of the 'Kurdish problem'. However, I could retrace my steps to Batumi, Georgia, and follow the Black Sea coast to Trabzon, and so on to Istanbul, thence to Eastern Europe.

Option two is to continue undaunted, treating the cries of 'Danger!' as no more than the natural concern of friends overinfluenced by the media. But, deep down, I know that to treat the Middle East from now on as the same place it was before September 11 would amount to self-deception. More than that, it would ignore my own history, which ought to tell me that when this region is sizzling with uncertainty I cannot sail through it unaffected.

Six or seven hours a day of CNN, with its constant coverage of the military offensive in Afghanistan, is not conducive to the calm atmosphere I need to make this momentous decision, and these past few days I can feel my sense of composure about the journey slipping away. So today I keep the TV turned off, rationing myself to one news bulletin in the morning and one in the evening. I must know what is happening but not be unduly alarmed.

DAY 171 (18 OCTOBER): YEREVAN

The first fruits of my calm approach come with a dawning realisation that the fallacy in my friends' urgings to come home, or at least stay away from the Middle East, lies in considering the whole region as equally dangerous.

How often I used to wish, when travelling in Africa, that people back home would distinguish between that continent's many cultures and see how being in Johannesburg was nothing like being in Lagos. Now it is I who have been failing to respect the diversity of the Middle East. By using my brain, and analysing each country in turn, I should steer clear of those where the risk of civil strife or something worse appears too great.

DAY 172 (19 OCTOBER): YEREVAN

After confiding my irritating health problem with delicacy and discretion to a long-term European resident here, I visit a clinic the expatriate population swears by. The doctor, a Muscovite whose nurse translates from Russian into English, recommends a special cream— and staying off my bum as much as possible.

With a list of Armenian terms for 'gauze', 'sticking plaster' and other items my first-aid kit ought to have had in abundance, I visit a puzzled pharmacist who equips me for a self-administered recovery.

DAY 173 (20 OCTOBER): YEREVAN

D-for-decision day.

In the West, people not only lump different Middle Eastern countries together—oh, they're all Arabs, they'll often say or at least think (although Iranians aren't)—they sometimes make the mistake of assuming that all Muslims think alike. As the first country I will cross is Iran, and Iran has a poisonous hatred of the Taliban (who torched the Iranian Embassy in Kabul, burning Iranian diplomats alive, no less), I am very sure Tehran will happily stand by and watch the Americans pound Kabul day and night until the Taliban are ousted, and only later turn overtly against Washington.

So I will proceed, cautiously, through Iran. And if the country drifts into hostilities with the US I will catch a flight from Tehran to Istanbul, and follow the East European route. This gives me until the second week of November to build flexibility into my plan.

After looking at the rest of the Middle East I discard only two destinations, and put a question mark over a third.

Yemen has recently succumbed to a spate of kidnappings (well, for the past 1500 years actually, but with special attention to Western targets this year) so it's off the menu.

Even though my guidebook says Iraqi visas can be issued to groups of five or more, I really don't think four other people mad enough to consider going there are likely to turn up: besides, its immediate future in Bush's 'war on terror' appears decidedly wobbly.

In Israel, suicide bombings are not an everyday reality, but the security situation will bear closer watching six months down the track, when I would be heading there. I feel mightily relieved to have this decision behind me.

DAY 174 (21 OCTOBER): YEREVAN

A visitor to Armenia can no more ignore than convey the horror of the genocide Turkey carried out against the Armenians living there at the very time the Gallipoli campaign brought this part of the world to the forefront of Australians' minds.

In 1915 (it is reliably estimated and only Turks themselves seem to be in denial) some 1.5 million Armenians were systematically massacred.

On a promontory just outside Yerevan sits the Genocide Memorial, preserve of concrete and basalt, clipped lawns and memories of a kind and scale far too horrific to grasp.

Pillars surrounding the Eternal Flame are separated by gaps wide enough to allow an outsider to take in the view but narrow enough not to disturb those laying flowers around the flame itself.

Just 25 days ago, a more famous traveller left a message in the garden. His sentiments, dated 26 September 2001, are freshly chiselled on a modest plaque:

O Lord, How the sons and daughters of this land have suffered, and grant Armenia your blessing.

FROM POPE JOHN PAUL II

DAY 175 (22 OCTOBER): YEREVAN

I now spend most of the night and hours by day lying on my side, like a Buddha-in-training. The abrasion is lessening. It hurts now only when I sit down. This is more than a bit of a problem when you've thousands of kilometres to go in a wheelchair, but the recumbent-Buddha posture is not practical in a crowded bus.

On this my last afternoon at the Hotel Erebuni, putting the woes of the world and my buttocks behind me, I sit in the cafeteria and sketch out in longhand an article for the *Age* travel pages.

It's a healthy diversion from doom and gloom to write a light-hearted piece about menu bloopers I've encountered these past few months. The most intriguing one was an item designated 'the cooked language of cattle'. It took me some minutes to puzzle out that this was probably a restaurateur's best stab at translating 'braised ox tongue'.

DAY 176 (23 OCTOBER): YEREVAN

At 8 am, right on time, our luxury coach pulls out of the Erebuni car park bound for Tehran. I'm getting off in the northern city of Tabriz. An hour out of Yerevan, the snow-mantled magnificence of Mount Ararat—on Turkish territory now but once part of Armenia—draws the passenger's gaze as irresistibly as a magnet. Soon afterwards we take a road branching off to the left, the beginning of a detour that will add hundreds of kilometres to the journey but one made unavoidable by the 'realities on the ground' after the Nagorno-Karabakh war of the early 1990s. The old bus route is no longer followed, the conductor and relief driver tells me cheerfully, because it's landmined. (And here am I reassuring people about how safe the Middle East is: if only they knew!)

Twice in the late afternoon our route takes us across the international border into Azerbaijan – for three minutes on the first occasion, four on the second. The driver assures us this bus does the trip three times a week and no one ever shoots at it. Travelling with optimists makes a huge difference to one's mood.

We reach the lonely border post of Meghri about 8.30 pm. In theory, the Christian Armenian West should bid me a fond farewell while the Islamic Republic of Iran—which has played hardest to get of all the visa-issuing countries on this entire journey—should treat me as a decadent Western infidel. Yet again, travel confounds expectations, with the Armenian officials playing hardball.

They appear to be angling for a bribe in exchange for an exit stamp in my passport. The Iranians, may Allah bless their souls, greet me like a long-lost brother. We are on the south bank of the Araks River, now inside the Islamic Republic. It will be five or six hours before any of us can lay our heads on a pillow in Tabriz, but I already feel as if I've arrived somewhere suspiciously like home.

Chapter 12

THE MUSLIM HEARTLANDS

*When one of the caliph's ministers was invited to Persia he refused
on the ground that he would need four hundred camels to carry
all his books.*

PETER MANSFIELD THE ARABS

OCTOBER-DECEMBER 2001

IRAN: 23 OCTOBER–10 DECEMBER

Having no choice but to live out of a suitcase—how else to carry the
urological gear that makes up a paraplegic's portable survival kit?—I
made a virtue of necessity and packed it even fuller with 27 books
before leaving home. Finding someone willing to lug it 100 or 200
metres from train station to taxi, or taxi to hotel is not an insuperable
problem, although at times I felt it would have made more sense to
travel with my own caravan. But in this part of the world camels are
expensive.

The Persians founded a civilisation in the true sense: a culture based
on city life. Persepolis pointed the way, and 2500 years later the city of
Isfahan still proudly calls itself 'half the world' (*nagsh-e-jahan*), an
instance of civic hubris that dwarfs even the Big Apple.

Whereas desert Arabs were, by and large, ascetic deniers of the 'good
life', keeping their gaze fixed on Paradise in the hereafter, Persians even
in ancient times were known for letting their hair down. The ancient
Greek historian Herodotus wrote about the Persians of his day:

If an important decision is to be made, they discuss the question when they are drunk, and the following day the master of the house … submits their decision for reconsideration when they are sober. If they still approve it, it is adopted; if not, it is abandoned. Conversely, any decision they make when they are sober is reconsidered afterwards when they are drunk.

The Persian genius is for artistic expression and theological speculation, but you would be wrong to assume they are a stern-visaged people after the fashion of Ayatollah Khomeini: the sense of humour here can be rich and sharp as a minaret. An Iranian I met in a Tehran museum told me of his experience in Williamsburg, Virginia, when he was the only non-American in a tour group being shown around the 18th-century colonial town. Noting that our friend was the only member of the group not asking questions, the guide approached him afterwards and said, 'Aren't you impressed with our fabulous culture?' Pausing to collect breath, the Iranian replied, 'It's very interesting, but my fruit-and-vegetable vendor back home has more culture in his cauliflowers than you have in this whole town.'

These people are mentally lively, historically aware and no cogs in anybody's Axis of Evil, whatever certain other fundamentalists would have you think.

Geography dictated that Iran—the only non-Arab country in this part of the world, apart from its mortal enemy, Israel—would be my first port of call in the Middle East. But the fact that Persians are not Arab was enough to focus my mind on what Islam had contributed to the world and whether they were a backward, dysfunctional branch of the human family, as you would believe from much of the West's media coverage, or just members of the human race, one and genetically indivisible, about whom we are remarkably ignorant (because for various reasons their minds and motives are a puzzle to us, as ours are to them).

At the time, when I was weighing up whether to heed my friends' warnings to abort this part of the journey, or at least put it on hold, I was convinced that—entering the region less than three months after the terror attacks on New York and Washington—my timing couldn't have been worse.

How Arab Muslims viewed September 11 and its consequences was obviously going to be a matter of some importance to me. One thing I could be sure of when travelling through their world in the closing months of 2001 and the beginning of 2002 was that Riyadh and Muscat, not to mention Dubai, were unlikely to be overrun by tourists. Even if they were, strict Muslims would probably find their view of Westerners as hedonists and materialists confirmed rather than confounded.

It helped to have a respect for Arabs and their contributions to global culture. It was Islam, in these lands, that kept the flame of ancient Greek learning alive throughout Europe's Dark Ages, and transmitted paper and gunpowder from China to Europe. Their artistic genius flowered in calligraphy and music: the oud, ancestor of the lute, is an Arab invention.

But these are superficial signs of a people's greatness: its essence resides in aspects of character that cannot be seen with any eye but that of sympathetic imagination. To exercise that imagination is to take a broader view of the race, and with no people can this perspective be more useful than the oft-maligned Arabs.

Islam was spread by the sword, it is true, and many of us in so-called Christian countries (forgetful of how Christianity was spread) regard the Muslim creed as barbaric for that reason. But I cannot think of a creed in whose name blood has not been shed, and Islam lays down a strong ethical foundation enjoining hospitality, charity and a colour-blind humanitarianism nobody can deny.

The first discovery awaiting the happy wanderer is that, contrary to what fearful friends back home may be thinking, the Muslim millions don't go to work every day armed with scimitars, the better to hack down infidels who cross their path. There are 'holy warriors' (I would soon meet one in Qatar) and indeed madmen with knives (ditto Syria) but they are a minority. No one was waiting to kill me, although more than a few were eager to convert me. But, wherever I went, most Muslims regarded me first and foremost as a human being, and respected the differences between us.

Anthrax may come and sarin may go, but politicians are constantly infecting the thought supply with such historically reckless statements as George W. Bush's declaration of a 'crusade' against militant Islam.

(That the first three or four Crusades were not a string of brilliant successes ought to have deterred any historically aware Western leader from mounting his steed and charging into a 'war on terror'.) Fortunately, Bahrainis and others in the region with whom I discussed this statement tended to regard Bush as a danger not because of his rhetorical excesses but because of the historical ignorance they revealed.

DAY 177 (24 OCTOBER): TABRIZ

A chill is in the air at 3.30 am as our bus pulls into Tabriz. A taxidriver overcharges by a factor of five to take me and my small baggage mountain 400 metres to the modest Ark Hotel. But it's too late and I am too tired to argue. There is also the fact that he has no English and I no Farsi, so he drives off before I can go through the usual argy-bargy.

Somehow I find a nightwatchman not actually asleep who shrugs helplessly but courteously unlocks the door. His shrug makes perfect sense when I see that all the rooms are up a narrow spiral staircase. I sprawl out on an armchair in the dimly lit foyer like a mannequin left overnight in a department store. Morning will rouse me to life.

DAY 178 (25 OCTOBER): TABRIZ

Tonight I kill two birds with one stone. After installing myself in Room 304 of a more habitable hotel, the Azarbaijan, I take local advice and search out a crowded coffee shop on Ferdosi Street, just off the city's main avenue, predictably named Imam Khomeini. Here two passions will be on display in a country often thought of as repressed. One is what the Egyptians call a hubble-bubble, the Indians a hookah—a water pipe, for the smoking of *shisha*, which Westerners always assume to be marijuana and Iranians (not to mention Gulf Arabs) always diffidently assure them is something far less thrilling, like apple shavings. The 'high' is definitely in the head, but whether it's physical or mental no one cares to speculate after a couple of satisfying draughts.

The other passion is soccer. Tonight Iran play the Emirates in a Dubai qualifying match for next year's World Cup. Through thick smoke I can make out an Iranian goal as it catches the inside corner of the net, and a split-second later the coffee shop erupts with the roar of 200 (all-male) voices in full-throated battle cry.

DAY 179 (26 OCTOBER): TABRIZ

Here is the Shi'ite Muslim equivalent of a mission statement, from a framed poster in the first-floor conference room of my hotel. Under the arresting title 'In the Name of God', it declares:

> As long as a tourist is in an Islamic country, the Islamic government is responsible to guarantee his safety and comfort. If a tourist in an Islamic country loses his properties, the government should support and provide him with the lost property.
>
> IMAM ALI (PEACE BE UPON HIM).

In this corner of Iran, seeing another tourist is something of an event in itself. So, over breakfast at my hotel, I fall naturally into conversation with a young English family who are also staying there. Later, on our way to the medieval brick-tiled bazaar that is the glory of this former Iranian capital, Rebecca Hathaway impulsively asks whether I would like to stay with her family when I get to Tehran. After months of hotels and guesthouses, the offer comes like manna from heaven. I arrange to ring her when my bus gets in on Sunday night.

This afternoon I cannot shrug off the suspicion that some intruder to my room (it can only have been someone sanctioned by the hotel authorities) has spirited off two or three film rolls. Should I take management up on the God-given replacement guarantee? I think better of it.

When I comment on the harum-scarum quality of the local driving—notorious even by Iranian standards—Pouria Taghavi, a Tabrizi assisting a travel agent with whom I hope to do business, tells me, 'It is easy to get a driving licence in Iran.' 'What do you have to do?' I ask. Taghavi replies with just the hint of a smile, 'Park the car.'

DAY 180 (27 OCTOBER): TABRIZ TO TAKHT-E SULEIMAN

Salve alone does not bring salvation: my gluteus maximus is now red-raw, and this morning the skin over my right buttock breaks open. Even a medical ignoramus like myself knows that I am suffering what the nurses warned me so fearfully about in the hospital spinal-injuries ward ten long years ago: a pressure sore. As the day wears on, my backside wears off and it dawns on me that what was so recently just an irritation now poses an inevitable check to my travel plans. If the skin is broken, so must my journey be.

En route I show the driver my guidebook, with its sketches of Iranian leaders. Ayatollah Khomeini elicits a tight grimace; President Mohammad Khatami an approving nod; but when he sees the 'hated' Shah he pulls the book from my hands (at some cost to his steering control) and kisses it. This is how you have a political conversation with someone who doesn't speak your language.

Dusk is gathering as we arrive at the entrance to Takht-e Suleiman (the Throne of Solomon), an archaeologist's Paradise on Earth. Here the rubble of four mighty epochs is scattered across remote rural slopes, a ruined palace here, a ramshackle temple there. The taxidriver urges me away, bemoaning the lateness of the hour and anxious to renegotiate the agreed price even as we roam around the site.

DAY 181 (28 OCTOBER): TAKAB TO TEHRAN

I cause a near-riot in the bus park at Takab. This is a town so remote that the sight of a wheelchair, let alone one whose occupant is determined to board a bus, is so alarming the police are called. Only with great difficulty and after thorough examination of my passport are they persuaded that I have the right to be on this planet. Even then, I suspect, their decision to let me go is made in the interests of public safety rather than because I have a ticket. This is the only place so far where I have become an object of hostility, but then I have a long way to go.

Into Zanjan province we ride, through a pelting downpour that brings the first rainbow of the journey, and as darkness falls we squelch our way through the suburbs of Tehran, city of 12 million, the appreciation of whose splendours must wait on sleep. Hopelessly lost after a taxi ride from the bus station to the city centre, I phone Rebecca Hathaway, who patiently rides to the rescue, and by mid-evening I am out of the rain, into the welcoming surrounds of a comfortable home in the suburbs.

DAY 183 (30 OCTOBER): TEHRAN

It is embarrassing, but I have to tell my hosts—who, I am sure, were expecting to put me up for just a few days—that my arrival has coincided with something of a medical emergency. All my travel plans

89

are in limbo until this skin rupture heals.

Rebecca—who, after just a few months in Tehran, is well connected to the expatriate community—calls in a Dutch doctor, Jorik, whose career history tending elderly patients in the Netherlands makes his prognosis less than reassuring. 'You must stay off the affected area, rest on your side for hours a day. This must be for weeks until we see how you improve—but in my experience once the skin is broken this will always be a problem for you.'

Suddenly I want to hear more about his current work with Afghan refugees.

My worn-down square of foam rubber has now been replaced by a round inflated tube resembling a large orange Life Saver. Sitting on it minimises pressure on the buttocks but I cannot imagine travelling like this. Still, I am under doctor's orders and there is no alternative: the journey must be put on hold.

DAY 184 (31 OCTOBER): TEHRAN

Hallowe'en in Tehran. After spending most of the day lying sideways on my bed staring alternately at a book and the bare wall, I balance myself on my orange tube and accompany the Hathaways—oilman Tom, Rebecca and their two sons—to the Hallowe'en party at the British School. As I wander around the schoolgrounds, carefully avoiding pumpkin-headed kids playing dead beside makeshift crosses, I meet some longer-term residents of Tehran. One of them, the wife of a Canadian diplomat, gives me better advice than I am to receive from the much-too-knowledgeable but under-analytical officials at my own embassy. 'You should realise,' she bends down to tell me, 'that if you go on to the Gulf states in the current climate the odds of anything calamitous happening to you have just risen from one in a million to one in a hundred thousand. How do you feel about that?'

WHAT WOULD HAVE BEEN DAY 185 (1 NOVEMBER) TEHRAN

To go, or not to go? I see now that the international and internal situations—or, in plain language, al-Qa'eda, Afghanistan and my bum—have made the decision for me.

I recognise that, although al-Qa'eda has warned Westerners not to set foot on the Arabian Peninsula, *jihadis* are unlikely to waste bullets or bombs on a lone itinerant when they could be out perpetrating massacres. I make a mental note to keep out of tall buildings and away from large groups of Western party-goers around New Year.

DAY 185 (13 NOVEMBER): TEHRAN

My gel-filled cushion, a superior solution to the orange tube, has arrived by courier service from Melbourne, and with Jorik's all-clear, accompanied by a less gloomy pronouncement on my health prospects, I resume the journey where I left off almost a fortnight ago.

Regional flights are so cheap in Iran I decide to break my surface-travel rule and fly to Isfahan a week from today. Tehran has plenty of sights to disclose, which two weeks on a bed has deprived me of seeing. This is catch-up time.

Two decades ago, the kidnapping of 52 Americans inside their own embassy became the longest-running news story of my life. To Americans it was an outrage; to Ayatollah Khomeini and his fervent followers it was a fitting humiliation inflicted on a neocolonial tiger trapped in his own lair.

From 4 November, the anniversary of the 1979 embassy takeover, until tomorrow, a commemorative exhibition is being mounted under the grandiose title '13th Aban Great Exhibition, Shattering of the Glassy Palace' (13th Aban being the equivalent of 4 November by the Persian solar calendar).

The Great Exhibition comprises 20 smaller exhibitions, each filling a single room of this squat red-brick building that looks like a high school but is, in fact, the old US Embassy itself, now re-branded the Den of Espionage. The 'glassy palace' derives from a ceiling-high glass cube in which a diorama shows William Sullivan, the last US ambassador to Iran, talking to two unidentified 'spies'. According to my tour guide, Reza, 'the glassy room for top-secret negotiations' was a bug-free retreat for these parasitic enemies of the host state. A 1970s telephone switchboard, telex machines and cipher equipment, now primary exhibits in the Eavesdropping Room, are similar reminders of the Americans' sinister intent.

From one point of view, all embassies are spy dens, so there is something comically melodramatic in making an exhibit of a typewriter, perhaps the very one allegedly used to falsify staff identity documents.

Behind the embassy building sit the rotor and metallic spine of the helicopter that crash-landed in central Iran in April 1980, dooming a mission to rescue the hostages and, many analysts believe, Jimmy Carter's presidency along with it.

DAY 186 (14 NOVEMBER): TEHRAN

This afternoon I visit Vanak Shopping Mall, a slice of the West. In a city where the whole side wall of a 20-storey building is covered with an eye-riveting mural of the Stars and Stripes being dive-bombed by torpedoes under the banner 'DOWN WITH THE USA', this is a haven. Here, a coffee shop attracts a cross-section of Iran's rising generation, who pay just enough attention to their malted milkshakes to avoid spilling any on their American-style youthwear.

Today there is a buzz of excitement as a woman in her early twenties spreads the word that females of her acquaintance are going to risk a beating with police truncheons by daring to sit in the men-only grandstand at Azari Stadium for tomorrow night's soccer qualifier against Ireland.

Although the chador is common on the streets of this bustling metropolis, conversations during my stay have revealed a clear division of opinion between those women who welcome it for shielding them from unwanted male advances and those—generally younger, in their teens or early twenties—who spurn it as a symbol of conformity and repression. Even those women who reject the chador are careful to dress in clothes that do not show too much flesh; and a colourful, raffishly worn hejab provides an excellent sartorial substitute for any woman who dares show her face.

DAY 188 (16 NOVEMBER): TEHRAN

Every holy Friday, when the weekday market shuts its doors, people with leisure and shopping money throng the Juma Bazaar, an underground car park crammed from end to end with everything you could imagine being bought or sold, and that includes kitchen sinks. Gold and silverware, 78 rpm records, embossed Korans, chessboards, spices from the East, TVs from the West: here is a cornucopia too rich and varied to take in at a glance.

Needless to say, this visual feast is more than matched by the assault on your eardrums. So, when I emerge from a tight knot of people crowded around a space at the far end of the cavernous room, even the sight of a tall merchant smiling agreeably, as if expecting me, takes a startled moment to register.

'Hello,' the lips move, but surely the words cannot be addressed to me, 'I'm Osama bin Laden.'

My eyes confirm his claim but, at a rare loss for words, I dip my right hand into my backpack and, after frantically rummaging through its jumbled contents, produce my camera.

'Uh, may I take your photograph?' I ask. Osama beams his approval. 'I mean, you know, George W., $1 million he will give me for this'— and then, on a sudden inspiration, I mime the sign for a half, striking one hand across the knuckles of the other like a karate blow—'half for me, and half for you.'

Osama's smile is now a broad grin, and I prepare to get my official photographic proof of what is either a significant victory in the war on terror or an imposture to dine out on for years to come.

By now, Tehrani shoppers are in on the joke, and hamming it up themselves. One stout matron who speaks English cups a hand over her face, eyes bulging with mock fright as she says to me in a stage whisper, 'Do you know who that is?'

'Yes, it's Osama bin Laden, he told me so,' I reply, to general laughter.

'But,' she adds, 'do you know who is the old man behind him with the grey beard?'

I haven't had time to give that one much thought. Seeing that Osama is selling a fine array of Persian and Afghan carpets, and assuming it to be a family business, I blurt out, 'His father?'

'No,' she lowers her voice—but by now the flow of shoppers has stalled and 50 pairs of ears are hanging on her final chilling disclosure— 'that's Mullah Omar!'

Just yesterday, I surmised to someone that the world's most famous caveman appeared to have just two options apart from staying to get himself martyred by the Americans. One was to escape to Pakistan, the other to head for Iran. I deemed the latter more likely because, although the Iranians and Taliban were deadly enemies, going to Pakistan while it was acting as a staunch ally of the Americans would probably seem like courting the greater of two evil fates.

DAY 189 (17 NOVEMBER): TEHRAN

Rebecca Hathaway has intrigued me with talk of another 'Shell wife', a Dutchwoman who has completed a gruelling trek overland from Damascus with a team of camels. I must meet her, was my response. Today is the day.

Lilianne Donders was born Dutch but has long looked upon herself as a Bedouin. A self-described nomad, she is both a mover and a Sheikha, having been honoured with that courtesy title by the al-Janabah tribe in the Sultanate of Oman.

Her solid European-style mansion in Tehran's plush northern suburbs lurks behind a steep flight of stairs so, this warm autumn day, we sit outside in her garden. Those who know her better inform me that the interior décor is dominated by a camel motif: camels in the carpets, camels on the walls. I can easily credit it—a pair of silver earrings, miniature ships of the desert, do not go unnoticed.

Donders has actually undertaken *two* camel treks. The one everyone talks about, though, traversed 1600 kilometres on foot and cloven hoof. The middle part was done by truck—'they're desert camels, they couldn't cross the mountains'—but the successful expedition amounts to a triumph of the will nevertheless.

Her acceptance by the Bedouin (under the tribal name of Laila) had been public knowledge for years when I worked in Oman in the late 1980s, but she was also known as a well-connected businesswoman. Her Muscat boutique bristled with Bedouin bowls, baskets, bric-a-brac and carpets, giving hundreds of Bedouin women a toehold in the cash economy.

In 1999, when a London specialist diagnosed her with a malignant breast tumour, Donders—far from cancelling plans to make the trek—christened her endeavour the Caravan for Cancer.

Others in Tehran's expatriate community tend to describe her as an eccentric. Ask why she loves camels, and the response sums up her character to perfection, 'They go their own way. Camels will never follow someone else's track. That says everything about me.'

DAY 193 (21 NOVEMBER): ISFAHAN

The sublime and breathtaking beauty of Iranian art is largely due to the strict interpretation of Islam's taboo on any depiction of the human form as a blasphemy against Allah, who alone has power to create, change and destroy his creatures' features.

That prohibition has resulted in such a concentration on the aesthetic possibilities of non-figurative art that calligraphy and abstract geometric design have long flowered in these climes. Indeed, they have reached such a pitch of intricate perfection that they bedazzle the onlooker.

Imam Khomeini Square, formerly Nagsh-e-Jahan Square, is the largest in the world after Beijing's Tiananmen. Five hundred metres long and 200 across, what is technically a quadrangle rather than a square is best navigated at clip-clop pace in a horse-drawn buggy.

At the 'city' or Mecca end of the quadrangle, we pause in front of the Masjed-e Emam (Mosque of the Imam). Before 1979 it was—surprise, surprise—Masjed-e Shah.

Yesterday evening, with another Melburnian met at a small but Internet-equipped hotel around the corner from mine, I defied the attempt of a gate guard to keep us out (simply because the ticket office had decided to close early). We took a chance on clambering through the 30-metre-high portal, and even the guard, though incandescent with rage at our audacity, respected the sanctuary by not pursuing us into its interior for an unseemly showdown.

Thus undisturbed, we found a vaulted hall deep within the mosque and, as I sat next to him, my friend stomped on black paving stones (as recommended by one and all), producing seven distinct echoes. When the seventh had died away, utter tranquillity reigned once more.

DAY 195 (23 NOVEMBER): ISFAHAN

It's Friday morning and Imam Khomeini Square fills with what must be an assembly numbering in the tens of thousands. Today marks a special commemoration, as the loudspeakers broadcasting a sermon from the great mosque make clear even to a non-Farsi speaker by constant repetition of the term 'basiji Isfahani'. The basiji—lest we forget—were Iran's child soldiers, twelve years old when sent into battle during the war against Iraq in the 1980s.

In conversations with even quite open-minded Iranians about this, I have found that whenever I question the dispatch of thousands of children to certain death I risk being thought a blasphemer. If that is how a detached intellectual reacts, I am going to keep my trap firmly shut today, having no desire to court an attack by a frenzied relative of one of the fallen.

In the afternoon I visit Golestan-e Shohada, the Rose Garden of the Martyrs. Located on Isfahan's outskirts, here are thousands upon thousands of extensively inscribed tombs. This is the closest I can come to absorbing the enormity of that eight-year war in which a million people perished. Each tomb is watched over by a photograph, except those where presumably none could be obtained. In most of these cases, Ayatollah Khomeini or Supreme Leader Ali Khamenei takes his place. More occasionally still, a portrayal of the Twelfth Imam of the Shias, Ali, superintends the grave.

An old man sits on the end of a shiny slab intoning verses from the Koran; a middle-aged woman mumbles in grief from behind a corner of her chador; a worker applies paint to whiten the loving inscriptions chiselled on another tomb. On yet another memorial to yet another life cut short, the family themselves rub the stone with water, the great reviver.

It is early evening and I am back in Isfahan. The city is justly famous for its bridges—there must be as many as in London or Prague—but one glorious example, the Bridge of 33 Arches (Pol-e Si-O-Se), outshines them all. After dark, its illuminated span sets off the Zayande River like a giant necklace. The arches are used to roof teahouses, where shisha is smoked and the herbal brew consumed in style.

Under one arch my Melburnian friend and I are welcomed like long-lost relatives to a table of young Isfahanis eager to hear about the outside world, of which the Internet has given them an enticing view. Grateful for a chance to speak English and show their goodwill, they contrive to pay for everything before we—who can far more easily afford to—have a chance.

DAY 196 (24 NOVEMBER): ISFAHAN
I couldn't help noticing that Iran's mobile-phone numbers carry the prefix 0911. What would the White House make of this?

DAY 198 (26 NOVEMBER): KASHAN
This craft centre and oasis on the edge of the Great Salt Desert has seen

conquerors come and go for two and a half thousand years. Today, though, it offers antique charm as a counterweight to monumental Isfahan.

In the afternoon I visit the Fin Garden. Its chief delight is the *qanat* (canal) runnels that crisscross it. The gentle flow of water reticulated on a grid pattern combines ancient know-how with a sense of beauty seldom equalled by the designers of Western fountains.

This evening I hear on the BBC that George Bush has called for a crusade to defend civilisation. Let him at least come here first, I tell myself, so they can get acquainted.

DAY 199 (27 NOVEMBER): ISFAHAN TO AHWAZ
On arrival in this town, a mere 50 kilometres from southern Iraq, the BBC informs me Bush has demanded Iraq re-admit weapons inspectors and Baghdad has refused. I watch and listen to learn whether this presages the use of Kuwait as a launchpad for military strikes against Iraq. It is disturbing that, this close to leaving Iran, I cannot be certain whether at the last minute Kuwait must be dropped from my itinerary.

DAY 200 (28 NOVEMBER): CHOGHA ZAMBIL
Having negotiated a round-trip taxi to Chogha Zambil, site of a ziggurat from the 13th century before Christ, my excitement is palpable. Built by the Elamite civilisation, it lay buried beneath the sands until an oil explorer rediscovered it in 1935.

Karim, my driver, must attend to practical matters first. Before leaving Ahwaz, he requires a police permit. Whether this is because of general security worries, or because he's an Arab and the Persians have always liked to make them feel small and inferior, I have no way of knowing.

We pass still-flaring fires from the oilfields first developed by the British almost a century ago but that's almost postmodern compared to our UNESCO-listed destination where reconstruction of the great ziggurat is proceeding under a hot desert sun. This man-made mountain was the pinnacle of a royal capital, a city complete with shrines to its chief gods and goddesses.

Next to the ziggurat we linger by a sundial, which has been telling the time for over 3000 years. Iraq is just over the horizon, and the year might as well be 640 BC, when Chogha Zambil was flattened by the Assyrians.

DAY 203 (1 DECEMBER): YAZD

Tonight I am reintroduced to Ali Heidari, a Yazdi I met in a Tehran museum. It turns out that Ali lives a good way out of town, so he has arranged for me to stay the night with a friend of his, whom I will call Musavi, and his family. Dinner is typically overgenerous—I stopped counting the courses at seven, but the pick of them was *eshkangh*, a rich stew-like soup—and it is all I can do not to demand the immediate presence of Musavi's wife, who never puts in an appearance and whose name I never learn. Ali conveys my gratitude to her through Musavi, but says this is the traditional way and I mustn't embarrass my host.

After dinner, Musavi shocks me with an offer. 'He says, "Would you like to smoke opium?"' Ali tells me a second time. My life passes before my eyes. In Australia I would no sooner try hard drugs than walk. But, hey, I've survived 47 years without opium and, if the gods smile on me, I may last another without a second invitation. 'Why not?' I say through a forced smile.

Five minutes later, a friend of the friend of my friend knocks on the front door, and Musavi and he lug a silver brazier into the living room. They begin heating the substance they will later tamp into the bowl of an outsize bong worthy of an American Indian peace parley. I ask no questions: this is Islamic Iran. I exhale a cloud of smoke long and slowly from my nostrils, pass the pipe and wait for the 'high'. But not until the bong has circled its way round a second time does it hit me— a mild but pleasantly delirious concussion as if I had been tapped between the eyebrows with a rubber-topped mallet.

DAY 204 (2 DECEMBER): SHIRAZ

In this southern city of grape fame, I learnt this afternoon that George Harrison had died. Apparently it was common knowledge in the West that he had terminal cancer but, not knowing this, my immediate reaction was that my informant was perpetrating a sick joke. Komeil Noofeli, a lively tourist guide in his mid-twenties, found out about it only because a 50-year-old woman from northern England—a tourist with whom, improbably enough, he has fallen head over heels in love—emailed him.

Noofeli, whom I frankly sought out for curiosity value after reading in my guidebook that he spoke Australian, is happy to show me over Persepolis in the morning. We seal the arrangement with a handshake. 'It will be bonzer, won't it?' he beams.

DAY 205 (3 DECEMBER): PERSEPOLIS
Komeil, who doesn't drive, has chartered a taxi for the half-day round trip to Persepolis. This is where the glory that was Persia began, with the construction before 500 BC of its summer capital.

You do need to bring a vivid imagination along to furnish and finish the ruins, as robbers have made off with much of what time hasn't eroded. But with bas-reliefs of kings and courtiers, sturdy granite columns and beckoning doorways, as well as still expressive sculpted horses' heads, there is enough material left to do the trick.

DAY 210 (8 DECEMBER): BUSHEHR
Partly because I've come this far but mainly because Bush's battle with Saddam is in the war-of-words phase, I recommit myself to visiting Kuwait.

Valfajre Shipping Co. confirms that its regular ferry service to the emirate will leave on Monday afternoon. A fax of my hotel booking is accepted as a substitute for a Kuwaiti visa (to be issued on arrival), and my return to the Arab world (Saddam and Bush permitting) should now be smooth sailing.

KUWAIT: 11–17 DECEMBER

DAY 213 (11 DECEMBER): KUWAIT CITY
Boarding yesterday was at 3 pm. Our ferry, which normally plies to the mouth of the Gulf but has been diverted to the Kuwait run, roared to life two and a half hours later, and pushed Iran away from us like the remains of a dinner that had left us feeling overfull.

We left directly after the *Iftar* meal: this is Ramadan, so not only must we fast by day—a good discipline, and one I followed in Iran too—but we must break our fast as soon as the sun has set. As the crossing to Kuwait should take eighteen hours, I was fully ready to continue fasting if there were no accessible toilets, but while waiting on board I checked out the 'facilities' and saw my fears on that score were unfounded.

Farouq Shah, the officer in charge of saloon passengers, is open-faced, a master of delightfully quirky English, and quite willing to speak his mind once out of land's view. He solemnly predicted that within five years there would be a 'small revolution' in Iran, seemingly unaware what an oxymoron that really is. What I think he meant is that trying to apply an overcoat of Islam to the surface of Iran's sense of self and culture—which is older, and believes itself superior—is, like any job of painting, one that will never be a complete success. In time it peels away.

The tension between pure Iran and pure Islam has its humorous side. Under a revolutionary edict, parents must give their children Islamic names, not Iranian ones. 'The man [official] says to me, "You cannot name your son Kourosh (Cyrus),"' Farouq told me. '"You must name him Mohammad or Ali." I say, "Mohammad is a nice name, but not for my son."'

Speaking of names, I remarked that our ship was Iran-Hormuz 24. 'Why don't you call her something like Queen of the Gulf?' I asked. 'We wanted to do something like that,' Farouq replied. 'But since the revolution we cannot make our ships have interesting names. So the managers decided that because all these ships go from Iran to Hormuz they would use numbers to make them different. Not so interesting, but different.'

We dock right on time—and then lose two hours at Customs. Not through meanness or hostility, I hasten to add. Kuwaitis are happy to see Western visitors (there are all too few of us), but somehow the visa-validating papers from my official host, the Hotel Carlton, have not arrived.

Phone calls are made, I must be patient. Everyone's baggage is being opened and searched in a vast concrete bunker, and tempers flare as there is no airconditioning. Eventually, a driver from the Carlton arrives to collect me.

Upon arrival I am comforted by the old-fashioned formality of the sign over reception, 'The hotel policy is to give satisfaction in every way and upon this the manager's endeavours are concentrated.' Late at night, men pass eagerly down the corridor with women clearly not their wives, bringing fresh meaning to this missionary statement.

But by day, on the streets, sex is blacked out. Full-length chadors, even the *burqa*—with that beak-like face shroud associated with Afghanistan under the Taliban—give immediate notice that Islamic rectitude is fiercer here than in, say, Tehran.

DAY 215 (13 DECEMBER): KUWAIT CITY

The National Assembly—designed by Joern Utzon—architect of the Sydney Opera House—is set in parklike grounds and it was only luck that the guard wandered off just before my arrival, enabling me to roll unhindered past the flowerbeds to an excellent vantage point about 50 metres off to one side of the building.

But these same guards must be given full marks for athletic prowess and devotion to duty. This one bounds across the lawn, quivering with affronted dignity, and hollers in my face, 'Stop!' followed by a string of Arabic words whose meaning leaps all language barriers. When he covers my camera lens with his hand, I roll away to get a clear sighting. Clearly I am up to no good: he clamps one palm over the lens again, while radioing for assistance with his free hand.

Eventually, his superior arrives and, after a quick inspection of my backpack and with extreme reluctance, allows me to take one photo of the empty but strategically situated building.

Kuwait City certainly boasts the most sumptuous shopping malls I have seen anywhere: the brand spanking new al-Sharq mall is strictly for those who have shopped until they dropped and gone to heaven. (But, during the 2003 invasion of Iraq, Scud missiles fired by Saddam's troops will narrowly miss the kilometre-long shopping centre, a reminder that luxury attracts the demon of envy.)

The West has always had a stereotypical view of Arabs. Contemplating a tour of the Arab world immediately after September 11, I wondered how much had changed in the way *we* viewed *them* and, more important from my point of view, how differently *they* now regarded *us*. Kuwait would provide my first clue.

Desert Storm was fought to right a wrong, to declare once and for all that the invasion of a sovereign state 'must not stand' (George Bush senior's words). As the war clouds gathered prior to the liberation of occupied Kuwait, Bush senior also spoke—it seems improbable now, but he did—of bringing democracy to the emirate. Western democracy, with its multi-party elections, would have been a second blow to Kuwaiti traditional society. Kuwait is an absolute monarchy. Three times in its modern history—in 1976, 1986 and 1999—the Emir has dissolved parliament, although you could hardly argue that the people's representatives had been dismissed, because women couldn't vote. The ruler's consultative councils had merely advisory powers.

But you couldn't deny that Kuwait had democratic institutions of a kind, even if parliament wasn't one of them. The *diwaniya* (or 'sitting circle', from the Turkish *divan*, whence we get the English 'divan') is where men regularly gather to chat about anything from football to politics. It's the Kuwaiti equivalent of a pub. A pub with no beer, certainly, but one with those water pipes that make life such a heady pleasure from Morocco to Oman. That, and good strong coffee (arabica, of course).

Tonight I push out to the old city *souq*, where a high-ceilinged market building is now occupied by neat boutiques opening onto an inner courtyard. This is filled by, yes, divans, where gentlemen of leisure sit clad in white robes, on their heads the distinctive Kuwaiti quoit-like rope circlet. Ever-obliging waiters hover discreetly, filling coffee orders and refilling hubble-bubbles. Here, everyone has an opinion and no one is afraid to voice it.

Mordi, a journalist in the foreign-media monitoring division at Kuwait TV, says, 'The Americans helped us [in 1991], we are grateful for that. But we know since then they do it for money. For Americans and Europeans, everything is money.

'America only is like this' (he rubs two fingers together) 'with Israel, and in Srebrenica [Bosnia] more people died than in New York [on September 11] and nobody does anything.'

Mordi likes Americans for their openness but distinguishes between the people and Washington. 'The [US] government wants to control everything everywhere, it doesn't respect the traditions of other peoples.'

DAY 216 (14 DECEMBER): FAILAKA ISLAND

Today is the fourth straight day on which it has rained. Rain is so rare in Kuwait no one will believe this. The newspaper says this is the heaviest December fall since 1934. Through a soft drizzle I wheel through a ghost town, on this island in Kuwait Bay which I have reached after an hour's ferry crossing from the city.

This was the scene of some of the worst pillaging by the Iraqi invaders during their eight-month occupation in 1990–91, during which they trashed the town and torched the museum.

The whole town is a museum now, and the ex-museum is part of it.

Back on the mainland I see a man wearing a red-and-white chequered kaffiyeh, a Saudi with a gap-toothed grin and a falcon on his wrist. I am told he has been appointed Chief Falconer by Sheikh Hamid, the Deputy Prime Minister, and his bird is from the Rolls-Royce of breeding grounds, Failaka.

This afternoon I visit Kuwait's Grand Mosque, surely without peer in the Gulf. The more I travel, the more I appreciate these spiritual retreats, where the eye instinctively looks up in awe.

DAY 217 (15 DECEMBER): OUT OF KUWAIT CITY

Thirty kilometres west of the capital, I ask the taxidriver to stop. I offer him the camera, and say 'al-Khaleej', pointing to a light-blue horizontal trickle that tapers to a tip about 500 metres in front of our eyes. Pointing the camera at it, he snaps. I'm satisfied. 'The end of al-Khaleej,' I exult. This is as far as the Gulf goes. From here, due west, lie land, and sand, all the way to the Suez Canal.

In 1920, the year my father was born, Kuwait was invaded by its larger neighbour. No, not Iraq. Back then, it was the newly emerging nation of Saudi Arabia that violated what was not formally a nation but a Turkish domain under British protection. British troops turned a decisive battle against the Saudis here at al-Jahra. The Red Fort (or Red Palace) was the prize. Comprising 33 rooms, six halls and two diwaniyas, as well as stables for the cavalry's mounts, it also—as the official brochure breathlessly informs the visitor—has a gate 'used as a woman exit and called the secret door'.

Back in the capital, Kuwait Towers attracts long queues of people, mostly families, buying tickets for the observation deck. I will never know whom to thank, but the ticket-seller waves me through, insisting my admission has already been paid for.

Having been up towers from Sydney to Tashkent, it would sound jaded to say there is nothing special about the view from here. But it is, to tell the truth, a familiar fairyland of bright lights, albeit glorified by a full moon rising. What is different, it strikes me, is the thought that must be inspired in a Kuwaiti surveying the scene, namely, 'This is all we have.' As virtually the whole of this small country beyond what lies below us is sand, Kuwait Towers gives viewers an opportunity usually vouchsafed only to astronauts: to take in a country at a glance. Look at it that way, and you can understand the passionate will to defend the home, the uneasy readiness to make allies of alien Western powers, and the never-diminishing throng of Kuwaitis longing to scale this landmark.

DAY 219 (17 DECEMBER): BACK TO BAHRAIN

Packing, in my room at the Carlton Hotel, I catch a BBC bulletin that includes the following priceless line: 'New York is usually a mecca for Christmas shoppers.'

The dream was to take a passenger ship halfway down the Gulf to Bahrain, but no such service operates, and I have been warned that cargo-ship owners in these edgy times will be wary as hell about taking me on board. So flying is the only way into Bahrain. In the departure lounge at Kuwait International Airport I fidget, unable to concentrate on my magazine, but by the time we are airborne the rites of passage—safety demo, food service, temperature and time announcements from the captain—have steadied me.

It is 11 minutes after the 11th hour when the plane taxis to a stop at Bahrain—and 11 years since everything came to a head for me in this teardrop-shaped island state. Other passengers rise to their feet, haul their hand luggage from the overhead lockers and proceed to the front. Let them go forward. My papers are in order but I will be entering the tunnel marked 'past'. For me, Bahrain must always be different. 1990 made it so.

Chapter 13

FALLING FROM THE EDGE

His thoughts, more incoherent, dragged him more unmercifully after them—as if a wretch, condemned to such expiation, were drawn at the heels of wild horses. No oblivion, and no rest.

CHARLES DICKENS, CHAPTER LV *DOMBEY AND SON*

AUGUST 1990-MARCH 1991

Contrary to conventional wisdom, one of the great lessons of our new age, typified by the 'war on terror', has to be that there is no great security in numbers. It is a lesson that should be taken to heart from September 11. A terrorist attack on civilians is likely to kill the huddled masses and leave the loner unscathed. This is not a reason to stay home; it's yet another reason not to entertain exaggerated fears about your fate when setting forth into unknown lands.

But if the 'war on terror' is being waged in your head and nerves, as mine was in 1990–91, being alone can develop into a definite disadvantage. Sullen, unwholesome brooding drives away the world and alienates you from your best allies, your friends. As one who lost that battle, I know that now.

I was 36 when this crisis struck. Elsewhere it might have happened sooner or, more likely, years later. Undoubtedly, though, the collapse of confidence that spun me out of control in Bahrain was triggered by a real-world event, the invasion of Kuwait. This rolled the first boulders down my mental mountainside and, once that process had begun, it precipitated a landslide that was scarcely perceptible at first but gathered unstoppable force as it went.

One other factor primed me for disaster. It had been my good luck earlier in life to suffer no great calamities, apart from the setbacks and challenges that are our common lot. Sheltered from the first, and from the worst, I lacked all prior acquaintance with what a nervous breakdown entails.

The battle was entirely mental and, after what happened to me in Bahrain, my defences were down. My enemies ranged themselves in dispersed formations, ready to attack from unexpected angles. As the months dragged on I would come to know them intimately, from fighting at close quarters.

But all that lay ahead of me the day I was released from the Bahrain Psychiatric Hospital and flew away from the Gulf bound for Hong Kong. I was confident I had escaped the worst and planned to rest and recuperate before collecting my scattered wits. The lithium carried deep in my bags was secreted where I could find it if I had to, but I had made a silent resolution to throw away the pharmacological crutch and stride away from my demons.

When the plane touched down in Hong Kong at the end of that horrible month of August, I would have described my nerves as frazzled rather than shot.

Little time was wasted in getting from Kai Tak airport to the Hong Kong Island terminus for ferries to Lantau. Two hours after touchdown I was in a taxi skirting the coast of that delightful outer island in the South China Sea. It had been six years since I'd stayed there but memory is a remarkable thing and, after taking one wrong turn-off, my mental route map directed me unerringly to the Cheung Sha restaurant-hotel.

Fronting the sandy beach of a picturesque cove, the Cheung Sha was one of those inns where you're instantly put at your ease, no matter the absence of any language in common. So, returning to the restaurant-hotel held no fears for me, and indeed promised an easing of those that had so unsettled my recent life. The plump, squat grandmother who ruled the roost there received a hearty hug and her ascetic, ever-smiling husband an equally hearty handshake. That they remembered me at all, given that we had 'known' one another for just a few days back in 1984, was gratifying. Grandma showed her remembrance with a simple homespun gesture, placing a basket of fresh apples on the table outside my door. All in all, I couldn't imagine a more likely place in which to regain my equilibrium, and this thought dominated all others that first evening as I sat overlooking the beach and listening to the timeless reassurance of the soughing waves.

Fatigued from a potent mix of the long air journey and jet lag coming on top of my recent ordeal, I drew deep sighs and looked forward to a long and restful night. The first hint that healing would be neither swift nor steady came when, with every reason to sleep through and greet the new day refreshed, I lapsed into two or three hours of troubled unconsciousness, only to awaken just after 9.30 pm. I remained awake until dawn.

What to do? Whatever I was reading at the time would have been in my backpack, beside the bed, but so great was my weariness that I couldn't even summon the concentration necessary for that pursuit. What could require less effort than that? Watching TV. There was one at the end of the bed. I reached over and turned it on. Delighted at first to discover that, even in this remote part of a remote island, satellite TV was available, I tuned in to CNN. Now there was no dozing off. The news was the same here as it had been in the psychiatric hospital, all talk of human shields, the rape of Kuwait, the gathering of a coalition determined to confront Saddam and, if necessary, retake his vanquished neighbour by force. In the fullness of time, this would come to be known as Operation Desert Storm.

Delight soon turned to fascination. That I couldn't avert my eyes, or staunch the stream of disturbing information, was understandable enough in someone who had been a self-confessed news junkie since childhood. But, to one newly arrived from the danger zone where the talons of fear had gripped him with fierce intensity, the continued infusion of alarming scenarios both thrilling and chilling could not help but make my waking hours—of which there were many more to come—ones of high anxiety.

Of a morning I would head downstairs to that quiet table by the beach, and try to concentrate on a book over my breakfast noodles. But the shockwaves proved as remorseless as the more visible tide. One morning I noticed my hand was trembling like that of an old man. Any dexterity I had achieved with Chinese eating utensils was immediately lost (although anyone looking in my direction would probably have mistaken me for just another Westerner unable to master chopstick technique).

Reading the same sentence in a book ten times over without taking any of it in, I soon abandoned the effort to lift my mind out of its rut that way. In other circumstances Cheung Sha is an ideal place to chase away your cares, but this time I found them hounding me. A daily walk, up along the coast road skirting the sea and back, perhaps 8 kilometres in all, certainly beguiled the hours, but then the night closed in.

Having attained a promising level of physical exhaustion, I would return to my room and turn on the TV. My inability to screen out the horrors for very long, day or night, ensured I was continually confronted by the cataclysm that had befallen my life.

Although sensing myself at the sharp end of this change, other people's perspective on those times reminds me that, objectively speaking, there was a seismic shift in the world order between mid-1990 and the end of the year. The invasion of Kuwait, with its accompanying and calculated spike in the price of oil, triggered the worst recession of the late 20th century. The 1980s wave of confidence dumped all who surfed it with a concussive thud on the desolate beach of a new decade. For many, this new world disorder fed people's worst forebodings. Having always been cursed with a lively imagination, I was a prime candidate for dislocation in a time of worldwide uncertainty.

Prior hopes that this would be a week of recuperation, even triggering a resurgence of confidence and mental agility that would prime me to turn that last leg of the flight ticket round and spend more time in England, faltered at the hurdle of every new day. The hopes had been founded on the fact that the last place I had been gainfully employed and happy in, before personal disaster struck, was England. Now, towards the end of the week in which these hopes fled, I concluded that the mental effort required to turn my life round once more was beyond me. I would go home to Australia instead.

My body was in a quiet holiday retreat, but my mind was all over the place: mostly accusing me of cowardice, of personal failure. As the week drew on, I was frightened at the prospect of reconnecting with family and friends, all six years older than when we last saw one another. Fear lobbed taunts at my febrile brain: *Will they see I've fallen apart? Will they think I've been hiding this lassitude and mental confusion for years? Will I end up in another psychiatric ward, drugged or—even worse this time—given electroconvulsive shock therapy?* Pummelling me like a bare-knuckle boxer being slugged by his opponent, each question was a well-aimed blow.

Unless there are events on the mental horizon that open up some prospect of achievement, or even good luck coming our way, there is no basis for hope. As an old proverb has it, humans can live three months without food, three weeks without fluids and three minutes without hope.

Hope and fear contended yet again, as I mentally previewed my return to Australia. Far from the way I had ever envisaged this odyssey ending, I saw my aspirations turned to ashes. In the mirror of my mind I gazed on myself and beheld a failure. Not only out of touch with Australians after such a long absence, but remote from the attitudes of even my own family, I was a poor prospect for reintegration into society.

On 5 September 1990 I set foot on Australian soil for the first time in a little over six years. The first night I spent with my younger brother and his wife, and this was as good a homecoming as I could have dreamt of, in the circumstances, since a few years earlier they had bought the home we grew up in. Yet that night I lay wide awake, attributing my sleeplessness to jet lag and the excitement of being home. What I couldn't explain so easily was the loud thumping of my heart, and the cold sweat on my chest.

This was a long way from the Middle East and, as if I needed reminding, back in a place where the concerns of the great world, however momentous, were kept in proper proportion. Switching on the radio next morning, I shook my head in amazement at the news bulletin leading with the latest on a footballer's strained ligament and only then turning to Saddam's human shields.

Later that day my parents greeted me with the effusive demonstrations of welcome any prodigal son might reasonably expect. Living on a large block in semi-rural Corinella, down on Western Port Bay, they did everything but kill the fatted calf. But behind my brave face was an overstrained mind contorted by carefully camouflaged private dread:

They mustn't see how I really feel. Can they or can't they? Who can tell? Who can I tell? I can't impose this terror on them. Terror is contagious. This is driving me mad. It'll drive them mad. I've got to stay long enough to let them know everything's all right, but not long enough for them to see it's not.

My interior world was evicting reality, closing the window of my perceptions while opening the front door to chilly blasts of fear. I was losing hope, with no structure to cling to. My closest friend from childhood, to whom I could have disclosed everything, had drifted apart from me during my long absence. I would sometimes find myself on the freeway passing the turn-off to his family's home, but I resolved not to visit, thinking that in my current state of mind I would be sparing him the burden of seeing me as I now knew myself to be: a mental and emotional wreck. This foolish thinking was based on a desire to be self-denying, to appear (to myself) more heroic than I truly was.

In retrospect I regard the self-denial, being too hard on myself, as one of the cankers eating away at my very instinct for self-preservation. I should have given myself a holiday. Physically arrived home, I was still trapped in the tentacles of trauma, unable to escape without assistance. As the brief bursts of euphoria at being back in my homeland subsided, I soon found myself thinking that the longer I spent by the bay the more surely my mental vegetation would become apparent to that small family circle around me. The restlessness that had fired me with so much positive energy that I had ranged far and wide across the world for most of the 1980s was about to drive me from home after a mere matter of weeks.

Fortunately my severance pay from Bahrain, and accumulated savings from previous work, had left me with enough money to tide me over a few more months. But getting that sum from the bank in Bahrain to the nearest Commonwealth Bank branch, in Wonthaggi, required an effort that seemed to me a gargantuan drain on my overworked mental resources. No doubt the paperwork was normal for one who, long absent from the country, had to establish a credit rating when that was not a straightforward process—but moving a mountain might have felt easier.

This all took time, and time was something I had far too much of. It dragged; it weighed me down; my feeling of failure was now compounded by one of uselessness. My uncle and aunt visited me; I visited my brothers. Sometime in early October, sensing my uncontrollable restlessness (now I can see that's why he made the suggestion), Dad proposed a car trip all the way up to my great aunt's, on the Darling River in Wentworth. She, too, must have noticed my unsettled state but, as someone who had taken me in when I 'went bush' as a youth, Auntie Ivy had a bluff acceptance of who I was. She did her best to reassure me that, at least somewhere in the world, all was well and normal. What she couldn't know was that, by now, my cast of mind was keenly attuned to any signs of abnormality or negativity. If she mentioned that her neighbour had been taken ill, or had been the victim of a robbery, my mind added that to all the great disasters of the day, until the whole world appeared to be painted a dark and threatening hue.

My parents lived opposite a bowls club, a sort of divine dispensation granted to Dad, who could combine sport and socialising. Dad took me over one day and, although not likely to be converted to his enthusiasm for the game, I spent some time in the bar chatting to these people who knew him. I remember a 90-year-old bowler sitting in the corner nursing a beer. One of the regulars told me the old geezer had been diagnosed with cancer and how everyone admired him for pitching up. Instead of being inspired by this intelligence, it merely reminded me how everything, and everyone, was on a one-way road to decay.

Despite what many will see as a clear-cut case of depression (though to this day I think the term itself simplistic, disguising more than it explains), I did put up a fight for my sanity. I forget how, but I managed to get a ticket to the football Grand Final which, being Australian Rules in Melbourne, was akin to unearthing the Holy Grail. Because of a draw during the finals, that year's match was being played a week later than usual—on the first Saturday in October—and offered Collingwood their best chance to break a 32-year hoodoo. That they did so, turning the tables on Essendon in a memorable display of power and grit, enabled me to participate vicariously in scenes of jubilation and excitement. It was an important attempt to reconnect with the society from which I had cut myself adrift.

That September and first half of October in Melbourne I spent meeting family and friends I hadn't seen for years. From what I can recollect, they seemed to marvel at the adventures I'd undergone which, since I scrupulously avoided concentrating on the recent collapse of hope, I was happy to let them do. I regaled them with dramatic tales from other years of my time away—close scrapes and bureaucratic battles in my African, Russian and Chinese travels. For many of those friends with whom I'd kept in contact only by the occasional letter, those experiences were as fresh as if they had occurred a week, rather than years, ago.

On the whole, and with such meetings to look forward to, my mental terrain began to develop recognisable contours. In the mornings I would meander through the valley of purposelessness. The afternoon would be marked by something to 'make the day', be it a meal or a reunion with someone from my old life. The evening might reconnect me with the news (that unfolding televisual horrorworld from which I couldn't find the will to escape); and then the long, unsleeping night would set in.

Dwelling on thoughts that revolve around the same mental track, of course, offers no release. You cannot escape from your thoughts, as the saying goes. My metabolism was a broken-down system feeding off itself: no refreshing nutrients were in prospect. The greatest achievement in the world is to be able to sit still, but the person to whom I had been reduced simply couldn't. The world had turned on me; now I was destroying the world, mistrusting all that was good, exaggerating all that was bad.

As masters of terror tactics from the KGB to the US military at Guantanamo have known, sleep deprivation is the royal road to madness. If you're not already unbalanced at the outset, you will be headed that way before 48 sleepless hours have passed.

My insomnia-induced stupor translated into an inability to carry even the simplest plan into being. Vacillating, increasingly in two minds, I found myself ringing at the last minute to announce I wouldn't be able to keep an appointment noted down in the diary days before. Often, as the weeks wore on, my legs felt like dead weights, and my formerly obedient body grew lethargic, as if magically transferred to a planet with three times Earth's gravitational pull.

The growing gulf between what I would do and did do further reduced my already battered self-image. Unwilling to impose too much of myself on people ranging from old workmates to casual acquaintances, I decided to travel interstate, seeking fresh vistas and the odd reunion with old friends there, too. So I headed north by train, to Sydney, staying with a good friend, a journalist with whom I'd worked closely in years gone by. He lived in the inner suburb of Glebe, in bachelor digs, but was a captive of romance and in fact not far off getting married.

Most of the time there, I was too scared of my own mental disarray to speak of what had happened. We went to the local pub, we watched TV, I heard him say—with the forced casualness of a mate—that it had finally struck him, this was the love of his life. But I held back, a tightly coiled spring, from revealing any of my own, quite different, disturbances. The imbalance between confidences shared and confidences withheld created a strain between us, at least from my perspective. This was the first time a thought occurred to me that would recur with increasing intensity over the next few months: *Whatever I say, no one can ever know what's happened to me, and even someone who did understand it all couldn't repair whatever has broken down within.*

After a couple of days in Sydney I resumed my northward journey. Having been away from home so long, and finding no calm there now (though there was no calm within me wherever I went), I remembered a couple met years before, with whom I had kept up intermittent contact during my time abroad.

Despair was edging closer to me and, the more desperate I became about my own future, the more 'confessional' I grew in my exchanges, feeling that the more of my sorry self I talked about, the more people who knew me might hit upon a solution to my inner woe. And those good friends in northern New South Wales were especially creative in helping me battle my demons.

His name was T—, hers D—, and they lived in Mullumbimby, near the heartland of the counter-culture, Nimbin. Although not dedicated followers of that or any other fashion, they were open to various ways of combating the one thing that was driving me mad (or, should I say, keeping me mad): the inability to get any sleep.

D— knew something about aromatherapy, and introduced me to a variety of fragrances that certainly packed a power of soothing. One Saturday we three went to a local agricultural show, and had a fine time sniffing the flowers. But, come the night, I still couldn't sleep. They both suggested warm milk before bed, which is a very pleasant drink. But not a wink.

T— introduced me to his parents and siblings, who made me feel as if I were an integral part of the family. For hours of an afternoon I soaked up the sunshine, reclining on a deckchair until the plastic straps left red marks on my bare back, reading most of the time, willing myself to feel better. Evening came on. The sun disappeared. It was back to T— and D—'s. We talked until 10: I retired to the front room they had generously let me use. And there I lay awake, staring at the ceiling, until at long last the sun returned.

D— was equally indefatigable in seeking out treatments. One I recollect was a greenish jelly known as Japanese magma. The effect, if I have this right, was supposed to be invigoration of the spirits. And I must have felt better for a time. But when that old lassitude returned, as it inevitably did, my fears would resurface and I would try to tackle them one by one.

A new terror sprang up in me: *Why am I not well? What can be done about it?* No one had the answer. No matter how outgoing and understanding anyone was, I felt the need to stop burdening them by my useless and downcast presence. Shortly afterwards, I moved for a few days to a rambling rural house, not far from Mullumbimby, owned by one of their relatives.

Those few days reminded me that even those families that appear the best adjusted have their own dramas. In my frenzied imagination, every little disagreement I overheard (and there weren't all that many, but spend a few hours around anyone's hearth and the family dynamics will reverberate clearly enough) was magnified into a divisive force that would set everyone against each other in the end. On the fourth day I made my excuses, returned to my good friends T—and D—, announced it was time I headed back to Melbourne, and consulted the departure times for buses heading south.

Now came November. I tried to fill up the pointless hours by seeing my hometown as if for the first time or, it would sometimes strike me, for the last. Voraciously I kept injecting the latest news of peril far away into my system direct via newspapers, radio and TV. The inability I felt to relate the enormity of what had happened to me in that frightening place was making me extremely tense and snappy. The need to avoid company was heightening my madness, yet I became acutely aware that understanding my predicament would not necessarily mean I, or anyone, could resolve it.

About this time came the first media reports of people returning from the Middle East with what was being diagnosed as post-traumatic stress syndrome. *That's me, I thought. That's exactly the label the psychiatric nurse in Bahrain gave me.* But again the afterthought: *They can name it but they cannot cure it.*

In East Melbourne, having found a nice anonymous psychiatric practice listed in the *Yellow Pages*, I made an appointment. The stakes couldn't have been higher: my sanity was on the line.

The appointment was for half an hour, maybe an hour, but in my compulsion to blurt out everything that had happened in the previous few months the awareness dawned that the sympathetic face of this health-care professional concealed an absolute inability to plumb the depths of my condition. Furthermore, if I told him everything with the full force of feeling welling up within me, it would sound like a tale told by a madman. I couldn't stand the thought of being committed to a clinic for the mentally ill where everyone who mattered to me would be visiting, or having my stress factored into the complex equations of their own lives. So I pulled my punches, kept my information general without being bland, and spared this busy professional the impression that the person sitting in front of him was desperately deranged.

Anti-depressants were prescribed. Another appointment was booked. I threw away the script—which makes more sense when you've already lost the plot—and never went back.

If I did energise myself with long walks, soon enough—and especially lying down at night—I would feel a tingling sensation in my extremities, way beyond numbness, that would remind me to breathe slowly. I believed that if I could control my breathing with deliberation my general anxiety level would drop. I also told myself that hyperventilation and tension in my limbs—sometimes my hands would become 'locked' like an arthritis sufferer's—could be precursors of a heart attack. Some nights I heard my heart skip a beat, and always felt a mild surprise when it kicked back into its normal rhythm.

Fright by night, skulking about the city like a cockroach by day: this was no way to live. I had plenty of time but was running out of meaningful things to fill it with. As November drew to a close, I recalled that the last time I had been happy was a year before, in England. Working in London as tumultuous events unfolded had been one of the most productive times of my life.

From old associates in Melbourne I knew that newspaper journalists were going through hard times. But in London not only were there several Fleet Street papers where I had contacts and was well regarded, I also knew the head of Reuters news agency's European division, Graham Stewart. No doubt it was optimistic to believe that a change of scene was all I required, but at home, where Treasurer Paul Keating had just announced the 'recession Australia had to have', all was gloom and doom. Going back to where I was before everything went sour seemed the best thing to do, and gave me the one thing I most needed. Hope.

That winter in London was as unlike the previous year's as anything I could imagine. On the Strand, where in 1989 a few beggars were to be seen, old tramps had been joined by young drug addicts, all with makeshift shelters constructed from cardboard boxes, huddling in doorways for shelter from the cold. Across the Thames, in front of Waterloo Station, the same phenomenon was writ so large the space had been christened Cardboard City.

Saddam's onslaught had triggered a global downturn that mirrored my personal downturn—two dark parallel lines without any foreseeable end. On the opposite side of the world, far from escaping gloom, I was surrounded by it, engulfed.

In England as in Australia, I sought out some friends—one among my closest—but avoided others. My internal battery was running down, and the energy I needed for seeking employment—anything to occupy my mind and drive out this endless nightmare—could not be entirely absorbed in gloomy reflection. I knocked on the doors of those newspapers for which I had worked twelve months previously, but they were no longer ajar. The recession had cut the hiring of casual sub-editors to the bone, and on some journals permanent staff were being laid off.

I remember spending the evening of 16 January in my room, by the

116

open fire but draped in a jacket and shrouded in all-pervasive gloom. The light was off; I wanted no false hope. Early in the morning, it must have been, I turned the radio on and caught a news flash. 'Operation Desert Storm has begun. Coalition troops have begun the battle to oust Iraqi forces from Kuwait.' Everything that happened was sucked into my own personal tragedy. I wasn't far out of danger now.

At the end of January 1991, I could see no future for myself in England. Good friends had done their best, there was no work or prospect of it, and my finances were beginning to mirror my inner resources (flickering). Having learnt the hard way that uncertainty was the only certainty, I had bought a round-the-world ticket in Melbourne, so that if I ended up staying in Britain the rest of the ticket could be used any time within a year of the first flight to London. This type of ticket is valid for two stopovers, so long as they are in the same direction—west to east, or east to west. London was the first, so I had one up my sleeve. A glance at the map, and a desire to use up all the time I could in finding a new life to replace my old broken one, suggested a halt in North America.

I had kept two friends from my days working on a newspaper in Athens: one an American, the other a Canadian. I have sometimes wondered since those days what would have happened if I had chosen to stop over in Los Angeles instead of Vancouver. But all such speculation is as idle as it is enticing: the probable answer is that, all things being equally dismal, I would have spun out of control in some other place.

Perhaps it was better this way. The Californian journalist was a close friend, whereas the Canadian journalist had remade her life in the Philippines. Neither could know what I had gone through or help me, of that I was convinced. But now, with Despair closing in, I felt that to fetch up almost unannounced on the doorstep of a friend with whom I'd kept in touch down the years by letter might be a bit overpowering for both of us, given my vulnerable state. It would be better to go the indirect route, as it were. I remembered that Penny had a brother, Greg, in Vancouver, and a phone call confirmed he still lived there and would be happy to put me up for a while.

Perhaps it was because I symbolised a living link with his sister who had lived overseas for many years that Greg welcomed me as if I were his brother, though of course we'd never met. He was living in a communal flat on the fashionable-arty South Side, and a sofa was set aside without fuss for me to doss on.

My nervous restlessness, though, was at such a pitch by now that, even without the slightest pressure for me to move out, I had become a virtual social isolate. Surrounded by new people—upbeat student types, fun characters getting on with life and ploughing furrows through those bleak economic times—I should have found their company stimulating and just the morale booster I needed. Instead, apart from one boisterous feast at a downtown *yum cha* restaurant to celebrate Chinese New Year, my time in drop-dead beautiful Vancouver was spent avoiding company, riding the ferry across to North Side and back, perhaps twice a day, ambling around aimlessly and observing the city's drawcards.

This avoidance of company and social gatherings—painful to me now that my thoughts were enmeshed in deepening mental torture—was another symptom of my constant stress. Sleep still came so rarely that I swear there could not have been more than two hours a night when oblivion claimed me, and still I would awaken unrefreshed. And now there were two new symptoms, closely allied to my rising unsociability. My overriding qualities, I may have said earlier, were an insatiable curiosity (which is why I became a journalist, after all) and an appreciation of the absurd that those of a friendly disposition have been careless enough to mistake for a sense of humour. Now I inquired after nothing, stopped reading newspapers, couldn't have told you how the Gulf War was proceeding.

I abandoned all interest in those events that had triggered my panic attack, persuading myself that since whatever was going to happen would happen I must not worry myself about it (the only glimmer of good sense to pierce the veil of my deepening detachment from the world). That sense of humour, too, had sunk without trace. Nothing amused me. It was as if the light had gone out of my soul. To crack a smile would have been deception on a grand scale. Laughter was for the truly insane, those who thought they were sane and didn't see what was all too obvious to me: Fear had gained the upper hand and Hope was on the ropes.

It was at the Chinese hotel in Vancouver's historic Gastown district, to which I moved with some excuse about living more centrally even though it was only a kilometre or so from Greg's pad, that I first saw where all this was tending. The two-storey hotel, its late-Victorian heritage fully restored, featured bright red banisters on which I placed my hands for balance as I ascended the staircase after saying goodnight to the family owners who were playing mah-jong in the downstairs parlour. The click-clack of tiles echoed up to the second floor where I stood, both hands now clenching the wooden stair rail that skirted an open rectangle of empty space. I was peering vacantly over the railing, down to the linoleum foyer two floors below, when the thought first occurred to me. *It would be so easy ...*

A couple of seconds and no more of this pain would exist. Even now, there were no voices in my head but my own thoughts, for crying out loud or suppressing as long as I could. With difficulty, I suppressed them. Low as I was, late in this bout with my demons as I found myself, there remained a residue of resistance in my fast-emptying soul.

Back in my room I spent the next few hours lying on the bed, unable to move a muscle, as if paralysed. Next day I didn't leave the room, couldn't see the point. Trapped within myself, trapped within the hotel, I didn't go down for breakfast and no one came up to inquire about me.

About four the following afternoon Vancouver was struck by a moderate earthquake (four on the Richter scale, I later heard). The jug of water on the period dressing-table teetered and toppled, crashing to the floor. Overhead, the light-globe swung like a corpse from a gibbet. Anarchy let loose in the political and now the physical world, coinciding with personal fragmentation, left me prey to the worst of forebodings. *Weird*, I thought. *Nothing in the world is the way it was.* My defences crumpled. The next blow would bring me crashing down. Where did I want to be when the worst came to the worst? I clutched my last ticket in the world. Home.

It was a decision taken with just enough willpower to carry it out. With my mind distracted by woes I missed the boarding call, couldn't remember the right departure gate, lost my boarding card and caused a whole lot of people (at the wrong airline counter, too, as it emerged) a few minutes of unholy panic while the transoceanic flight was kept waiting for its late late passenger. I think it fair to say that everyone in the plane was red-faced as I was shown to my seat, even if my facial colour was produced by shame and theirs by impatience.

Across the Pacific I flew on the last leg of my spin around the world, with a brief night-time stopover in Hawaii. February was almost over when the jet touched down in Sydney, where I decided to spend the night before taking a train south to Melbourne the next day.

For the second time in five months I had arrived home, but this time more close-mouthed, less brave-faced, than before. However, I still tried not to burden my parents with my black-cloud gloom, the hopelessly negative mindset that now made me feel physically as if I were carrying a ten-tonne weight on my back. I strove not to share with them the one certainty I had become convinced of in our ever-changing world: that I had come home to die.

Now, approaching the end of my fraying mental tether, I was absolutely convinced nobody and nothing could retrieve my sanity. Despair had knocked me to the canvas and all the noise of the world was a dull roar in my ears. I was down for the count.

One thing that must be said of the suicidal urge is this: the human being without hope is someone in chronic pain, and it is completely natural for any creature in torment to adopt the least painful course. I didn't choose to die. Choice implies a free rational decision when faced with two or more courses of action. Dying is a painful course, but if every minute of the day is torture, and there's every indication of this continuing remorselessly into eternity, then dying becomes the least painful course.

How my strengths had become weaknesses, and my mental resources had failed, made me embarrassingly aware that I was not the person I had been, and that my once sharp intellect was now a broken reed. The mind cowers in a corner of its old palatial mansion and mourns its loss, its forcible ejection from the throne of reason.

The constant motion of my body, and the motion in my battered brain, would not permit me to stay long at my parents' house. Not only were there no means of ending the torment at hand—and it was my wish not to be found by them—but the way I must go was not yet clear to me, and this I must find when the opportunity presented itself.

Running away from my intolerable life, I found precious few bolt-holes left. One was to go and stay with Anne, an elderly friend of my mother's who lived in the inner Melbourne suburb of East St Kilda. I barely knew her, but she welcomed me in. Plying me with food and sympathy, she seemed an understanding soul. Anne even had a piano there: it had been years since I had played, and that evening the little concert I gave her would have done David Helfgott proud, if feeling counted for more than virtuosity.

But my oppressive spirits pushed me ever closer to the precipice, and it required maximum restraint for me to give attention to what she was trying to tell me. Anne had family photos out on the settee and was leafing through them. A Holocaust survivor, she was pointing out her Ukrainian relatives, one by one, cherishing them in lamentations, losing them all over again. Losing me, too: at one point, politely but plaintively changing the subject, I refused to take aboard any more emotional ballast. I couldn't stay there another night.

The first weekend of March 1991 found me a temporary guest—no one set a limit, I myself didn't raise the matter—in Sydenham House, a tall neo-Gothic mansion situated in Hotham Street, East Melbourne, about 500 metres north of the MCG. It was accommodation that in better times I would have felt right at home in, shared as it was by a gaggle of journalists, most of whom were known to me. The one among them who was a particularly good friend of mine, Stephanie Bunbury, had been a colleague when we were both reporters for the *Age* a decade before. It was she who answered my obviously desperate call for somewhere to stay a few days. One of the communards was away for the weekend. I could have his room, Stephanie told me. I'd find it on the third floor. He wouldn't mind. This turned out to be good or bad luck, depending on how you view these things.

Of my first full day in residence I remember only three things. First is wandering down to the MCG and, incredible as this may sound, circumnavigating it. So central a place does the Melbourne Cricket Ground hold in Australian sporting memory that walking around its circumference could easily be a religious ritual. Perhaps that is why I did it.

Second was trundling a shopping cart through a local grocery store, hardly the way one would choose to pass the time, you might think. A packet of crisps and a drink really don't amount to much, but I did pause for an unnaturally long time beside the carton of rat poison, before deciding that I'd read somewhere people who swallow toxins tend to regurgitate a lot of them without much guarantee of achieving their objective.

Third and last memory of the day is of sitting around a long table in the evening with half a dozen housemates waiting for, and then enjoying to the full, a dish of steaming pasta prepared by Stephanie with the help of one or two others. Italian cooking, Australian wine: even with my jaded appetite, this was a night to remember.

After dinner, one of the residents responded to my curiosity about the mansion next door. Of the same Victorian vintage, it appeared to be deserted. Gingerly we entered it, and found that indeed it was unoccupied. I trudged up several storeys, inspected the cobwebs at close quarters, and thought it would make an ideal set for a horror movie. *I might or might not be back here*, I thought, but left satisfied that the visit hadn't been an utter waste of my apportioned time.

After the convivial atmosphere of Saturday night, Sunday at Sydenham House was as quiet as the grave. Our coterie had dispersed to the four winds, to visit family, walk in parks, admire the first flush of autumn, recreate, re-create and, for all I know, procreate—anyway, to live.

Today, through the last keyhole of sanity, this wretched silhouette walked around the backyard of an empty mansion in the city of his birth with not a thought in his head but that this wasn't life, and therefore you couldn't call transforming it into something else or nothing the ending of a life. He looked to his own resources, and saw a void.

He had roamed widely through his homeland, Asia and Africa, and for most of his life never craved rest. He had known the highest of highs and the lowest of lows; his spirit had thrilled in exultation and grieved over the tragic loss of one who loved him freely. All that was behind him now. Nothing could be recaptured. Believing that we each of us live in order to find out the meaning of our own life he confessed to himself that the seven months and this desolate day since 2 August were a travesty of meaning, a negation of sense.

He tried to calm his soul to prepare for the coming trial. Everyone was away until tomorrow. He knew full well that others would say he wanted to die. He didn't. Afternoon sunshine filtered into the shaded room. He lay on the bed turning the world over in his mind.

My life as it is now is worthless. Throwing away what is worthless must be right. Discarding the worthless is good. Don't fight it, fight the weakness and fear that would hold you back. I don't want to die but I can't go on like this.

The warming sun dipped below East Melbourne's leafy horizon as I looked to the west through the bedroom window. In the ordinary course of events I would have eaten about now, but the ordinary course of events had long ago stopped. My physical world was now dominated by an imaginary line of two metres separating the bed from the window. I paced that line to and fro, breathing deeply and slowly, thinking what it would be like not to breathe.

The time has come to act. A fall from the heights will be quick. Quick is good. But, even if I can summon the courage to go over the top, can I not decide in advance what I shall do and then, in my sleep perhaps, carry out my final order? But how to sleep, after months with scarcely any? There are pills in the room next door—the one I saw when being given a guided tour of the house upon my arrival here. Steal them, no one will notice a few missing, and then, so that no one alone will bear the guilt of 'supplying' me with these means, look for others.

Between 9 and 10 pm I rushed from chamber to chamber gathering up tablets from bedside tables. Most of them were Vitamin C capsules, I noticed with a twinge of regret, but there were sleeping pills too. Not enough to do the job on their own but enough, taken together, to blank my mind into non-resistance.

The night was balmy, rich in stars. After initial resistance, my thumb snapped free the window clasp and my two strong arms pushed the pane up. The trees looked like a painting, their leaves still-lifes, stirred by no breath of wind. I sat myself on the windowsill, overlooking the backyard, and downed a dozen pills with two gulps of water.

My breath was annoyingly regular. I launched myself from the ledge, back into the room. *No, I can't do it. Don't have the guts. What's stopping you? You'll be doing everyone a favour.*

Back to the sill. *Get used to it, it won't be so hard, just one small push, that's all it will take. And you go to the next level.*

The next level? In my tortured thinking I remember looking out, and down, and reckoning I might just survive a third-floor fall. The actual words? 'It mightn't work.'

I hurried into the empty hallway and bounded up the stairs to the fourth floor. There's a last time for everything. I didn't know whose room it was, if anyone's. The room was identical to mine, the furnishings as bare. The windowsill could have been the same, too, but the treetops were now below eye level.

I lay on this more anonymous bed, willing myself into unconsciousness with just one programmed command, a mantra I repeated until everything else was driven out of my distracted mind: *Walk to the sill. Fall off, fall away. Fall off, fall away.*

The still-life remained unchanged at 11 pm as it did, I suppose, three hours later. *It must be 2 am, 4 March, but that doesn't matter to me. What's the time when the time has come? The stars, the trees, the warmth of autumn, fall. Fall off, fall away.*

In silence no longer dread but serene, I arose from the bed and reclined on the ledge, nudging myself a little further out with my right hand cupped around the underside of the window jutting out above me.

Now I was right on the edge, willing the perfect moment to come. Rocking in and out of the building, side on, I tried to work up enough momentum to tip myself over, opening my cupped hand until I clung by just a middle finger to the window that hovered over me like a guillotine blade.

What will be or not will be or not. Don't care what. I slid my finger down to the edge of the window frame and let go. I cannot tell what happened next. I fell off. All thought fell away.

The drop was 15 metres.
Down to Earth.
Heels first, striking pitiless gravel.
The Earth broke my fall.
The bones of my feet smashed into
a thousand slivers.
Both legs fractured in several places.
My pelvis cracked.
Spine snapped.
Neck was dislocated.
The Earth is 13 000 kilometres thick.
It emerged unscathed.

Chapter 14

REJECTED FOR HEAVEN

To be or not to be, that is the question.

WILLIAM SHAKESPEARE *HAMLET*

MARCH-JUNE 1991

Imagine a million miniature arrows tipped with molten tar piercing each atom of your being with piston-like rapidity, and even then you can have only the most indistinct picture of the Hell that was going through me. I was not in Hell; Hell had taken me over, until there was no I, nothing but wild screaming endless terror. No sense that I had a body, no awareness of time, no past or future or even present in the ordinary sense of the word. The whole universe, all reality, filled up with metaphysical torment. Boundless suffering, disembodied pain.

By a stroke of luck to which I owe my life, Stephanie had arrived home not long before I jumped and, hearing the thud, rushed into the backyard, where she found my broken body sprawled in the gravel of the flowerbed. After phoning an ambulance, she had found my brother's number in personal papers among my belongings, and phoned him next. Bruce, of course, phoned my parents.

The ambulance sped me to St Vincent's Hospital, barely a kilometre away, where medics quickly realised my injuries were life-threatening. However, for one overriding reason, they ordered my immediate transfer. The Austin Hospital, where I went straight to Emergency around sunrise, was and remains one of the world's leading centres for the treatment of spinal injury. After taking my life out of my own hands, I had no responsibility for the fact that it passed into far more capable ones.

For two days, I am told, a quivering mass of agony that used to be me lay in the intensive-care unit, hovering this side of the fate it had tempted, the line it had dared to cross. In the next few weeks I would become unavoidably aware of how thin that line can be, of how easily it can be slipped across. One day, white curtains were drawn in haste around the bed next to mine, and a covey of masked doctors swarmed into that space in a desperate bid to revive the patient, a Japanese tourist grievously injured in a motorcycle accident on Victoria's Great Ocean Road. By then I could turn my head and, doing so, closed my eyes against the sight, even—I recall—praying for the life of this human being unknown to me but for now my neighbour. That night new sheets were laid out, and next morning a new patient occupied his space. Only upon persistent questioning did one of the nurses confirm that the man from Japan had died in this foreign land without regaining consciousness.

That could have been me is an obvious thought in such circumstances. But in the first few days, when it so nearly was my end too, no thoughts entered my mass of sensations, a state known to psychologists as anoesis. Later I would learn that the first sign I was winning the battle for life was, paradoxically enough, an action that could have hastened death: when I felt such extreme pain that, out of pure instinct, I ripped the intravenous tubes out of my arm. Of this I have no recollection.

Thanks to the extraordinary skills and expertise developed at the Austin over many years, the prospects of survival are many times greater than they were a few decades ago. In the 1950s a snapped spine was a (lingering) death sentence. But, even in these comparatively benign days, Death drives a hard bargain for each and every one of us.

It may have been the second day after my admission, or the third, when a primal awareness penetrated this mass of agony, awareness of an outside force trying to reach me in my suffering. Somehow divining that I was going to be operated on, I cried out for spiritual help. Even now it is hard to explain why the efforts to save my battered body spurred me to call for someone who could perform no such office. My action was not taken out of a belief in God but from a driving sense of terror that something beyond my body, something immaterial and so of transcendent importance, would be lost if the surgery failed.

I sought consolation ahead of that next obstacle on my road. The hospital sent me a Churches of Christ chaplain, George Warren, who spoke softly and reassuringly, while realistically preparing me as best he could to accept whichever of the two directions awaited me at the fork in the road ahead.

Pethidine was administered. I recall being wheeled into the operating theatre, even the conversational murmur of the surgeons, and wondering if my senses kept picking up such chit-chat how I could know whether I was alive or dead. Then, nothing ...

My vital signs were wildly unstable, I later learnt, for days after the surgery, which consisted of putting metal rods in my spine and temporary ones in my legs. (The rods in my back are still there today, and on the day of my death I expect to be worth a fortune on the scrap-metal market.) It was essential for the reconfiguration of my physical frame that the legs, indeed as much of the body as possible, be kept immobile for the next few weeks.

The most important, and paralysing, consequence of my self-willed fall was the 'incomplete' fracture of my spine at L1, the first vertebra in the lumbar region of the lower back. The 'incomplete' nature of this break, or what the medical profession calls a lesion, enabled signals from the brain—in those days almost all of them signals of pain—to register sensations from the south of the body to the north. This wholeness is a blessing: many spinal-injury sufferers feel nothing in their lower limbs so that routines the rest of the population take for granted put them in great peril. For example, while taking a shower they could scald themselves without any warning to the brain that the water is too hot.

Before any attempt was made to apprise me of the new terms on which my life would be lived, the doctors and nurses had to wait for the shock I had given my body to subside. For days I was 'fed' intravenously, and for weeks after that it was a lottery whether any food spooned into my mouth would be vomited up again, with the added risk of choking. My head had to be immobilised too. For the first twelve weeks in hospital I was staring at the ceiling because the fall had dislocated two vertebrae in my neck, and they took all that time to heal. Only when fed, and struggling to avoid the choking just described, would I incline my head to one side.

On the fifth day—again I must go on what others have told me—I returned to the world of the living. The first memory of my second life was that time had begun again. This was an odd sensation, precisely deposited in my memory bank by the sight of a clock on the right-hand wall just after my vision returned: 10.10, it read. Minutes more passed before the light streaming through the window at my right led me to another profound revelation: *It's morning*.

The pain was intense, my fright and disorientation were extreme. But I knew I was in a hospital, even though there were times in the next few weeks when I wondered whether this was the delirium of thought continuing beyond physical death. Reality soon intruded upon such philosophical rambles and reveries in the form of my parents, who visited me, driving daily for three hours—the round trip from Western Port Bay, more than 100 kilometres south-east of Melbourne, all the way across town to the northern suburbs.

Their devotion was constant, but that wasn't what struck me dumb and brought tears to my eyes. It was the recognition, looking them full in the face, of the grief I had brought into their lives. Yet there was no accusation mixed in with those looks, merely an inexpressible chagrin at my loss and gratitude that something of greater value had been saved from my personal wreckage.

But had life been saved? What sort of life was open to me now? Strange though it sounds in my ears now, the question that dominated my thoughts, and that I uttered to pastor Warren on his next visit, was: 'How can I do any good, or be any good, from now on?' To live for a purpose, or to live and find a purpose, is still what makes our lives more valuable than that of an amoeba. I could conceive of no purpose likely to be fulfilled by someone reduced to this lamentable condition.

The doctors told my parents early on, quietly and sombrely in a room set aside for just such a purpose, that they must expect this son of theirs would never walk again. Just as quietly, Dad told me the same. By then it wasn't entirely unexpected, but I couldn't focus my mind on what that would mean.

Probably as a result of perceiving how grief-stricken my mother and father were, my own thoughts turned on the hopelessness of my situation, and many a time I wished—for their sake now, rather than mine—that this personal tragedy would pass into the realm of eternal forgetfulness.

I recall secretively hoarding the heparin tablets that overworked nurses, following written orders, left on my bedside table. Those tablets, I knew, were to prevent the blood from coagulating due to shock. In my newfound depression and will to cross that line at a second attempt I thought, *If they don't see me take these tablets, but think I have, then my blood will clot, a clot will go to the heart or develop into thrombosis, and death will come swiftly and sharply, before I feel it. Yes, that would be for the best.*

The first unfamiliar routines in my life as a supine object centred on basic functions. There is no way of knowing which routine was administered first, after my transfer from ICU to the happily numbered Ward 13, home to spinally injured patients deemed no longer in danger of dying. Likely as not, it was a visit by one of the urological nurses to empty the bladder—in my case by the application of an indwelling catheter to be replaced in time by an intermittent one, which I would insert whenever I felt the need.

In those early days, when my system was still in shock, involuntary urination was one sign that, in this new life, I had reverted to infancy when it came to matters of personal care.

The second routine only confirmed this utter dependence and indignity. Every few hours—whenever their busy schedules permitted—a team of 'lifters' arrived to perform two services. The first was to clear my body of its putrid wastes (and I cannot have been the only one to find this humiliating). Then would come the second part of the process: turning me on one side—this after the leg bones had reset and the pins came out—so as to minimise the risk of bedsores from lying too long in the one spot.

To re-learn toilet functions at age 36 is no picnic, but the urologists one and all were models of perseverance. The first time a catheter was forced up my urethra, the pain was phenomenal and I nearly passed out. (Today I perform the function perhaps four times a day as if it were second nature.)

Another routine was the morning medical round. In my helplessness, it disturbed me to be an object of curiosity to these strange men in white coats, each armed with a clipboard. They seemed agreed on the importance of building up my calcium levels (which is indeed a priority

131

for spinal-injury patients, since the flesh directly around the damaged part of the backbone typically atrophies). But even in my weakened state I would argue the point with those distinguished visitors, saying that the urologist had warned against too much milk intake, because an excess of calcium built up bladder stones and similar obstructions (apparently, that's right too). Such hostility was essentially my way of telling them all to go away. Only when I came to accept my 'new body' on its own terms would I be ready to hear the wisdom they had to pass on about how to look after it.

Heading the team was Dr Gerald Ungar, an Austrian Jewish refugee whose compassion and patience soon won me over. Another of Australia's leading experts in the field of spinal injury was also on the team. A Singaporean-trained medic, his surname surprised, and brought a much-needed smile to the faces of people who had just lost the use of their legs: Dr Terry Lim.

They; another eminent specialist Doug Brown; and some of the nurses tried their best to brighten up my day, but estrangement from the stricken and disfigured frame stretched out along the bed—this body not me—prevented any sharing of confidences.

Thinking of my parents, but mourning the loss of my physical self, tears started to flow, sobs that would gush unbidden at any hour of the day or night. The sight must have been familiar to nurses on this ward, as they tended paraplegics and quadriplegics whose lives had been savagely interrupted by personal disasters ranging from car accidents and necks broken by mistimed dives into shallow water to unlikelier causes such as belly flops into mosh pits and being pinned under overturned tractors.

But my 'cause of admission' was different. Written without any ambiguity on the medical records kept at the ward registry— 'attempted suicide'—the judgment of society (so it seemed to me) was no secret to Ward 13 staff.

One morning in my first fortnight on the ward, my favourite nurse (a dark-complexioned Croatian woman who closely resembled the photo of Mum on her wedding day, a likeness that struck me as extraordinary) bent over my bed and whispered in words clearly intended to comfort my now guilt-ridden mind, 'Look at it this way. You've been rejected for Heaven.'

132

As soon as they felt I was well enough to explain myself, the doctors allowed medical students to bring their clipboards closer, plying me with insolent questionnaires. I treated them as a sick joke, since at this stage with the small store of heparin safely stowed under my pillow I knew all this quizzing was pointless. It was only a matter of time.

As they grilled me on why I had tried to kill myself, there were two points I was adamant on: 'No, I didn't want to die, I just couldn't go on living.' I hoped they could see the difference, but wondered whether it sounded too theatrical. And, whenever these psychiatric students would suggest that I must have been suffering depression to do such a thing, I let my anger show. No, I hadn't been depressed: my dominant emotion was extreme anxiety, terror, dread. 'I wasn't depressed before but I am now.'

Of course they then wanted to know if I regretted not 'succeeding'. The mortification on my parents' faces, the knowledge that this desperate deed had clouded the lives of loved ones with sorrow, meant that the true answer was yes. But, having interviewed a few people in my time, I could tell that a frank statement of my feelings now would be semaphored up the chain and either they would transfer me to Ward 15, the psychiatric ward—which I devoutly wished to be spared—or place me under round-the-clock surveillance. 'Well,' I told my callow inquisitors, stalling until the right words came, 'if I had succeeded you wouldn't be asking me that.' This bit of cheek usually did the trick. They went away.

As the weeks wore on, changes came. An overhead TV was fitted into place, but the moronic pap of daytime television gains nothing in interest simply because there is nothing else to look at. That wasn't quite the case, anyway, as there was always the ceiling to stare at. Counting the number of 'pinholes' in it (3025) could be quite entertaining ... up to a point.

Slowly but insistently, my sense of humour sloped back. In grim mood one morning as I craned to see the windowsill above and just to the right of my bed, I thought, *If I wanted to kill myself now by dropping off a window ledge, I'd need help to get up there.*

But, even as I lay there chuckling at this unlikely vision, I realised that a week had gone by, and my blood had apparently decided not to clot and endanger my stubborn life. So, later in the day, I furtively shovelled the heparin tablets from under the pillow into the wastepaper basket.

Self-understanding dawns slowly, and I wasn't there yet. It was April, and I had been almost a month in Ward 13 – almost a month, when the depths of my uncommunicative, teary struggle with this new existence were plumbed.

Had anyone then confronted me with the fact that I was submerged in self-pity, my reaction would have been one of anger and resentment. But that was the predominant wellspring of my depressive emotions.

The loss of a limb is no light thing. A part of one's body since birth is something to which one is attached—yes, there is humour in that—but vitally, in every way, not just physically. The loss is palpable, and the grief that flows from that constant sense of bereavement is initially overpowering.

It recedes over time—just as grief at the loss of a loved one does—but to absorb that loss and convert it into a sense that this is what you have come to while your self remains essentially unimpaired is the work not of a day, week or month, but of years. Because of this, self-pity—the ability to grieve with your whole heart at your reduced condition, your baby-like helplessness—is in my view a necessary phase in the grieving process. Advice is beside the point here but, if anyone were to ask how to treat this much maligned compassion for oneself in those days of self-mourning, I would offer this simple counsel: wallow in it. If recuperation is to come, however, you will eventually need to turf out self-pity, a guest always inclined to overstay its welcome.

It was one of the night-time lifters—the strongest of the crew, whom I'd come to trust from our brief but regular conversations—who, a few months into my incarceration, opened the first window onto my future. It came in the form of a casual remark, merely letting me know that he would be away in England for the next month, with an old Ward 13 patient of his who needed a carer with him on his touring holiday.

Two weeks into my stay, just when I was beginning to stabilise, Dr Ungar had calmly but gravely confirmed I would never walk again, triggering a new stage in my grief. Obviously he realised that the first time I had been told the cue had come too early. This time round the news appeared horrific. In the next few days I would ponder the loss inwardly, deeply, with renewed bouts of weeping, and about five times an hour I would miss walking. But now, months down the track, when this revelation came that a paraplegic could do something as normal, and to me desirable, as travel, I didn't think about walking, didn't miss it, more than once a day. Still, it seemed one of those things every normal person did.

My frame was racked by a single spasm. This information lit a candle of hope in my darkened brain. For the first time it occurred to me that I might travel again, though my rational blinkers immediately dimmed the light. I'd lost the ability to imagine a future beyond the helplessness and powerlessness I could see all around and within me.

Then my friend the lifter and turner, seeming to sense my mental struggle with this new perspective, added, 'Do you know what percentage of patients here go on to lead useful lives?'

'I dunno. Ten per cent?' I replied, not really interested in playing this game. 'Ninety-five,' he returned, to my obvious disbelief. 'Ninety-five. The rest vegetate.'

Chapter 15

THE GROWING GULF

C'est quasi le même de converser avec ceux des autres siècles que de voyager. (Conversing with those from other centuries is almost the same as travelling.)

DESCARTES, QUOTED BY TIM MACKINTOSH-SMITH IN *Travels with a Tangerine*

DECEMBER 2001-FEBRUARY 2002

Back in Bahrain, on Christmas Day 2001—which, of course, is just another day for the vast majority of the population there—I received the latest cache of mail from home. On opening a greetings card from the seven-year-old son of a family friend, I had to laugh. Above a hand-drawn Christmas tree, he had written, '*Dear Ken, Watch out for the bombs, And have a great Christmas were ever* [sic] *you are!'*

Second time round, Bahrain holds no fears for me. The reply to his greeting flows easily from my pen. *While I promise to watch out for the bombs, young Joash, the fact is that I haven't seen one yet. Maybe I'm blind to the danger but I prefer to think it is because so few people are carrying them.*

BAHRAIN: 17–26 DECEMBER

Despite the trauma that began on this island eleven years earlier, returning here was not like going back into the lion's den, getting back on the horse or whatever other analogy you might choose. Times had changed: whatever regional threats existed at the end of 2001, invasion wasn't one of them.

Among our unsung debts to the Arabs is a love of horseflesh, but race-day crowds at this course in the centre of Bahrain island play a numbers game that would be hardly recognisable on the Australian turf. Gambling is too un-Islamic to be permitted here, but punters must have their incentive so the Bahrain Racing and Equestrian Club runs what is essentially a raffle in its place.

At the grandstand window, a woman hands me a slip of paper headed 'Forecasts' and for one dinar (about A$5) I get to nominate the first- and second-place runners in any of the seven events on today's card.

I tip No. 5 in the fourth, and 5 again in the sixth. The winning dividend is not called a payout but a jackpot, the distinction between gambling and picking a winner appearing to me as slight as my chances of ending up ahead at this game. But No. 5 in the fourth flies home first, and my guide to the mysteries of Bahraini racing, Khalil Bakal, tells me that if my race-six fancy, Kuwait Bay, does the same I could wheel away with 100 dinars (A$500). My pulse quickens. Just last week I was on a ferry crossing Kuwait Bay, so what could beat that?

Persian Adventure (another name that should have struck a chord with me), that's what. Kuwait Bay crosses the finishing line second. There is no prize for second, no jackpot for yours truly.

A Bahraini-born Iranian, Khalil grew up in an equine world. His uncle kept stables and Khalil was just six when he rode his first horse—and that was not a pony, but a full-height Arab steed. 'I was scared but after I know the horse it was easy for me,' he says.

Children are naturally curious about wheelchairs. We are beside the parade ring now, and the young son of one of his friends tries to turn the tyres on my chair before switching his attention to Khalil's. You see few enough wheelchair users in the cities of Central and South-west Asia, and those you do see are more likely to be out earning a subsistence living than enjoying their leisure. Khalil, whose old life ended in a 1984 motorbike accident, admits he is lucky to come from a well-to-do family.

Attitudes to people in wheelchairs differ from culture to culture. In Australia, as experience has taught me, most people will seem casual and indifferent, as though they haven't noticed. (That's nice.) In England, usually when I'm minding my own business, total strangers will occasionally come up and ask, 'Can I help you?' ('No. Can I help *you*?' I sometimes answer, even though I know this is rude.) In southern Africa, concern can be indicated by bluff directness, when someone you've never seen steps up and asks, 'What happened?'

In Arab society, being different from the group is social death, and Khalil sometimes finds this hard to handle. 'One day I go shopping, these ladies say, "Look at that guy, he's in a wheelchair." My brother says to me, "Let them go. If you take care for that, you cannot enjoy this life."'

DAY 227 (25 DECEMBER): MANAMA

Do they know it's Christmas? Well, the Hotel Aradous has a huge fir tree with plastic needles reaching to the ceiling, and the Filipino jazz band have an extra spring in their step, but basically the answer is no. I spend the day writing. One of the advantages of not celebrating Christmas is that the post office remains open until 7 pm for the dispatch of ... belated Christmas cards.

QATAR: 26–30 DECEMBER

Mostly trackless desert, Qatar is a thumb jutting up from the Arabian mainland. Its main attraction is that it has no 'main attractions', although at this point in its history Sleepy Hollow is receiving a wake-up call, with the United States discreetly deciding to set up a military headquarters here. But the reason Qatar is now sticking its head above the sand, so to speak, is that it is home to al-Jazeera, the controversial Arab satellite-TV network that brought Osama bin Laden into the West's living rooms.

DAY 229 (27 DECEMBER): DOHA

Qatar's capital is a bright, modern but decidedly quiet city clinging to a horseshoe-shaped harbour. For once I have pre-booked accommodation, taking advantage of my youth hostel membership card, and Doha Youth Hostel is by any standards a spacious and welcoming home away from home. The 'war on terror' makes this an instructive New Year to be in the Gulf, and this evening the lesson comes into *our* living room, in the form of al-Jazeera's latest scoop: a video message from bin Laden allegedly made since the US campaign that ousted his Taliban hosts.

Seated in a semicircle around the hostel's TV are an Egyptian man, who never gives away his attitude to bin Laden; two middle-aged Sudanese men who take to backchatting the al-Qa'eda chief; and an intense European-looking man in his mid-twenties, but clearly a Muslim in his white *jellaba*, who strokes his goatee beard throughout the telecast. As bin Laden fades from the screen, the young, previously silent one—who it turns out is from the Balkans—stands up, points at the television, declaims 'He is the best man in the whole world' (in English, significantly, not Arabic, leaving no room for doubt that his words are meant primarily for my ears), and quits the room.

I follow him out to the porch, where he seems to be expecting me. We exchange names, and as the *Sydney Morning Herald* has already asked me to garner local reaction to the latest bin Laden tape I mention that his views would be of interest to Australians. The Slovene agrees to talk but will allow himself to be identified only as Abu Amr (Yasser Arafat's alias, no less). The obvious question comes first. 'So why do you admire bin Laden?'

'Like Tolstoy, he is a great man of faith.' Abu Amr astonishes me with this comparison. 'But he is also a man of action, like your Mad Max.'

Am I hearing right? Bin Laden, road warrior?

'When I was growing up, I always liked to look at those movies. Mel Gibson was a real superstar. But people forget why Mad Max became mad: because he had seen his woman raped and his child killed … now you can understand Osama. He's the only one today who stood up and acted on his beliefs without any fear and talked tough to the biggest hypocrite in the world. He's the only one of the Muslims who spoke the truth about injustice in Palestine, the killing of those poor kids in Iraq, and destroying the only pharmaceutical factory in Sudan.'

The scholarly 29-year-old is a computer technician, a refugee from the imploded Yugoslavia, who claims to have lived in Kosovo and Bosnia, and even to have taught at a summer camp in Missouri.

America's way of life and love of informality seem to have turned him into an old-fashioned Methodist. 'Stuff that is forbidden—drinking, prostitution, cursing, making jokes about the Prophets, even the Prophet Jesus, peace be upon him—they do it all. For the normal person who believes in God and the Prophets, there are limits. I heard them, "Tonight we speak to our Lord …" and they dance. A normal person cannot take it as worshipping; it's making jokes; for us it's blasphemy.'

The wounds of September 11 are still raw. Does Abu Amr accept that those who died in New York were innocent? 'The majority of them,' he says cautiously. 'Some of them, maybe, if they were still alive, would have embraced Islam. Some of those who died were Muslims. There was a small mosque in the World Trade Center, did you know?' (I didn't.) '… So this I condemn but, regarding the Pentagon, this is another case.'

His selective notion of innocence is extremely disturbing but Abu Amr immediately makes it clear he has given the matter deep thought. Unprompted, the young Islamist quotes *al-Maleda* (or 'Feast Table'), the fifth *sura* of the Koran. 'Killing one innocent person is like killing the whole of mankind.'

Unless we in the West think we're perfect, we must listen to what the Abu Amrs have to say, or ignore it at our peril. After all, the so-called clash of civilisations is really a clash between those who think all of us have some of the truth, and those who think some of us have it all.

DAY 230 (28 DECEMBER): DOHA

The 1991 Gulf War put CNN on the map. Ten years later the US bombing campaign in Afghanistan did the same for al-Jazeera, although that same campaign took its Kabul studio off the map.

Yesterday, when I rang up Osama bin Laden's channel of choice and said that as an Australian journalist I would like to come along and see just what al-Jazeera was all about, the last answer I expected was yes. In many American eyes the station is merely a mouthpiece for terrorists, while in many Arab ones it represents a free market of dissenting voices speaking without a foreign, specifically American, accent. Then there is the adrenaline rush of visiting a place that not only reports the news but has become newsworthy itself. Since September 11 the words 'al-Jazeera exclusive', flanked by the outlet's flame-like logo, have become familiar to TV viewers the world over.

Ibrahim Hilal, the station's editor-in-chief, greets me with a smile. He knows the way to a journalist's heart, launching forth on press freedom by recounting a phone conversation he had with the *New York Times* editor after that paper had accused al-Jazeera of reporting baseless rumours.

Hilal says he told the editor, 'We are on the same front [in this cause]. If the window of freedom in the Middle East is closed, everyone will be a loser. It's a big window, it's clear and it's open. Let's keep it open.'

Sadly, Hilal's simple and eloquent message will be tarnished later by what appears to be a lack of candour (to say the least) by his ex-Kabul-bureau chief, Tayseer Allouni.

Allouni, a hale and hearty man, is summoned to Hilal's office and, in the course of a long interview, tells me he has 'no contacts within al-Qa'eda'. What he doesn't tell me—but it comes out later—is that he met bin Laden, and that his interview with him was run as a 'scoop'.

Of course, if Allouni was doing his job of reporting Afghanistan over the past few years he *should* have had contacts within al-Qa'eda. What worries me is not the existence of such contacts, but his literally incredible denial of them. When he says more videos can be expected from bin Laden 'because it is very easy for the al-Qa'eda organisation to put them into DHL or another courier service', I wonder who he thinks he's kidding. DHL under the Taliban? Give me a break.

Of course the video trail leads to bin Laden and I'm itching to know where he is. But, journalist to journalist, I cannot demand that Allouni reveal his sources. Instead I ask Hilal his opinion on bin Laden's whereabouts. 'You can say he's close to God,' he answers. 'He may try to send some signals, but they will not be of the coded type [as the Americans have warned]. He is playing with Washington. He wants to die a martyr.'

What happened to the Kabul bureau on the night of 13 November was no mistake, Hilal says angrily. 'They avoided hitting it for 38 days. Then four bombs hit it.'

Allouni tells a dramatic tale of escape, to Pakistan after a long detour via Kandahar, including an assault by Northern Alliance soldiers who regarded him as a Taliban sympathiser. Humanly, one can see the man has gone through hell, but the last paragraph of my report says, '... perhaps he knows something we don't, and may tell it to the public after the holiday he has planned in Spain'.

Time will prove my prophecy half right.

Tonight I glean an insight into the conflict between Western-propelled mass communications and an older system, the faith of the world's billion Muslims. On the TV that yesterday brought us bin Laden, I see a particularly powerful commercial, which I'm told is being screened throughout the Arab world. It shows a youth of eighteen years seated at his computer, typing compulsively. He ignores his father's soft-spoken plea to go and pray. Presently a vision appears on the computer screen: it's his own funeral, with his parents grieving and him looking helplessly out of the grave as spadefuls of earth are tossed into it. The ad closes with a single line of white Arabic script on a black background. Youssef Bada, one of the Sudanese men who are staying here at the hostel, explains, 'The message is, "Do your prayer before you are finished (a looser translation would be "while there's still time")".' He adds, 'They need to say this to young people now at the Internet and spending hours and hours at the screen, neglecting their religious duties.'

UNITED ARAB EMIRATES: 31 DECEMBER-8 JANUARY

DAY 233 (31 DECEMBER): INTO THE UAE

A busload of travellers, rudely awakened by the glare of an unsleeping border post in the dead of night (3.10 am UAE time), rolls across the sand, skirting the southern shore of the Gulf: first destination Abu Dhabi, second Dubai.

The former is the capital of this collection of seven sovereign sheikhdoms one third the size of Victoria, the latter a glittering showcase of how Islam and advanced Western civilisation can coexist in harmony, despite a view abroad that they must inevitably clash head on.

Of course, this first New Year of the 'war on terror', I have been wont to joke to concerned friends back home that I will be careful to stay out of tall buildings and away from any large gatherings of celebrating Westerners. Once in Dubai, though, I tempt fate on both counts. In the early afternoon I roll up to the ubiquitous Irish bar, where an expatriate rock band is tuning up at the decibel level of a ship's boiler room. This, I muse, would be doubly unbelievable to the folks back home: that a deeply Muslim state should have any bars at all, let alone Irish ones.

The ancient year's last hurrah is a hauntingly beautiful burnt-orange sunset seen from atop the most stunning of skyscrapers, the Arabian Tower, symbol of the fast-growing Gulf and more familiarly known as the Jumeira Beach Hotel. What to do until midnight? I hail a taxi and direct the driver to Dubai's most modern cineplex. It is almost as though I am seeking out those places that one occasionally sees at the foot of the 'Briefs' columns on newspapers' foreign pages: '232 killed in downtown theatre explosion in Dubai'. But such is the draw of the box office that the temptation to see the first 'Harry Potter' movie in this exotic setting is too great to resist.

Unfortunately, so energy-sapping has the constant cycling around town been that, not long after one of the school scenes, I doze off. All I can remember of the rest of the film is the excitement of that bout of 'aerial football' (aka quidditch) where Harry's broomstickmanship lays his enemies waste.

Just after 11 pm I emerge into the warm night. Families, old couples, teenagers (but no skateboards yet, one expects them any time now) drift along the concourse beside the creek awaiting the change of the Christian year in what is truly a Common Era. Cometh the hour, come the fireworks: silver sparklers and blue fountains of light arc over the inky-black water. The *abras*, those long wooden floating taxis once poled now engine-propelled up and down the waterway, honk their horns to welcome in 2002.

DAY 234 (1 JANUARY): DUBAI
Sana Jedida Sa'ida '(Happy New Year' in Arabic), uttered in what must sound a weirdly uncultured accent, elicits fond indulgent smiles from strangers everywhere. As the years turn, the world may not be at peace, but here I'm among people at peace with the world.

DAY 237 (4 JANUARY): DUBAI
Afternoon on the water: I hire an abra for an hour's sailing past superb incurving gold-tinted facades of the, ahem, Twin Towers shopping centre and back again to Deira docks. Ahmed the abra pilot pours petrol into the engine and then sits back to enjoy a smoke (bit of a worry, that) but we are soon on our way, gliding on the gentlest of swells. With no language in common, my thoughts are totally absorbed in the scenery.

DAY 238 (5 JANUARY): ABU DHABI

First impressions often last, and this is obviously nowhere truer than in a city you visit for a single day. The oldest building in the UAE capital, the al-Hosn Palace or White Fort, dates back only to 1930 (which makes it an exact contemporary of New York's Empire State and makes it more than twice as old as most other structures here). Abu Dhabi is mostly boutiques and banks, but what state-of-the-art boutiques, what opulent banks!

DAY 240 (7 JANUARY): AJMAN

Hearing that the animal-and-bird market in the smallest sheikhdom of them all is in full swing, I arrive late in the afternoon unprepared for what awaits me, the impressive and the depressive separated only by iron bars. Falcons from the emirates fetch from A$10 000—a Sharjah man later tells me top price for the elite type runs to 150 000 dirhams, a price comparable to that for a classy saloon car. Australiana is predictably represented by kangaroos: two mangy grey wallabies are in a cage of less than one square metre (in contravention of market rules as printed on a wall sticker, I note) and offered for sale at 6000 dirhams (A$3300) each.

SULTANATE OF OMAN: 8–30 JANUARY

DAY 241 (8 JANUARY): MUSCAT

It would be grossly dishonest to say I'd forgotten the grandeur of this country's interior, but to be back here where I spent a year of my life (working at a newspaper in the late 1980s) is to see it as new, if somewhat changed. Jagged cliffs, ochre turning orange in the late-afternoon sun, vie for attention with the *wadis*—those dry riverbeds where expatriates and bronze-skinned Omanis alike can be found picnicking on Friday-and-Saturday weekends.

This visit constitutes a break with the purity of my journey, in that so far I have mostly looked after myself but here I have accepted the kind hospitality of Rosie, an Englishwoman from the Ministry of Information with whom I had dealings in those days. First she arranges for me to be put up for a few days at the five-star Muscat Intercontinental Hotel where the cheapest rooms are about A$300 a night. Then I move into her house, built on a beetling clifftop high up over the Arabian Sea, within what seems a stone's throw of the most perfectly formed cove.

DAY 244 (11 JANUARY): MUSCAT

An Arab society long cut off from others, Oman has a fraction of the oil reserves of nations to the north and west. So Omanis, I recall from my working year here, are less mercenary, gentler, than the Bahrainis, less worldly than the Emiratis but less strict than the Saudis. These, of course, are generalisations but, just as no one who had been to Britain and France would deny the existence of different national characteristics there, we should not lump all Arabs together in our thinking. Omanis have their own story to tell, their own pride and vulnerability, their own traditions.

Serving coffee to the guest is one of those traditions. The first sight that greets you upon entering the palatial al-Bustan Hotel is an old gentleman sitting cross-legged on a carpet, silver dagger under his belt, gaudy turban on his head, dispensing pure arabica from a silver beak-nosed coffeepot—another distinctive symbol of Oman.

Another tradition is the Omani bullfight, and it is a fairly safe bet that Hemingway, intrepid adventurer that he was, never witnessed anything like this. Here the bull fights its own kind: man, in the form of a handler or two tugging on the leash, restrains aggression rather than incites it. Every Friday afternoon in what is laughingly called winter (average temperature 28°C), the owners of these cloven-hoofed Sherman tanks converge on Barka, an hour up the Arabian Sea coast from the capital.

Once before, in the 1980s, I attended a skirmish here. Then your typical Brahmin owner arrived at the battlefield—a patch of dirt—with his charger in tow. Today a low-rise concrete stadium attests to the same type of modernising influences that have affected sports closer to home. Around the boundary, combatants-in-waiting take their stand. Iron stakes prevent them from upsetting the order of play, but unprogrammed bellowings (not to mention less decorous bodily functions) add to the ringside atmosphere.

Prodded into head-on confrontation, the two leviathans in the centre indulge in an engrossing tug of war which begins with their locking

145

horns and ends either with a knockout—when one forces the other off the turf—or when one of the opponents turns tail and runs. This is what, late in the two-hour card, one of these lumbering beefsteaks decides to do, and 'run' scarcely does justice to what ensues. Fed up with the spectacle at close quarters, this Taurus not only turns his rump on the whole affair but gives his handlers the slip and charges straight for the perimeter, gathering ferocity and velocity as he rages around the fence in what might have been a victory lap (if he hadn't been a loser with a mean streak) but what is, in fact, a frenzied quest for liberty.

Suddenly, he spies it, in the form of the stadium's only exit, just one life-saving metre to the left of where I have foolishly chosen to sit. Oblivious to my existence, the frantic beast bounds over the fence and scrambles down the embankment, leaving me to offer a silent prayer to the stadium architect who placed a bull bar just in front of my otherwise exposed vantage point.

The fugitive's dash for freedom is as short-lived as it is spectacular. The last I see, one of his 'controllers' (this being a three-handler bull, make no mistake) grabs his tail and holds on for dear life as they both disappear over a sand dune.

DAY 248 (15 JANUARY): MUSCAT

At Rosie's, I add BBC World TV news to my routine. At this point, my usually inviting itineraries are perturbing. Saudi Arabia is probably second only to North Korea when it comes to the difficulty of obtaining a visa: I know it's going to be almost impossible to get one even before I head off to the embassy.

Tourism is an alien notion, and a transit visa may restrict me to staying on a long-distance bus all the way from Dubai to Jordan. As that is said to be a 36-hour journey, and I can't use bus toilets the size of broom closets, a road crossing of the peninsula seems out of the question.

The Saudi visa application saga deserves a book to itself, but here is the condensed version. On six occasions between now and 28 January I will take a taxi to this embassy. On the fourth visit I become so desperate for a stamp in my passport that (I can hardly believe this now) having squeezed through the metal detector, which my chair of course sets off every time, and waited in absolute silence for an hour and a half, I dismount carefully to a low step and crawl—yes, crablike—along the corridor and into the chancery, to press my case.

Security is called and things look hairy for a moment, but this manoeuvre does result in my application, already completed in triplicate and drawered a week before, being retrieved and passed on to a higher level: Ali Shehri.

It is he, on my sixth visit, who in exchange for the non-princely sum of US$12 ostentatiously issues me with a transit visa, the number 7 written in (I insist on that). Armed with this, he assures me, I will be able to cross the kingdom within as many days, getting on and off buses, and staying at towns along the way, without let or hindrance.

DAY 250 (17 JANUARY): NIZWA

In spite of all my micro-planning, I must admit some of the best travel moments owe everything to luck. And today I'm in luck, for today is Thursday, and in Nizwa that means one thing: the goat market.

In the Bible, goats are separated from sheep: here, cattle get into the act as well. Being paraded around a circuit under capacious trees in the market square are goats and cattle—bulls, cows and heifers—and the only controversy attending the live sheep market here revolves around price, not morality. A small boy also circulates, selling peanuts and chickpeas.

An English-speaking Omani who sees I am a stranger to these parts talks learnedly of the spectacle before us, betraying a wicked and hitherto unsuspected sense of humour as he points out the meanest bull on the block—big, black and muscle-bound—and tells me deadpan, 'We call it Tyson.'

For a few minutes, I am absorbed in the hyperbole of haggling, the play-acting of disappointment and pleading that rivet the spectator at any market or auction. I look on at one veteran raising his cane as if to strike a grasping herdsman, wondering what will happen next, when a tremendous shove from behind nearly pitches me out of my chair. Grabbing the tyres, it takes me a moment to regain my balance, then I jerk my head around to find myself face to face with the goat that has just butted my personal transport (perhaps mistaking it for a hostile beast). The drama is over in seconds. With a dumb look and a snort of contempt, the horned one disappears through a parting knot of people.

DAY 253 (20 JANUARY): MUSCAT

I'm not done with bureaucracy yet. The visa prospects for Syria are dubious. So I return to the diplomatic quarter, to seek assurance from the consul, Muhammad Ibrahim. A breezy, mustachioed man in his forties, Ibrahim gives me his card and assures me that, as an Australian, I will be a welcome guest in his country and given a visa, cost-free, on arrival. Then he adds ominously, 'If you have any trouble, ring my number.'

DAY 255 (22 JANUARY): SALALAH

Having insisted on taking the overnight bus the whole 1000 kilometres through the Omani interior, I find myself on the Frankincense Coast—a couple of hundred 'clicks' from busy al-Qa'eda training cells, if Donald Rumsfeld is to be believed. At the Hilton Salalah they have changed my name to Mr Halev, but when landed in the lap of luxury a well-brought-up lad knows better than to complain about such trifles.

Greeted by officials from the Ministry of Information, courtesy of Rosie, a letter of official welcome is handed to me on behalf of the General Manager, an Austrian with the magnificent moniker of Franz-Josef Macho (I kid you not).

DAY 256 (23 JANUARY): SALALAH

BBC bulletin: A suicide bomber blows himself up in West Jerusalem. The blast leaves 20 civilians injured.

My principal guide, Abdul Aziz, troops around the central market as I negotiate for frankincense with chubby women whose faces are covered by black burqas. We are in the Land of Ophir from which that precious essence has been derived since the Queen of Sheba was a girl. I have been here before and know a thing or two about bargaining, but the vendor knows ten or 20, and only later do I learn that the price I have paid for a tin of the stuff is three times what the locals shell out.

OUT OF THE GULAG (Kazakhstan): Aboard the train from Qaragandy bound for Lake Balkash, the author takes up his seat—or, rather, has it taken up to him—in the vestibule, lifted by railway staff and the odd fellow passenger. Luggage follows.

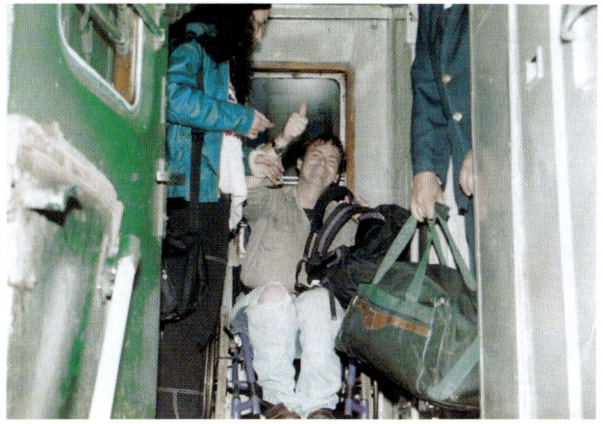

RED CARPET WELCOME (Azerbaijan): Lunch is served at Baku's Caravanserai Restaurant, a refreshment and recuperation stop for camels and their owners since the 15th century. The latest piece of excess baggage to arrive on this side of the Caspian is shouted to lunch here by the Deugro freight-forwarding company on his first day in the Caucasus.

THE EMPIRE STRIKES BAKU (Azerbaijan): As stately in its way as the Potala Palace in Lhasa, Tibet; more imposing by far than Yarralumla: Government House in the Azeri capital ought to be a world-famous landmark … but this is well off the tourists' beaten track.

CLASH OF CIVILISATIONS, WHAT CLASH? (Azerbaijan, September 2, 2001): Apple tea, boiled eggs and bread on a platter are shared with the taxi driver who has brought me to a 1,600-year-old church at Kish, not far from the border with Russia. Ilharna, in charge of restoring the ancient Christian house of worship, and her family offered us morning tea, quite out of the blue. They are Muslims.

THE OTHER CAVERN (Georgia): Facing a plaque 'dedicated to the Memory of Sir John Whinston [sic] Lennon', the author took this photo while bumming his way down to the basement of Tbilisi's Beatles Club.

HALCYON DAYS
(Georgia, September 11,
2001): Sun-dappled scene
in Tbilisi's Old Town quarter
which seemed idyllic enough
when it was viewed five
hours before the attacks on
New York and Washington
shook the larger world, and
even this apparently self-
contained one.

HOSTAGE TO HISTORY
(Iran): Behind the former US
Embassy, now the Den of
Espionage, is displayed the
wreckage of the helicopter
that crash-landed in desert
country in April 1980 while
on a mission to rescue the
Americans held captive here.

BROTHERS IN ARMS
(Bahrain): Sometimes people
in wheelchairs are thought
to have so much in common
they will just 'click'. Often
that's a fallacy, but this
sedate gentleman and his
daughter, encountered near
Manama's entrance gate,
Bab al-Bahrain, were
enjoyable company.

JIHAD IN THEIR VIEW
(Qatar): Tayseer Allouni
(right), al-Jazeera's ex-Kabul
bureau chief, embraces his
former cameraman from
Afghanistan days, Abdul
Ibrahimi, whom he hadn't
seen since 2000. At the time
of going to press, Allouni is
in a Spanish jail, convicted
of being an al-Qa'eda agent.

MY LOWEST POINT
(Jordan): Smeared with
green mud, a supposed
curative, in the shallows of
the Dead Sea, 400 metres
below sea level, the author
lets his mind do the floating.

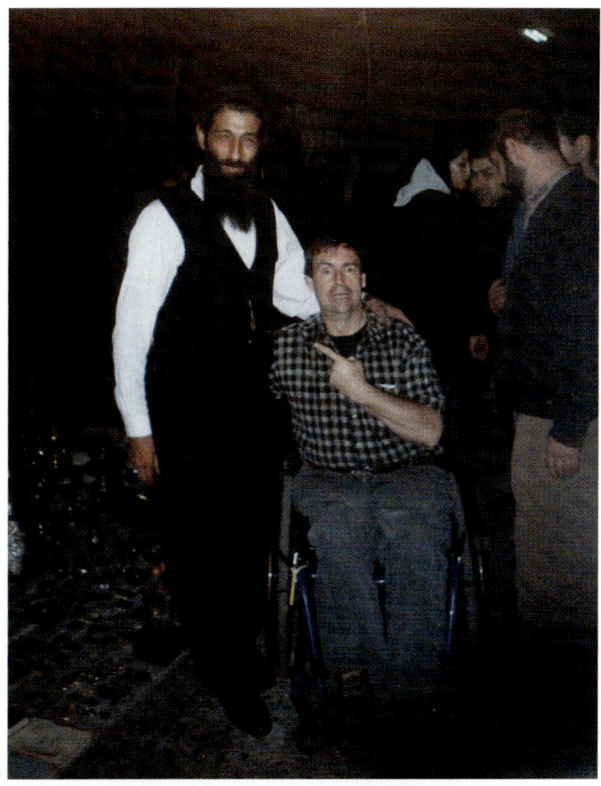

FINDING OSAMA (Iran): The author forgets to claim his reward for tracking down the boss of al-Qa'eda. Selling carpets in Tehran might have been plausible cover—the author himself was floored—if al-Qa'eda and the Iranians, whose embassy in Kabul they had torched to the ground with significant loss of life, weren't mortal enemies.

MASS SACRIFICE (Iran): A few of the tombs in this most personal of graveyards at Golestan-e Shohada, the Rose Garden of the Martyrs, on the outskirts of Isfahan, where 100,000 dead from the eight-year war between Iran and Saddam Hussein's Iraq lie buried.

DESERT NORM (Jordan): On a 24-hour bivouac made tolerable only by fasting, the author camps outside a Bedouin tent at Wadi Rum, where the older generation remembers Peter O'Toole as Lawrence of Arabia without ever having been to a cinema.

TERRORIST OR FREEDOM FIGHTER? (Syria): Kurdish activist and member of the PKK, regarded by Turkey and the US as a terrorist organisation, Abdul Latif Hussein Younis Ali stands defiantly against the backdrop of Turkish terrain, not much more than a kilometre from the border town of Qamishle.

HAVE AGENCY, WILL TRAVEL (Lebanon): Having spent the past half-century making other people's holidays more enjoyable, people like the gentleman standing beside him here— a satisfied customer for 35 years—Afif Abdul Malik makes his own getaway to the South of France every August.

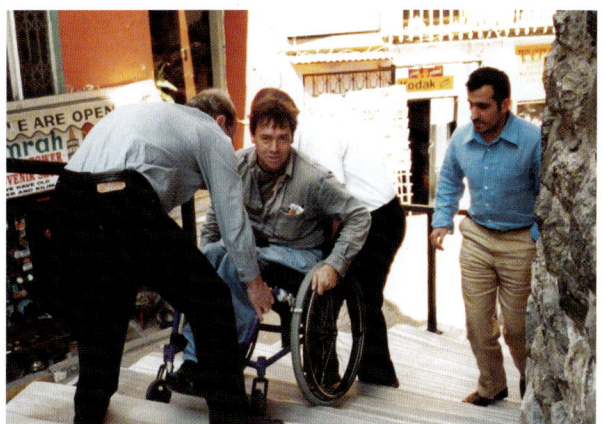

KINDNESS OF STRANGERS (Turkey): Turks from the Asian side of Istanbul turn the task of mounting the steps of the city's famous Galata Tower from one that looked impossible into the merely difficult. (Photo credit: Emilie Binnerts)

ABANDON HOPE: (Poland) All who pass through the chilling entrance to Auschwitz under the cruellest slogan imaginable: ARBEIT MACHT FREI ('WORK MAKES YOU FREE').

OLD TIMERS' SAKE
(Latvia): Two men of a
certain age face daily life in
the post-communist world
with a certain resignation.
Seated on a bench in the
provincial town of Kuldiga,
they could, on the other
hand, have been rehearsing
Waiting for Godot.

RIGHT ON QUEUE
(Estonia): Waiting in sub-
zero Tallinn for to top up
her financial reserves,
fellow journalist and friend
Stephanie Bunbury, snug as
a bug in her bunny rug,
makes the most of her
Baltic break.

TURNING POINT
(Finland): At 69°N, 25° E,
just north of Inari, Finland
—and thus unarguably
above the Arctic Circle —
the author gazes up the road
to the point where it veers
off towards Norway, and
feels his journey complete.

DAY 257 (24 JANUARY): JOB'S TOMB

Up into the hills our Mercedes climbs until eventually we come to a site that leaves me at once sceptical and reverent. Beyond a simple mosque, an uphill push of 100 metres brings me to a sunlit room with just one piece of furniture (if that is the word for a three-metre-long tomb draped in silken green fabric).

Mournful-looking women in black enter the room, dropping to their knees beside the tomb. My scepticism—how could Job, however patient he was, have made it here from Palestine?—is also silenced. They believe: this is more important, this is enough. Enough to remind me that Job is a prophet revered not only by Jews and Christians but by the God-fearing faith of Avraham/Abraham/Ibrahim's other spiritual descendants, the Muslims. To Muslim Arabs everywhere, this site is sacred. Job's Tomb. *Nabi Ayyub.*

DAY 258 (25 JANUARY): SALALAH

Believers in the clash-of-civilisations theory must be feeling vindicated today. Another suicide bomber has blown himself up, this time in Tel Aviv: casualties number nineteen.

You can almost feel East and West drifting further apart, the gulf growing by the day. That seals it. Much as I would like to see the world entire—and much as I know 99.9 per cent or more of Israelis go through every day without any untoward incident occurring—the idea of visiting Israel or Palestine now defies my rule of not visiting countries at war or on the slippery slope to it. Let them get their house in order: I will go another day, another year. (And, come March and April, when Bethlehem is under siege, my caution will look positively clairvoyant.)

DAY 260 (27 JANUARY): RAS AL-JINZ

By bus to Sur, and thence to the easternmost shore of the Arabian Peninsula by hire car, paid for by the Ministry of Information. I am the proud owner of a turtle permit, but dusk has fallen and a precious hour is lost when our driver, well off the nearest paved road and unfamiliar with these backblocks, misses the turn-off to the coast.

For another half hour it seems possible that, despite the best-laid plans, we are going to miss one of Nature's more reliable spectacles:

the nightly waddling ashore of giant (one-metre-long plus) sea turtles to lay their eggs. The turtles, who don't wear watches, nevertheless time their arrival between 9 and 10 pm every night of the year, and it is 9.15 when our car parks near the beach.

A ranger, who has been expecting us, treads across the sand in front of what must be a strange sight in itself: three people, one perched on a chair while two carry it over sand impassable to its wheels, we move in sedan-like procession beneath ghostly moonlight.

Our ranger stops, having found one of the turtles. He spews out statistics the way a geyser gushes water: 95 kilograms to 155 kilograms, mature at 25 years, 70 to 140 eggs buried at a time, the turtle can live to be 100. Exhausted though she must be from her haul out of the sea onto the broad sandy strip, the mother, with her pleading eyes reacting to the glare of torchlight on her face, hunkers ever more closely over her eggs. Forget the statistics, this is a sight to warm the cockles of the heart, one that amply justifies my own hard trek to this magical rendezvous.

DAY 263 (30 JANUARY): BACK TO THE UAE

Thank God for the BBC. Now it tells me George W. Bush has called Iraq, Iran and North Korea the Axis of Evil. I'm glad I went to Iran when it was just a 'rogue state'. To be roguish is kinda cute but from evil, we pray to Heaven, deliver us.

SAUDI ARABIA: 31 JANUARY–4 FEBRUARY

DAYS 264/265 (31 JANUARY/1 FEBRUARY): UAE–SAUDI BORDER

I'm on the night bus to Hofuf, an oasis town in Saudi Arabia's Eastern Province. Owning that hard-won visa only because I persuaded those reputed hearts of flint that it would be impossible for me to stay on a bus long enough to cross their vast land, I am now fasting—as always on long bus journeys—so as to avoid an all-round embarrassing emergency.

By the time we cross the border, February is 50 minutes old. Wait a minute: no, it isn't: there are ten minutes of January left. Saudi Arabian time is one hour behind the Emirates.

We are still at the border post when February comes round for the second time. Normally, at borders the bus driver explains my non-ambulatory status to a more or less understanding immigration officer who lets me stay on board while my paperwork is processed. Not here. The officers are insisting I get down from the bus.

I'm tired and a bit cranky. 'Why?' I protest. Because, they say, pointing to a row of eager-looking Alsatians, these dogs are so new we haven't had time to train them for restraint, only for aggression. I'm down those steps in a flash.

DAY 266 (2 FEBRUARY–02.02.02): RIYADH

On arriving in the Saudi capital, I notice for the first time that the bus-ticket collector's right hand consists of a solitary thumb and four bleached knuckle stumps where the fingers should be (or were). I ask no questions.

Modern tower blocks don't surprise. A swimming pool with a sign saying 'NO SWIMMING' does. As does a diversion sign on a four-lane highway advising 'CAMEL OVERPASS'.

Heading off to dinner at the Riyadh youth hostel, a Saudi hostel resident inconsiderately leaves the refectory door wide open. I am about to call out 'Hey, were you born in a tent?' but, just in time, remember where I am.

Perhaps it is not so strange, considering the vast inequalities of wealth distribution in this oil-rich kingdom, that it is in Saudi Arabia where buses seem to have risen most effectively to the challenge of air travel. From a new terminal in Riyadh, which has its own supermarket and whose arrival and departure lounges bristle with security guards, to the coaches themselves in which refreshments are served, this is a bus system with its wings outspread.

And, as we barrel north into the heart of Arabia, the view is not as barren as I had envisaged. Were it not for the Arabic script on the side of the wheat silos, you could mistake the irrigated farmlands of central Arabia for the cultivated drylands of the Wimmera. Solar-powered telephone booths stand, lonely roadside sentinels, hundreds of kilometres from towns and villages. Whoever uses them?

The bus drops me in Taima, a piddling 230 kilometres from Madain Salah, the ruins of my dreams. No public transport goes anywhere near it and, as luck would have it, my visit coincides with the *hajj*, just when a million Muslims are coursing through the kingdom bound for Mecca.

What to do? The likes of Sir Richard Burton and Charles Doughty, the first Westerners to clap eyes on this lost city of the dead, in the 1880s, joined the pilgrim throng in Arab disguise. This gives me an idea: gingerly, I approach fellow diners at the Taima Hotel—North Africans who, I have heard, are leaving today for Mecca—and cadge a lift with them to a highway roundabout the size of a space station. From there I plan to hitchhike my way to Madain Salah.

The highway junction has a name (al-Jawrah), which is somewhat astounding given that it is in the middle of nowhere. I cycle round to the east-west road and spend an hour unprotected from the broiling sun. Just as I am conjuring up the headlines that will inform my furthest and dearest of my demise ('Antipodean Culture Vulture Gives Thumbs Up to Death') Providence sends the first vehicle for what?—hours? days?—along my chosen road. Saudi student and Formula One aspirant Sami Musa must be shocked, too. With a screech of brakes he reverses his utility, and agrees to drive me to al-Ula, in the western Saudi province known as the Hejaz.

This speed freak, who freely admits he is driving home after a night without sleep, somehow gets both of us alive to the modest town just 22 tantalising kilometres from my objective. Knowing that no one may visit Madain Salah without a police permit, I proceed immediately to al-Ula's constabulary headquarters, guarded by swaggering types with Mexican-style bandoliers, holsters and live ammunition.

Just as I am wondering where all this is leading, down the front steps of the station comes a portly aristocrat to whom all bow low. I am briefly introduced to Prince Ahmed, son of King Fahd. No sooner has his Cadillac borne him away than I am told that the Prince, on hearing of this rare arrival's wish to see the local 2000-year-old ruins, has signed the permit with his own right royal hand.

And that's how I meet Sultan. As near as I ever make out, he is a police detective gone to seed: flatulent, fulsomely friendly and unashamedly uncultured. We make an odd couple for the outing to this open-air museum.

As Sultan drives the police pick-up out of the compound, he mentions for what will be the first of a dozen times that I should not forget (and he makes me write it down) that his full name is Sultan bin Hamud bin Salhan al-Thawab al-Bedawi. This impressive pedigree does not prevent him dropping into the local mini-mart like any pleb and stocking up with three kilos of rice and a similar quantity of grilled chook, water and Pepsi, for what he regards as a first-class picnic opportunity.

Followed at a discreet distance by our police Jeep shadow, we take the Madain Salah turn-off and present our precious permit to the soldiers at the Department of Antiquities hut outside the wire-fenced site.

Ten minutes later we are seated in an empty chamber carved out of the rock, featuring ledges halfway up the interior wall where dead bodies lay nineteen centuries back. To picnic here would be an act of desecration, I reflect, had they not been dispossessed of their resting places long ago.

In this ancient necropolis raised by the Nabataean civilisation, most of the chambers—including the one where Sultan and I dine alfresco—were mausoleums for the exalted rich.

Sultan, I sense, has no idea of, let alone interest in, this fact as he tosses his Pepsi can onto the sand in front of the cave.

First stop after the picnic is Qasr al-Farid, a tomb whose impressive frontage thrusts 30 metres skyward and which is carved in its entirety from a single majestic outcrop of sandstone.

Altogether, there are 110 tombs here. And that is not all: you can explore a reasonably intact Islamic castle from the 13th century and marvel at a rusty locomotive in the 1906 Hejaz Railway sheds, although the tracks have long since been swallowed by the sands.

Madain Salah is so remote that after dark I have to beg the police to extend their escort duties to guaranteeing my safe return to Taima, ready for the next bus to Jordan.

Prince Ahmed's writ runs further than I would have guessed. But then Sultan drops his guard and tells me that Prince Ahmed—despite his resplendent black robe lined with gold braid—is not a prince of the realm, merely the Mayor of al-Ula. Calling him a prince was a sneer, a leg-pull, a desert mirage. I return the prankster's smile good-humouredly: at least Madain Salah was for real.

Chapter 16

YOU ARE WELCOME IN JORDAN

The Arabs are a proud and sensitive people ... some appreciation is
needed of how much they have in their past of which to be proud, and
how much in their present about which to be sensitive.

WILFRED CANTWELL SMITH *Islam in Modern History*

FEBRUARY-MARCH 2002

If Israel–Palestine lies at the crux of conflict in the Middle East, it is
Israel's neighbours Syria and Lebanon, and the shadowy groups that
fight for sub-national causes there—Hezbollah, the Druze, the Kurds—
who have given the region much of its reputation as a no-go zone.

Those who read only the latest disasters in the news pages could be
excused for dismissing the cities of Damascus, Aleppo and Amman as
destinations of choice. But, whether or not you buy the idea that we
are taking part in a war on terror, those who shun the region are cutting
themselves off from a pillar of wisdom we can all lean on: the wisdom
of how to recover from the loss of one's known world. Six thousand
years after humans settled down in west Asia and started growing
crops, these people know something about continuity. Believe me.

JORDAN: 4–18 FEBRUARY

DAY 269 (5 FEBRUARY): AMMAN

It's 3 am and our bus, whose journey began in Dubai and which I
joined in Taima, draws to a stop in Amman. Against my better
judgment I let the co-driver stow my wheelchair in the hold of the bus
and, now as it comes back with him holding one of the brakes up

155

separately from the chassis, my patience snaps. If not quite a frosty parting, it is as cool as the damp night under this leaden winter sky.

Knowing that the late hour means I must hastily find a place to stay, I am grateful that the night-duty receptionist at the first *funduq* we come to is understanding enough to charge me a half rate for an empty room.

I've reached the far edge of Arabia, but the article I filed after my visit to al-Jazeera's studios in Qatar has stalked me across the desert. An email from the foreign editor of the *Sydney Morning Herald* informs me that wire services are running a story that Tayseer Allouni, the ex-Kabul-bureau chief, actually interviewed bin Laden. The foreign editor is speculating that the Americans would have known about this and waited for it to be aired. Maybe the decision to bomb al-Jazeera's Kabul centre was linked to this.

He asks me to activate my al-Jazeera contacts to get their side of the story. I spend most of today phoning Doha from the crowded cubby-hole of a phone-call vendor but, by evening, I'm in an Internet café writing for publication:

> Qatari-based al-Jazeera television has muzzled its staff amid renewed controversy ... 'I cannot give you any details about this matter,' Allouni said.

My dream of becoming a foreign correspondent has never died.

A year and a half later, Allouni will be arrested in Spain over his al-Qa'eda links. In October 2005 he will be jailed for seven years by a Spanish court that ruled he was an active collaborator with the Islamist movement.

But even now I can see the amusing side of things. For months I have been telling the folks back home how I ran into 'Osama bin Laden' in a Tehran bazaar, while the more dramatic meeting was with a television journalist who had met not a look-alike but the man himself.

DAY 272 (8 FEBRUARY): AMMAN

Amman, known to the ancients as Philadelphia, is a rabbit warren of narrow streets linked at crazy angles. As a wheelchair user I find that this city, like Tehran before it and Minsk yet to come, is one where the old adage 'If you can't beat 'em, join 'em' applies. When there is no way to cross a street by waiting for the ceaseless flow of traffic to clear,

I take up position by the kerb (facing the oncoming traffic, an important safety precaution) and 'row' against the tide.

The local citizenry is almost unfailingly friendly, a phenomenon I have come to conclude is directly related to the scarcity of foreign visitors.

DAY 273 (9 FEBRUARY): SUWEIMEH, DEAD SEA

An hour's ride by minibus from Amman and I'm deposited at the Dead Sea Rest House. It's what you might call a going concern: going to be demolished, to make way for a more upmarket resort by the shores of the lake that occupies the lowest point on Earth (398 metres below sea level).

Just a few kilometres from the River Jordan, where Jesus once turned the tide on John the Baptist, the Dead Sea is famous for its salt content, which turns the body into a flotation device, and for its curative properties: those associated with the green clay that is smeared on bathers' skin. This day, though, is no seaside frolic for, as it happens, my plan for a private dip in the water coincides with the arrival of another, far more famous visitor: Her Highness the Princess Alia, sister of King Abdullah.

But all I know as the minibus pulls into the Rest House car park is that the phalanx of 20 or so green jackets, not to mention another score of tourist police, all of whom greet me as I alight, seems just a tad excessive. As do the metal detector and table for the reception of luggage. Nevertheless I deposit my two bags and address one of the green jackets, who, I later learn, is a Royal Guard. 'Please inspect,' I invite him.

'Why have you come here?' his commanding officer quizzes me with an unmistakable edge of hostility.

'To float in the Dead Sea,' I reply, trying not to sound like a smart arse, but I might as well have said, 'To view the flying saucers.' Unimpressed, the chief of the Royal Guard counters, 'You will not be allowed to.'

At this point, perhaps sensing the need to lower the temperature, the head of the tourist police, Sergeant H. Magdidi, blurts out that familiar refrain which is music to the ears, 'You are welcome in Jordan.'

'Somehow I don't feel it right now,' I say, turning to the Royal Guard

157

leader (whose name I am later given as Tariq). Keeping my voice as measured as possible in the circumstances, I continue, 'I've come 16 000 kilometres to be here, my papers are in order, and I *will* be entering the Dead Sea.'

My jut-jawed determination is too much for Tariq's *amour propre*, and he shouts at close quarters, 'Fuck you. Fuck you ten times.'

To his credit, Tariq immediately apologises, but remains tight-lipped about the royal visit, which is common knowledge among Jordanians.

Hasty whispers are exchanged with hotel staff, and 20 minutes later I am triumphantly offshore, watched over by a Royal Guard marksman in possession of a semi-automatic and (I hope) no orders to shoot.

DAY 276 (12 FEBRUARY): AJLOUN, JORDAN VALLEY

Most of today was spent on a wild-goose chase, but it ends in the lap of outstanding hospitality, if not luxury.

The idea was to visit Pella, a northern archaeological dig being supervised by Australians (an embryonic 'Email from the Edge' article beckoned). However, by the time we find Pella's excavations (at dusk) we learn that the Australians won't be back until May and the site itself is locked up. So I rely on the driver to find me lodgings for the night and, as this isn't his part of the country, that's a tall order. About 7.30 pm, we pitch up to the only hotel in Ajloun, and—as best I can estimate it—the only one within an 80-kilometre radius.

A less propitious abode for the wheelchair-inhabiting guest it is hard to conceive of. Two long flights of stairs separate the street from the three-storey hostelry perched on one of the town's two hills (a castle occupies the other). Nor can the two brothers who manage the hotel have been expecting any guest, let alone one in my situation, this cold February night. But, within seconds of the driver explaining my predicament, they bound down the stairs, ask what they can do to help and, despite an expenditure of energy that would put an Olympic weightlifter to shame, proceed to make me feel at home.

Once safely in the foyer, I discover that the guestrooms are on the third floor and even I quail at putting mein hosts to further trouble. No problem: they bring a bed down *from* the third floor and set it up in the ground-floor restaurant. The restaurant toilets are accessible.

So thankful am I for this extraordinary welcome I stay an extra day.

158

This time the stock phrase is not trotted out, but the truth of it is deeply felt: I am welcome in Jordan.

DAY 278 (14 FEBRUARY): PETRA

Majestic Petra is your answer to those who would say that Arabs are shiftless, unproductive nomads. For desert dwellers, survival comes before everything else—but look at what these Bedouins built here in 'the rose-red city half as old as time', and such stereotypes crumble before your mind's eye.

Yesterday I travelled south to overnight at a rest-house in the town of Wadi Musa, separated by a rift valley from Israel, a bare 15 kilometres distant. As luck would have it, heavy rains fell yesterday, and the resulting flash floods forced the authorities to close the site. So I set off this morning not knowing whether my once-in-a-lifetime chance to see Jordan's most popular tourist attraction is about to sink without trace.

Where the taxi drops me off, by the entrance at which horses—carriages in tow—wait patiently, water is rushing down a normally dry wadi but the ticket-sellers reassure me Petra is open again. I breathe a sigh of relief.

Spurning the horses (BYO transport is my rule), I push off down a long road that will take me further than I can see. But the morning sun is pleasant, and this is not a race, so I lapse into a leisurely rhythm.

The Nabataeans built Petra originally, in the third century BC, as a refuge from hostile desert warriors. Over the decades it grew into a city— today we can make out houses, temples, tombs and theatres— but retained the character of a fortress, being carved entirely out of the massive sandstone rock formations that dominate the area.

Each marvel is named as well as we moderns can accomplish on the basis of what has been dredged up from antiquity: here is the Winged Lions Temple, over there the Roman Soldier's Tomb. Then the road forms a long defile. Tectonic changes have created this fissure in the rock, a path along which every visitor to Petra must travel for more than a kilometre. This literal rite of passage cannot be taken quickly, even on foot; if you're on wheels, it is excruciatingly slow. As if forcing my way over pebbles weren't hard enough, I soon find they give way to irregularly shaped rocks, and at times passing from one to the other leaves me teetering perilously. The passage, called the Siq, seems never-ending. At one point another traveller retraces his steps to ask if I need help. I do, but am too proud to accept it. Traversing the Siq is something I'm determined to do in my own time, at my pace, if it takes my last ounce of energy.

Half an hour later—just as I'm ruing my stubbornness and wondering why more fellow travellers can't see the straits I'm in—the roughest surface I've travelled on since leaving home twists to the left, and the sight that makes the Siq worthwhile lies straight ahead, in all its celebrated glory. This is al-Khazneh, the Treasury, the city's most impressive public building, familiar from the film *Indiana Jones and the Last Crusade*.

DAY 279 (15 FEBRUARY): WADI RUM

One spontaneous moment is worth a month of plans. Reading up about the Arabs had sown in my brain the dream of spending a night under the stars, Bedouin-style. But, given the practical difficulty of being 24 hours away from any Western toilets, I had consigned it securely to the brain cell labelled 'Dreams Never To Be Acted On'.

This morning the dream bursts into a realistic prospect. As I am leaving the rest-house, I find my fellow passengers in the minibus are a mixed assortment of Australian, New Zealand and English backpackers. They have all booked a night in a Bedouin tent out in the desert near Wadi Rum, and are happy for me to become a last-minute extra paying guest. Deciding that if I can fast 20 hours to survive a long-distance Kazakh train journey this challenge should not over-extend me, I dispel all misgivings and abandon myself to the adventure.

A four-wheel drive awaits us by the roadside, and the driver is equally welcoming. As we pause for breakfast at the tourist centre just off the Desert Highway, I head off to do my ablutions (and incidentally to avoid the too tempting sight of others eating).

We speed past the Bedouin shanty dwellers and out into some of the most pristine desert imaginable. Across the sands we bounce, to the northern side of a *jebel* (Arabic for 'hill'), where my fellow passengers troop off with the guide to inspect Bedouin rock carvings and Kufic inscriptions in its cool interior.

Our next halt is Lawrence's Well. These days it is stagnant but once it was fed by springs cascading from another jebel high overhead. To general amusement, our guide tells us that even today older Bedouin can clearly recall meeting Lawrence, who retains a legendary place in their memory. Only the Lawrence they recall is not the Englishman himself (that was before their time) but Peter O'Toole, whom many of these people—not cinema-goers even now—saw bestriding Wadi Rum when it was converted into a film set back in 1962.

As the sun approaches its zenith we head out into the desert, lunching (well, *they* do, and there is no escaping the sight this time) in the shade of a convenient hollowed-out rock, before driving ahead to the shade of a larger rocky outcrop. Right next to it is an imposing dune, 20 metres high, and with some trepidation I let the two strongest members of our party lift my chair—despite the sands shifting under our combined weight—so that the promised rich orange sunset can be enjoyed by one and all.

By now, I am steeled against hunger pangs well enough to endure close-up observation of the evening meal. The organisers have barbecued a goat, and a local Bedouin who plays the oud has joined us for the occasion. A star field as rich as any in Africa or Central Australia mesmerises our party, so you could hardly say it's lights out, but we all manage to sleep soundly in this desert idyll.

SYRIA: 18 FEBRUARY–1 MARCH

In the days when Bill Clinton ruled the roost, Syria was branded a 'rogue state'. For all I know, it still is. Certainly, at the time of writing it remained a state that supported terrorism (according to the US Congress). But there are good reasons to go there, quite apart from the hospitality of the ordinary people—which comes as less and less of a surprise the further this journey takes me.

Assyria was one of the earliest powerful nations, and Damascus lays claim to being the world's oldest city. Here, history breathes.

DAY 282 (18 FEBRUARY): THE BORDER, OR THEREABOUTS
They manhandled me, were on the point of roughing me up, and nearly ruined my nice continuous line on the map. I was shaking with anger and powerless to stop them.

161

Backtracking, the first blow to my keen anticipation was struck at Amman railway station. At 7 am, in the process of buying a ticket to Damascus, I couldn't get over the fact that today I would be travelling on the Hejaz Railway that al-Aurans (Lawrence) and his merry band blew up when the Ottomans were the nominal ruling power round these parts.

The ticket vendor, to give him his due, tried to let me down gently. 'They will not let you into Syria,' he cooed. But the Syrian consul in Oman had promised there would be no problem, I replied, and showed him the relevant passage in my guidebook: 'Australians and the Irish are [two] of the few nationalities that can cross into Syria from Jordan without a visa [in advance]—it is issued at the border ...'

Not only would it be issued, it would be free of charge: I had the diplomat's word for that, too. Knowing better than to argue, the vendor sold me the ticket. As porters lifted me aboard I was happy to see that the carriages were 'open-plan' so I didn't have to spend the journey crammed into the vestibule. I settled down for a leisurely journey north.

My luck held out even beyond the country's last railway station, where Jordanian immigration control argued earnestly over whether I should be allowed to continue. My what-the-ambassador-told-me-and-the-book-says routine prevailed despite much shaking of official heads. There was a brief attempt to levy a departure tax. 'A departure tax by train?' I protested. 'You must be joking.' They did not insist: sweet reason had prevailed again.

But then along came Syria. Our old rust bucket rattled to a stop at De'ra railway station, a couple of kilometres over the border. Here, I had been told by helpful passengers with little English but a gleam of compassion in their eyes, everyone must change for the train to Damascus.

This I hadn't reckoned on. After a five-minute wait, the surliest-looking young soldiers I had clapped eyes on in a long time bustled aboard and indicated I must disembark. I pointed to the wheelchair, made it obvious despite any language gap between us that I couldn't get myself onto the platform, let alone into the Customs building, and handed them my passport.

'Australian passport,' I thought, a trace smugly. 'They will see I'm not a rogue American, but one of the good guys—perhaps they'll think

I'm Irish?—and, their China-wall faces will crease into grins normally reserved for reunions with long-lost relatives.'

Ten minutes passed, fifteen. Alongside us, not a leg's breadth from our train, another had shunted down the track and everyone else in our compartment was swapping carriages. So I lowered myself to the floor and crawled and shuffled onto the Damascus train.

Five minutes later I was poised for the onward journey, along with my luggage, which had been brought over by the other passengers, when a frowning military officer with a moustache that would have done the Führer proud towered over me and spoke briskly to a young woman translator. 'He says you must leave the train, and you must leave the country,' she told me.

'Please inform him that I was told by the Syrian ambassador to Oman,'—I fumbled for his card—'Muhammad Ibrahim, that I would be issued a visa on arrival.' The officer dismissed his translator: this was an ominous sign.

A minute later, the same four strapping young soldiers stepped aboard and, following their superior's command, took hold of my limbs and lifted. Anyone in a wheelchair will tell you that the rest of the population is often awkward when it comes to relating physically to you. A hug is difficult, even if one feels the urge; a pat on the shoulder is all most people can manage. But violent or forcible entry into one's personal comfort zone is so unexpected that this bodily removal came as a shock. Fortunately, I had the presence of mind not to go stiff or resist. I let them lift me, shouting, 'I'm in a wheelchair, you can do medical damage!' but, of course, they couldn't understand a word and wouldn't have altered their conduct if they did.

Looking back, I concede that they did not use undue force, and carefully deposited me on the seat of the train I'd arrived on—the one that was shortly to head back to Amman—followed by my luggage, piece by piece. But at the time I was embarrassed and, as soon as I was free to do so without provoking them to drop me, gave vent to my fury, shouting in their wake as they retreated to the Customs house.

The consul's assurance was an empty promise. I slumped in the corner of the carriage, a spectacle of distress that other passengers tried to sympathise with, but, for all they knew, the authorities were well rid of a dangerous individual.

The same train that brought me to Syria bore me away again, back to Jordan. I don't know the Arabic for 'I told you so' but it was written all over the Jordanian immigration authorities' faces. I turned to an English-speaking passenger to ask why the Syrians wouldn't let me in.

'It is because they have no computers at the railway station,' he explained, 'so they cannot check you. They think you may be an Israeli agent, or a terrorist.'

Being deported from Syria as a terrorist is one of my few claims to fame. The irony didn't dawn on me at the time, though, I have to say.

Sometime after 4 pm I arrived back at the Syrian border—this time by road. A taxi dropped me there, and my plan was to get that elusive visa before hitchhiking, if need be, to Damascus. It took me a full hour among the Jordanian paper-shufflers to explain my cancelled exit stamp and get a new one. With no one to transport my luggage those few hundred metres to the Syrian border post, I was contemplating the risks of mounting some kind of bag relay when I saw a passenger coach boarding. It was certainly pointed in the right direction so worth a try.

Did the driver have room for a traveller going to Damascus? He nodded. I clambered aboard, another passenger moved up, and suddenly my fortunes had changed.

Just one obstacle remained: when we came to the Syrian post, the authorities demanded US$30 for the visa. At this point, it was obvious, no one was going to be ringing Muscat to give me the benefit of the doubt so discretion was called for. Politely, I told them this visa should really be complimentary but I would pay the US$30 if he issued a receipt. He obliged. I held my peace. No one is ever going to be able to say I was deported from a country twice on the same day.

DAY 284 (20 FEBRUARY): DAMASCUS

This city harks back to the dawn of civilisation but, for the most part, it features abominable architecture from the early 20th century, tending to Stalinist monumentalism. As is possible anywhere the French colonised, you can get a decent baguette here, but the overriding impression these days is of a police state. I soon locate the capital's only Internet café—situated opposite the security police headquarters—and its young manager confides that all messages are monitored by the police, and there's nothing he can do about it.

Everywhere, in posters of varying size, one sees the stern visage of Bashar al-Assad, the thirty-something dictator who took over when his father, Hafez, died, and who runs an equally tight ship. There is no point in pretending that Syria is a Western democracy, or even that it aspires to be. It takes only a few heart-to-heart conversations with the young and the intellectual—curious about the West, sceptical, not in the market for any cut-and-dried belief systems—to know that the Syrian military and police rule through fear.

Nothing has essentially changed since Lawrence said of the Syrians at the end of World War I, 'They were discontented always with what government they had; such being their intellectual pride; but few of them honestly thought out a working alternative, and fewer still agreed upon one.'

Down to the Immigration Office: they shouldn't have charged me for that visa and I am out for administrative revenge.

Here, in this three-storey building that looks as though it hasn't been cleaned since the 1940s, hundreds of people crowd into the downstairs hall, clamouring for the right to speak to someone in authority. But those in authority are on floor three—up three flights of stairs. After an hour or so, a man in a buttoned-up white shirt descends the stairs and asks what I'm here for. When I explain, and hand him my passport, he asks me to wait downstairs. What choice have I? Another half hour passes, and he returns. 'The high general handles these matters, and he would like you to come upstairs.'

'Please tell the high general,' I say, barely containing my frustration, 'that he must come down low because I cannot go up high.'

'But,' he counters, 'you are wasting your time. The visa is paid for.'

'Did the Syrian consul in Muscat lie to me when he told me the visa was free?' I challenge him.

'No,' he replies with studied equanimity, 'he was right. For Australians, the visa is free—but you must pay.'

This apparent contradiction throws me for a moment, but then I see Syrian-style reason. 'Do you really mean that the visa is free but, because I have paid at the border, you're not going to give me my money back?'

'Yes, that's right,' he beams, clearly impressed by my quick grasp of Syrian crisis management.

'Oh well, that's all I wanted to know,' I say. Business is completed: it's time to see the city.

DAY 285 (21 FEBRUARY): DAMASCUS

Much of Damascus may be architecturally undistinguished but, boy, does the Old City live up to its name. On the edge of the CBD, it sprawls over little more than a square kilometre but inside it are bazaars, ancient Roman ruins, *hammam* baths and mosques.

Opposite the great covered bazaar, Souq al-Hamidiyya, is the Umayyad Mosque, which suggests most powerfully that if I didn't know better this could be the third century before or after Christ. Accompanied by Bachar, a Syrian museum attendant steeped in his country's history, I wait calmly outside while the Umayyad's senior mullah is humbly asked whether I may intrude with silent reverence into the courtyard of Damascus's holy of holies. (My wheels enable me to do silence better than pedestrians.)

Despite Islam's forbidding image in the West, I know from experience (most recently in Kuwait and Bahrain) that Muslims welcome respectful visitors, believing that we are all creatures of Allah. But error creeps into all human organisations, and hierarchies are like bread, growing crusty at the top. So, already branded a terrorist in a land to which so few Westerners come, I feel only a dull disappointment on being told, 'The mullah says you cannot enter the mosque because it is forbidden in Scripture to enter the House of God on wheels.'

I hand the camera to my learned go-between and ask him to be my eyes in the House of God.

Sensing my disappointment at being excluded from the inner sanctum, Bachar points to one of the pencil-thin spires that grace the mosque's south wall. 'That is the white minaret of Damascus, which we also call the Jesus Minaret,' he urges my gaze skyward. Instantly I recall that the Christian Lord is also revered in Islam as a prophet.

'It is believed by Muslims that Jesus will appear there on Judgment Day—to make all people Muslims. We don't believe that Jesus is dead, but we believe Judas was crucified in his place.'

Damascus, as St Paul was the first to admit, is a place where all previous beliefs are seen in a new light.

166

George W(armonger) Bush can talk about Crusades all he likes: it was Saladin who sent the Crusaders packing, defeated Richard the Lionheart and captured Jerusalem (in 1187)—and here the all-conquering Arab hero was buried.

In the shadow of the Umayyad Mosque stands his marble mausoleum, draped in a green Islamic banner, much too new to have occupied its place of honour since 1193. I ask Bachar about this, and it turns out that even here one cannot quite escape Lawrence of Arabia: on conquering Damascus in 1918, his forces are believed to have stolen the coverlet from Saladin's sarcophagus.

Next comes an even bigger shock: the mausoleum itself is barely a century old, a gift to mark Kaiser Wilhelm's visit here in 1898. Saladin represents the pinnacle of Muslim conquest, so it is a tribute that eight centuries after his death would-be mighty men jostle to claim his mantle.

Oh, and here's a quick way to win money. Ask someone, 'Who was the most powerful person ever to hail from Tikrit?'

Odds are they'll answer 'Saddam Hussein'. But it's no contest, really; even Arabs will give the prize to Saladin. After all, Saddam (who sometimes compared himself to the great man) never captured Jerusalem.

DAY 287 (23 FEBRUARY): PALMYRA

Another day, another empire. To the central Syrian desert, hundreds of kilometres north-east of the capital, I have come on a public bus occupied mostly by bored soldiers. Here amid a copybook oasis lies Palmyra, alias Tadmor. A smallish town now, it was a rich and flourishing centre for the first two centuries of the Christian era. Its world-acclaimed historic site lies a good quarter hour's push (by chair) from the modern settlement. Rebuffing the offer of a camel ride—do these tourist touts lack imagination or eyesight, I wonder—I pass the hours rolling up to the *agora*, then down to the ancient city theatre, and explore as much of the breathtaking Temple of Bel (AD 31) as I can.

DAY 289 (25 FEBRUARY): QAMISHLE,
ON THE SYRIAN–TURKISH BORDER

They have lived in the Middle East for 5000 years, probably longer than the Arabs themselves. They are a people with their own language and culture, yet have never had a nation to call their own. Today 65 million strong, they are a substantial minority in four lands, but say the word 'Kurdestan' and shivers run down spines all the way from Baghdad to Washington, not to mention Tehran and Ankara. To the media they are a 'problem', even the UN won't encourage their hopes of nationhood. In the 'liberation' of Iraq, they were an afterthought. Who are the Kurds? And what do they want? I am here to find out.

Here in the heartland of their 'homeland', 'authorities' cannot ignore them, only try to subdue them. As I am way out of tourist bounds, I have to be very discreet in seeking out the half persons of Qamishle, or my rough welcome to Syria's southern border may turn out to be a modest prelude to what awaits me on its northern frontier.

Force is more obvious in such places: it wears a uniform; is armed; it struts and swaggers. Trying to make myself inconspicuous as a waiter brings my thick Levantine coffee, I bend over the book I have brought with me. It is the 19th-century explorer Sir Richard Burton's translation of *Arabian Nights* and he is writing about Aladdin. 'Soon he entered a coffee house, a fine building which stood in the marketplace, and which attracted many people to play at dice, backgammon, chess, and other games.'

I look up. Facing each other, a metre in front of my face, are two ancient men. At their elbows lie their coffees, steaming, forgotten, as one raises a playing card tremulously for a moment before slamming it on the table, face up, in triumph. His opponent grunts in admiration.

This could be 2002 or, if my name were Aladdin, 1002.

My reverie is broken by the presence of an earnest-looking man of about 40 years. I throw out what I hope will be a hook that doesn't impale the fisherman by saying, 'I am just here looking for a Kurdish person.'

'I am a Kurdish person,' he replies. 'My name is Hussein Ahmad.' Bait taken.

Two hours later, I am seated cross-legged on the floor of a house in Hellalia, surely the poorest suburb of Qamishle, in the company of Hussein Ahmad and friends. We sip cardamom tea, and dine on goat and rice prepared by Hussein's sister, Shamsa. When the main course is finished, she presents us with a plate of *kulitcha*, a Kurdish shortbread.

Over the border, no more than a kilometre away, we can see a Turkish hillside. Kurds are also numerous there, where power flaunts itself even more menacingly, because that is where guerrillas of the PKK (Kurdish Workers' Party)—terrorists or freedom fighters, depending on how you view them—lurk.

It is not news to me that the Kurdish world is divided into two camps. The first subscribes to Lawrence's philosophy that 'freedom cannot be given; it can only be taken'. The other believes that the path of violence cannot lead to liberty.

Hussein refills my cup, and assures me that Syria's not-so-secret police would never dare disturb any gathering in this neglected, unsewered quarter of town. Opposite me, nibbling on his kulitcha, is a one-eyed 'terrorist', Hussein's younger brother Abdul Latif Hussein Younis Ali.

'How did you lose your eye?' I venture, hoping my curiosity will not be taken for impoliteness. During a gun battle in the Lebanese civil war, he tells me. 'You remember the bombing of the US Marines?'

The death of more than 200 Americans in a single blast in 1983 is not something a journalist is likely to forget. I nod. Younis Ali smiles toothlessly: his mouth has closed.

Now in his late thirties, Younis Ali—head wrapped in red-and-white kaffiyeh—says he remains an active member of the PKK. He looks classically volatile, out to impress. At one point, without warning, he reaches into the inside pocket of his jacket and pulls out ... a wallet. With another deft movement he proffers a small photo of Abdullah Ocalan, the PKK leader sentenced to death by Turkey. Suddenly he is on his feet, pumping the air like Atlas on speed. 'I love him too much,' he gushes with the excessive zeal of the single-minded.

Younis Ali's English is threadbare. 'Do Syria's Kurds feel better treated than their brothers and sisters in Turkey?' I ask his brother.

'If a Kurd try to open a business [here], they will take away the permit,' he says. 'Here they don't make this' (Hussein gets to his knees and looses off an imaginary Kalashnikov volley), 'they make do like this' (he now leaps across the refreshments to play-act at strangling me). I get the point.

'Youths I have spoken to here—Kurds who live in Canada and England, home for the feast of Eid—say that the refusal of Iraq, Iran,

Syria and Turkey to give up any territory for Kurdestan means you have no alternative but to fight for it. Is that how you see things?'

'If other people don't give you this, you must be fighting, the same for any country. Any people will fight for their freedom: you see Cuba, you see Vietnam. Too much talk, they give you nothing. If fighting, I think this is better.'

'And if you die fighting …?'

'Die together.'

Time to confront the fighters. 'The world calls you terrorists. How can you win through terror?'

'We are not terrorists. If this is your house, and someone can come and stay in your house and not go away, where is the terrorism? This is our home, not for another people, not Turkey, not Syria. Three thousand years ago in this land you call Medea, we Kurds live here …'

LEBANON: 1–17 MARCH

Bad reputations cling to disaster zones like the lengthening tails of comets. Today your chances of being blown up in Beirut are probably less than those of being shot on the streets of America, but the 1980s civil war still makes this a no-go zone in the minds of most tourists. However, countries that have been to hell and back, like people who have been through the fire of experience, have stories to tell. And, even if we couldn't learn from them, perhaps it would deepen our sense of common humanity to make their acquaintance.

Time was when I flattered myself that, since we are born on the same planet, anywhere we go should feel like home. The experience of passing through many places has made me somewhat more discriminating. Now I would add that it is in the aftermath of human upheaval, where the local inhabitants have come face to face with what ultimately counts in life (shared human experience, not lost traveller's cheques), that the visitor with an open mind and heart feels most at home.

Like any civil war, Lebanon's was a struggle for power. But somewhere along the line the car bombs and hostage-taking diverted Western TV viewers from the root causes, and the mercenary motives of the warlords who posed as politicians.

Oddly enough, the fratricide ended with the unity of Lebanon but under a pro-Syrian government so that, for many Christians, the country when I visited was regarded as a colony of Damascus by the sea. But Beirut, with its openness and pumping neon nightlife, couldn't be less like Damascus if it tried.

Psychologists know that aggression stems from insecurity, and there we have a clue to Lebanon's volatile recent past. Within their own communities of belief, the dominant Muslim and Christian groups (Shias and Maronites) are regarded as minorities, with tales of persecution to tell. So are the Druze, the mountain-dwelling Muslim sect that even most of the other Muslims have little time for. Lebanon is a small, fragmented country. About the only thing fiercer than the forces pulling it apart is the attachment each of its minorities feels to the 'idea' of Lebanese unity. After a few days here, Lebanon appears to me like a priceless Chinese vase that has been cracked but, because of the brilliant scenes depicted on it, no one wants to replace.

For most of its history, Lebanon has been a successful example of the 'live and let live' philosophy. To remember it at its worst is unfair.

DAY 293 (1 MARCH): BEIRUT

The early morning bus from Damascus pulls into Masnah, the Lebanese border post, soon after 9 am. I stay on board in Seat 3, while an obliging fellow passenger, a Lebanese doctor, takes my passport into the immigration building, together with a request. I've heard that Australians get fourteen-day visas on arrival but, as I hope to stay sixteen days, could I have longer?

Ten minutes pass, and a blue-jacketed official approaches the bus, my passport in hand. Here comes trouble, I think. He smiles, keeps me in the merest moment's suspense, and tells me how I'm in luck arriving on today's bus rather than yesterday's. From 1 March, Australians get a month-long visa upon arrival. He hands my passport up. 'Welcome to Lebanon.' I thank him, and when he is gone turn to the doctor and say, 'Aren't I lucky 2002 isn't a leap year!"

Beirut is as I imagined it, one never-ending housing project sited between pine-forest cathedrals and that turquoise jewel, the Mediterranean. The search for an accessible downtown hotel takes time, and pauses only long enough for me to take in the somewhat unbelievable sight of the portly Prime Minister, Rafiq Hariri, waddling into a seaside restaurant, flanked by a bevy of bodyguards.

Two years later, Hariri's bodyguards won't be able to save his life from a bomb detonated near this very spot. An old score will be settled, but not an old war revived.

The sensible response will not be to cancel travel to Lebanon. When the IRA let off bombs in London randomly during the early 1980s, tourists still flocked there. When shadowy Muslim immigrant groups brought carnage to the streets of Paris, no one seriously advised travellers to avoid the city of love. And when home-grown terror came to London in July 2005 the shock was palpable, yet life went on. But, of course, different—double—standards apply to the Middle East.

The best accommodation option I come across is a 'cheapie'—the Hotel Regis—one block in from the beach and, although up a brief flight of stairs, staffed by friendly receptionists. The place is run by Syrians (like hotel, like country) and my chair is such a tight fit in the lift that a staff member must run upstairs and joggle the backrest until I shoot out of the elevator like a cannonball, nearly crushing him in the process.

The Hotel Regis's greatest drawback turns out to be its chief asset: it sits alone on a large urban block that would be known in Belfast as a 'bomb site'. Down at heel, it must once have been down at hell: anyway, its splendid isolation means I am simultaneously in the heart of a vibrant city yet shielded from the worst of the noise.

Come evening, it's time to explore the neighbourhood I've just moved into. Only a couple of minutes away is the *corniche*, that Lebanese–French pavement where lovers stroll by the Mediterranean, their gaze on the winking light of an oil tanker out to sea. Peanut-and-cool-drink vendors solicit custom, while old men smoke shishas under a balmy night sky.

DAY 295 (3 MARCH): BEIRUT

After pushing through West Beirut, from the dowdy but still fashionable district of Hamra, I emerge on a road that takes me to the coast. Rearing over the road, confirming the guidebook map, is Luna Park. Will this be too strange for the gatekeepers at the palace of fun? I ask whether it will be possible for me to ride the Ferris wheel. No trouble at all: my wheelchair is carefully moved clear of the apparatus as I settle myself in the wire cage.

At the top of the ride, the operators stop for a full minute and I go snap-happy photographing the high-rise apartments, the Mediterranean, the football stadium protruding like a green lozenge beneath my feet and the entire expanse of Luna Park beneath me.

In an open-air café a few metres away, half a dozen patrons are kicking up their heels this Sunday afternoon in a collective dance step, to the rapt attention of not only myself but everyone else present. Recorded music it may be, but the sense of a people who know how to enjoy themselves, and are gobbling up life by the hungry mouthful after years of denial, is inescapable.

DAY 297 (5 MARCH): BEIRUT

Afif Abdul Malik has a low opinion of travel agents. 'In this business you have to be a liar,' he says as if speaking to an apprentice. With 53 years of satisfying other people's wanderlust, he should know. We are sitting in the CLTC—Centre Libanaise de Tourisme Culturel—in the quarter they call Ras Beirut, just up the hill from the American University. The once raffish neighbourhood became a cockpit of urban jungle warfare in the early '80s. However, Abdul Malik's agency has been on this (highly exposed) corner for 44 years and it will take more than a civil war to shift him.

'There's not enough business here, you cannot make money. The Lebanese are called good businessmen not because they are geniuses: they are liars and opportunists,' he tells me, as thick coffee arrives in two small cups. 'It is a matter of ethics: you have to choose the low road.'

'Aha! Then Abdul Malik, as you are still in business after all these years, you must be an exceptional travel agent, or else you are lying to me.'

'Not at all,' he chuckles. 'Believe me, I lose much work because of my ethics.'

Abdul Malik's office has two computers, but he seldom turns them on. At 76 he is not lapping up every new gadget that comes along. Anyway, he is devoted to real customer care, not the god of speed. For flight information he telephones the airlines, taking care to get the name of the person who handles his call; he totes up considerable distances walking to their offices, collecting and checking the tickets in person. Arduous as that is today, it must have been downright hair-raising during the civil war, which he touches on as if it were a trifling inconvenience rather than a catastrophe.

In May 1984, when Ras Beirut was turned into a free-fire zone, Abdul Malik was offered 150 000 Lebanese pounds to sell up, 'leave the area', as it was put to him. He refused point-blank. 'When the street fighting started to get very heavy I had to close down some days, but when it died down I opened for business again.

'One night, though, there was heavy gunfire along the street, between the Syrians here and the Falangists. I live just nearby but they were shooting ceaselessly late into the night, so I slept here on these stairs.' (Abdul Malik gestures towards a narrow stairwell that would be difficult enough to stand upon for any length of time, let alone rest on.)

In a country where until recently the religion you were born into could get you killed, Abdul Malik knows the secrets of survival. Hailing from the Chouf Mountains, a stronghold of the Druze sect, he has been content all these years working in majority-Muslim West Beirut to let his customers think he himself is a Druze, although his family background is actually Maronite Christian. But, he hastens to add, 'I am not a partisan, I am a Lebanese.' And he's not a liar either, even if he is one of the world's most durable travel agents.

'There is the conscience to please, and I am happy,' he says as I depart. 'The most important thing is to sleep well.'

DAY 301 (9 MARCH): JOUNIEH

Wear and tear on my chair is like hair falling out: the loss of wheel spokes is something one must expect over time. Happily, the remedy is simple: bicycle spokes are exactly the right length and any mechanic worth his salt can replace them. (It's remarkable, though, how often a cycle-shop assistant will tell me, 'Sorry, we don't fix wheelchairs.')

But will there be a helpful shop here in a town this size, where I haven't seen a single bike? No sooner have I posed the question than the answer appears, in the form of another wheelchair user leading a busy life. Roy Jaja, who runs an optical-goods shop in the heart of Jounieh's tourist quarter, is a reverse immigrant: brought up in Sydney, he returned to his parents' homeland a few years ago. 'The social atmosphere, being among your own people, nothing could replace that for me,' he explains.

'No regrets?'

'None really. I go back to Sydney now and again, and catch up with my old friends.'

Roy knows where to get wheelchair parts, spares, add-ons. Off we go to a service station where trusted hands replace my spokes. Roy and I meet as strangers, part as friends.

DAY 302 (10 MARCH): BYBLOS

Byblos is my Jericho. As I won't be getting to the world's oldest town—which is about to be occupied by Ariel Sharon's troops in a drive to stop suicide attacks against Israelis—this mere stripling of 7000 inhabited years will have to serve as a substitute. And it's quite an acceptable one, as Byblos (Book City) is the birthplace of the alphabet.

So what is there to see today? A Roman colonnade from the third century after Christ; a nymphaeum from the century before that; an obelisk-shaped temple from the second millennium BC; a typical local home from 2800 BC adjoined to a temple for the worship of Baal; and all in a grassed-over field in the shadow of a Crusader castle entered via an indestructible-looking keep.

DAY 303 (11 MARCH): CEDARS OF LEBANON

I travel by shared taxi to Bcharre, Kahlil Gibran's hometown. It's an oversight to come here on a Monday: the museum in his honour is closed. But at least, in this high country where the predominant element appears to be raw oxygen, I will see Nature's answer to Byblos. This is the only place, it is said, where you can see the cedars, these symbols of Lebanon that stood in biblical times. Some of the specimens are 1500 years old (a little young for the Bible, but the experience is invigorating).

DAY 304 (12 MARCH): BAALBEK

Nestling in the beautiful Beka'a Valley, Baalbek is famous for its World Heritage-listed ruins, but this is no motley collection of marble stumps: here are awesome full-scale temples (this one to Venus, that one to Jupiter) from the glory days of the Roman Empire.

DAY 305 (13 MARCH): TYRE

From Beirut it's a sunny, relaxed morning drive down the coast to south Lebanon. In Sidon the taxi picks up a second passenger, a young, unshaven university student heading home. To avoid politics makes sense in this part of the world, so I chit-chat about the historical ruins he has seen. But Hamid's mind is fixed on more recent times. Out of the blue he tells me, 'My brother chose the road of martyrdom. He exploded a bus in Jerusalem.' He awaits my reaction.

'Can you make peace this way?' I ask (privately wondering whether he thinks I'm an Israeli).

He looks out to sea, ignoring the irrelevance of the question, and adds, 'I would do exactly the same.'

Like Byblos, Tyre was a Phoenician port, famous in King Solomon's day, but its modern history is every bit as riveting as the ancient stuff. Wheeling along the coastal road, I cannot help noticing the serried ranks of beach palms, systematically shot out (Hezbollah target practice?). Opposite the al-Mina excavations is a sign in red paint that reads, 'Ali H. killed by Zionist pigs, 27 April 1997'. Terror breeds terror.

At times like these, when the distant past is far more appealing than the present, there is no place like a hippodrome. Horseshoe-shaped, this stadium where second-century Romans held chariot races is so well preserved that footraces could be held there today (and, for all I know, are). I do a full circuit, a victory lap for the absent crowd.

DAY 308 (16 MARCH): TRIPOLI

Alternative name Trablus—and for me instantly troublous. Of all the halts on this journey, this triply famous one (not to be confused with its namesakes in Libya and Greece) is perhaps the least suitable for a wheelchair user.

If the Old City's charm belongs largely to centuries past, the same could be said of its hotels, all of which are up narrow flights of stairs. I find the best resting place close to the sea, in this case a 5-kilometre taxi ride to Tripoli's port. But here is the strange thing: the grand hotel overlooking the Mediterranean can find me a room only on the fourth floor. This means dismounting from my chair and bumming my way up all four levels, pausing on the landings to catch my breath.

The maître d' appears put out by this, although his assistant understands. Tired out from the quest for a room, I cling to this half empty hotel as if it were a life raft. Somehow the durable grand staircase, with its broad expanse of carpet, spells W-E-L-C-O-M-E whereas the rickety splintered boards of those dosshouses in the Old City screamed F-U-C-K O-F-F. The sight of someone shuffling down to breakfast on his posterior doesn't seem to disturb my fellow guests (though what they say in Arabic over their falafel sandwiches I can only imagine).

SYRIA REVISITED: 17-25 MARCH

DAY 312 (20 MARCH): KRAK DES CHEVALIERS

This castle's French name translates literally as Castle of the Knights (Qasr al-Hosn in Arabic), 'the finest castle in the world' according to Lawrence. Normally a castle, with its steep stone staircases, vaulted cellars, forbidding ramparts and lofty bastions, is the last place a wheelchair user would think of setting footplate, but today I am in luck. Some English backpackers whom I've met up with in Hama are happy to let me join them on their tour, and even volunteer to do the heavy lifting.

Construction began in 1031, when it was intended as a Kurdish garrison. At the end of the 11th century it became a target of the Crusaders, under Raymond de-Gilles of Toulouse. From 1142, Christians occupied the fort, holding out against even the most determined assaults of our other recently visited friend Saladin, and succumbing only in 1271 to Sultan Beybers—sometimes called the last man standing in the Crusades—a Muslim sultan who swept the Christian fundamentalists out of Syria.

The see-saw of conquest is reflected in an assortment of Arabic and Latin inscriptions chiselled into the clammy walls of this gigantic stone-and-brick labyrinth. We spend an hour testing its echo-chamber effects, sunbaking in its courtyards, and generally acting like carefree children on the last day of term.

DAY 313 (21 MARCH): HAMA

The Orontes is only a stream, but wending its way through this peaceful-looking town it passes the medieval waterwheels that symbolise Hama and remain its most enduring memory. Tremendously powerful, they creak like mechanical monsters from the Industrial Revolution.

The Basman Hotel makes me feel at home, but not in a patronising, charitable way as if my being in a wheelchair made a difference: the Basman makes everyone feel at home. This turns out to be just as well, because I am on the eve of a painful episode, and the hotel's capacity for TLC is about to be stretched to the maximum.

DAY 314 (22 MARCH): APAMEA

This morning finds me tied to another knot of day trippers, in a taxi headed along backroads two hours north-west of Hama. Our destination is Apamea, an excavated granite city from Roman times that flourished from the second century BC until AD 540, when the Persians overran it.

After Palmyra and the ancient wonders of Lebanon (not to mention Persia), I am becoming something of an ancient-world buff, and promise myself to add this to my résumé. I love the thought that here, where my wheels are but passing through, other people once lived, scarcely giving a thought to the notion that 2000 years later someone would pass by, looking in pity or awe at the residue of their daily lives.

This day is ideal for such sobering reflection: dark clouds rumble, threatening rain. Indeed, the evidence of a solid downpour overnight is at our feet for the marble strip of road is hidden here and there by puddles.

Those puddles prove my downfall. As my wheels wade through one of them, with considerably more effort than usual, I cannot see that the next marble slab in this ancient paved highway is slightly higher than the ones around it. The impact of my casters hitting the exposed slab pitchforks me head over heels. Instinctively I roll myself into a ball, going with the flow, to lessen the risk of breaking bones.

Even as this emergency unfolds, I recall being embarrassed that it is taking place in front of a tour group (French, from the exclamations I hear them utter), or indeed in anyone's presence. A Syrian man comes to my assistance, considerately lifting me back into the chair.

By the time the taxi returns me to Hama, the dull soreness that followed my fall has sharpened into a throbbing fusillade of pains emanating every few seconds from my inflamed big toes. The driver and fellow passengers offer sympathy; and I try to deflect their concern by making light of the whole affair, wondering aloud how the ancient Romans ever acquired such a good reputation as road builders.

Back in Hama, Abdullah from the Basman Hotel swings into action. After detailing hotel staff to lift my sorry sedentary form, in the chair, up to my first-floor room, he arranges a relay of tin basins filled with water to soak my feet in and ease the swelling.

Perhaps an hour has passed when there is a knock on my door and in walks Dr Mustafa Abdel Jawad. The details of his treatment need not detain us: anti-inflammatory tablets and a couple of days' rest do the trick.

But Dr Jawad is no ordinary medic. On his second visit, when he sees I'm on the non-Roman road to recovery, he hands me a written report and a CD outlining a most remarkable surgical operation.

It is a case study Dr Jawad clearly hopes will establish his medical reputation worldwide, and I see he has already presented this report to an obscure medical congress. In 1998, Jawad informed the congress, a patient of his, Mr M.K., presented with what X-rays showed was a small abdominal mass which turned out to comprise fourteen metal items: seven wrenches, two long needles, three long paperclips and a needle in two parts. 'All these instruments were oxidised and black because they have stayed more than three months in the stomach and the colon,' Dr Jawad told delegates, who no doubt received this intelligence with an amazement equal to my own.

Reporting his 'rare surgical management for metal instruments in the digestive system', the pioneering Dr Jawad reported that, following his 'very good diagnosis and very careful operation, the patient became healthy'.

What he didn't tell them or me, and apparently didn't bother to inquire, was how Mr M.K. came to have so many spanners in his works, so to speak.

Was he a motor mechanic with an iron deficiency? A circus performer? We may never know.

I can now claim to have crossed the Arab world. Aleppo, or Haleb as they call it here, is laid out in a European-style street pattern, with its own Christian Quarter sporting more than a few shop signs in Armenian. These facts reflect, respectively, the town's historical ties with East–West trade and its proximity to Turkey, from which a sizeable Armenian community fled here after the genocide last century.

But the Arab world is here, too, and for me this is its last outpost. Aleppo's vast covered souq provides more adventure than I bargained for.

Grot and grime and even odd tufts of grass overgrowing the mortar serve as a reminder that traders have spent their working lives in this vast, sprawling market since AD 1500, in some cases earlier. 'Fabulous' is the term applied by the guidebook and, although brochures always rhapsodise in such terms, Aleppo's souq merits the description.

Wheeling a few metres down the main corridor, I spy an interesting sign above the butcher's shop that occupies a recess on my left. Backing into a corner, I take out my camera and train the lens fractionally above the horizontal, aware as I do so that the result should also capture a nice, busy bazaar crowd at the same time as the wording on the sign.

'Click' I go. No flash, but an almighty shout, a whoop of rage, issues from a bearded man in a dirty jellaba about five metres in front of me. His livid face is not mollified by my pointing to the sign above his head. He is clearly accusing me of taking his photo without permission.

In his fury he makes a sudden move to the butcher's block, picking up a carving knife and waving it samurai-like in front of my face. I must have blanched but there is no obvious escape route. If I wheel backwards, I could easily tip up the chair and be at his mercy. Reversing and scurrying down the avenue involve turning my back, not exactly a smart alternative.

Fortunately, others in the crowd have seen the danger and quickly form two human cocoons: one closes around me, the other around my would-be assailant. Two of its stronger members pin the man's arms to his side, forcing him to drop the knife, which is large enough to have given Crocodile Dundee heart failure. After a few minutes my cocoon has moved me away from the scene, to a jeweller's shop close to the souq entrance.

The jeweller, after the situation is explained to him, arranges for that staple of Middle Eastern hospitality, a cup of tea, to be brought to me. His idea is evidently to calm me down. But now, removed from imminent danger of being slashed, I become brave and vociferous myself. Only after some quiet persuasion by an English-speaking member of the cocoon do I concede the pointlessness of calling in the police.

I'm only a short time in Aleppo but it is unthinkable not to drop in at the grand, colonial-era Baron Hotel, even if it doesn't offer the budget traveller best value.

Old photographs in the lounge room opposite the bar portray some of its most distinguished guests, most of whom stayed here when the French ran the show. The list includes Kemal Ataturk, Lady Mountbatten, Charles Lindbergh, Mr and Mrs Theodore Roosevelt, Sir Hugh Knutchbull-Hugessen (don't know who he was but obviously worthy of inclusion in the A-list on the strength of his name alone), Agatha Christie and Dame Freya Stark.

After dinner I share a convivial hour on the terrace with other remarkable, if less illustrious, company.

One of those present is an Australian woman in her mid-twenties who briefly manages to make me feel envious when she relates that just a month ago (when I would have been there if I'd judged it safe to go) she was in Yemen.

We all sit spellbound as she recounts how magnificent the tall houses of Sana'a were; what a friendly reception she got from the female stallholders in Aden's bazaar; and how everywhere she went she felt safe. She even had her own armed escort while journeying down the Hadramaut coast, the most lawless part of the country, where al-Qa'eda sympathisers and operatives walk around in broad daylight unmolested.

After the envy has subsided, what do I think of this? I cannot criticise her: she has taken a risk and arguably shown it to be exaggerated. But the question remains, if ten people follow her lead and only nine come back to tell the tale, where will I be?

The first time I met St Simeon, a fifth-century holy man, was years ago in the pages of the *Guinness Book of Records*. He is the man who, without even meaning to set a record, earned his place in history's Hall of Fame by sitting on top of a pillar for 36 years. And it is here, an hour by road west of Aleppo, that he did it.

After Simeon's death in AD 459, the biggest church in the Middle East was built around his sacred stele. In our age, when freak shows have largely crowded out the idea of pious devotion, I arrive expecting to see crass mass commercialisation of his 'memory'. However, I wander around the basilicas without once being disturbed by trinket touts. And, yes, there in a grassy field stands an indented marble stump, barely three metres high, which a nearby sign assures the world is where St Simeon of Stylites sat ('stylite' being the name for this singular form of worshipper).

Strangely for one who has been told he has an overdeveloped sense of the absurd, I come away with something approaching awe. Even if what the mystic was on about remains beyond my intellectual grasp, I can see that Simeon exemplifies pure dedication, an admirably steadfast refusal to be diverted from his goal.

But the convulsions that racked my life in 1990 and 1991 have freed me from the esteem in which I used to hold people who stick to a plan. History is littered with examples of sticking to plans, and many of them feature stacks of corpses: Gallipoli, the Somme, the Khmer Rouge plan to remake Cambodia and China's Cultural Revolution – all carried out with faultless dedication.

Beside these catastrophes, a mere travel plan seems an unlikely means of semaphoring Fate. But, where chance plays a part – and it was by chance I saw and answered an ad, with consequences that took me to Bahrain in 1990 – it is asking too much of Fortune to favour players who never fold their cards and walk away. Perseverance in a good cause is one thing; stubbornness in the face of unpleasant facts, merely a form of stupidity. This wisdom I have learnt at a cost.

Chapter 17

KNOCK, KNOCK, KNOCKING ON EUROPE'S DOOR

I have always depended on the kindness of strangers.

TENNESSEE WILLIAMS A Streetcar Named Desire

MARCH-JUNE 2002

It is said that we live in an age of specialists rather than Jacks and Jills of all trades, and the trend has now spilt over from the world of work to our leisure pursuits. The grab-bag term 'tourism' has begun to split up into its own specialities: we now have eco-tourism, extreme tourism, even responsible tourism. (What does that mean? Staying at home?)

Having never felt comfortable with the term 'tourist'—it smacks too much of the cocktail lounge at five-star hotels or the most expensive shoulder-slung video equipment—it ill becomes me to suggest a new term. But there must be many people like myself who have found that, even though we fill our itineraries with places to see, it is the people we meet who endow us with our most cherished travel memories.

Perhaps travellers who defy the prophets of doom and venture to see the world as it is, who delve behind the lines and read between them, are a new breed of tourist, the pioneers of 'humanitourism' (for want of a better word).

TURKEY: 25 MARCH–16 JUNE

Turkey marked the halfway point of my Eurasian crossing, the point at which I took my longest 'time out'—six weeks to reflect on how far I had come, how far to go. It also marked the dawning of my awareness of why it is so satisfying to visit a country not just for its sights but for the experience of becoming acquainted with its people, however fleetingly, and the chance to understand how their view of the world differs from ours. Even where people are poor, you will find yourself reminded that in their appreciation of the good things in life they have a better sense of proportion than you, and that their concerns are real, not based on what might happen or might never happen.

Simply put, such travel can enlarge our view of what it means to be human. Each day filled with new insights, we can 'exercise humanity', free to be our best selves but without the effort normally associated with being on our best behaviour. Free, most significantly, of the work-related stomach tightening, the family-based anxieties and the personal fears that drag us down.

Where Asia comes knocking at Europe's door, the result is not clashing cultures but a hybrid richness stemming from mixed soils. Modern Turks are Asians who want to be Europeans, or Muslims who, according to the great modern founder of their state, Kemal Ataturk, might have been better off as Christians.

I wonder if it isn't because Turks are a mass of living contradictions that so many visitors fall in love with this society at first sight. They are at once the least strict and hidebound of Muslims, and yet so proud of their heritage, reflected in the Islamic crescent on their national flag. And that's not surprising, given that in their glory days, from the 15th century to the 19th, the Ottoman Empire held sway all the way from Central Europe to North Africa, Mecca and beyond.

The yearning to be accepted as part of the civilised world was a driving force for Ataturk who (you will only upset Turks by reminding them) wasn't a Turk himself but a Macedonian born in Salonica, now part of Greece. Many believe modern Turkey wouldn't have come into being at all or survived as long as it has done but for Ataturk, despite his authoritarian stamp not exactly being a prescription for democracy.

Turks know how to enjoy the good life. Istanbul is one of the great cities of the world, and Efes beer is up there with the best. Yet, while they are wannabe Europeans, it is the Turks' very lack of sophistication (meant as a compliment) that many visitors find attractive. They are not slaves to the clock, and will while away the afternoon puffing on

184

a hookah with you rather than strain themselves to keep appointments of dubious importance. The Turks are ever ready to welcome you into their richly carpeted homeland and make you feel as if you belong there. Before long, you will.

DAY 317 (25 MARCH): ANTAKYA

A cross-border bus link with Aleppo makes it the easiest thing in the world to get to Antakya (the ancient Antioch) but, once there, finding a ground-floor hotel room defeats me. For starters, the town is of modest size these days. Then I realise that obtaining Turkish lire is as big a challenge as finding a hotel, because without some I won't be able to pay for a room anyway. First things first.

In a country whose currency unit trades at a rate of 1.3 million to a single US dollar, an appearance on *Who Wants To Be a Millionaire?* would be an invitation to poverty. I'll need tens of millions but it is evening now and the banks have closed. As for ATMs, they are a foreign concept round here.

In these situations, while keeping a close eye on four items of baggage—wait a minute, one, two, three … oh no, my sports bag is still on the bus! Everything is falling apart! Where was I? Oh yes, first things first.

With some help from observant bus passengers who see I can't make it alone over the step into the offices of the bus company that brought me here from Syria, I front the desk. After a couple of minutes' confusion I convey my troubles to the office manager who, luckily, is willing and able to help.

He phones the bus driver and, after an anxious wait, receives a call back to say that a bag matching the description I gave has been found and will be given to a taxidriver in the next town along from Antakya. A price is mentioned that sounds a bit hefty but this is no time for bargaining. I agree to terms, and check that off my mental list of worries.

An hour later the taxidriver arrives and reunites me with the bag, and by that time—amazingly—I hand him over enough millions to give him a brief spell of quiz-show fame.

How to get money when banks are closed? Well, I would have thought the US dollar spoke all languages but not in Antakya on a

Sunday, let me tell you. If the owner of the only shop open in the vicinity of the bus park hadn't been a personal friend of the bank manager, and the manager hadn't agreed to open up the bank out of hours, that sports bag might be back in Syria by now.

Next priority being to book a seat on the earliest possible express coach to Istanbul, I find that most of the buses are full but cadge a seat on the 1.15. Good, I think, that will give me the night to rest—it's been a long day—and the morning to mosey around town.

Only after two hours' exploration do I discover the lack of suitable hotel rooms within wheeling distance of the bus station. More problems pile up. By this time, mid-evening, it has started raining—heavily—and I'm soaked as well as unsheltered. I decide to park myself all night in the bus company's waiting room.

About 10 pm I'm called over to the ticket counter. The bus will be ready to board in an hour, I'm informed. Incredulous, I shake my head. How can that be? Slow, patient explanations are dispensed for the ignorant foreigner's sake. Turkey has adopted not only the Western workweek but also the Continental preference for the 24-hour clock. The bus I thought was leaving at 1.15 tomorrow afternoon departs at 1.15 in the morning—and it terminates at Ankara, forcing me to wait for a connection to Istanbul. But this is a good outcome, and I thank my lucky stars that I couldn't find a place to stay in Antakya.

DAY 318 (26 MARCH): ANATOLIA TO ISTANBUL

Last night's rain has given way to the first snowfall of this voyage. We are passing through the uplands of Anatolia, and even through the windowpane of a bus the sight is bracing, pure.

At 4.30 pm on this, the last day of my travel before calling a halt to the journey, our bus joins the peak-hour crawl across a bridge that takes me out of Asia, the continent where I have lived for the past eleven months. For the first time in five years I am in Europe. It is one of Istanbul's magical aspects, this fact that it straddles the continents, like a giant with one foot in the East and the other in the West. Here you experience the same type of intellectual thrill as you do standing on the Equator.

A helpful taxidriver (quite contrary to the type Istanbul has an unfortunate reputation for) says he knows just the hotel for me. As his small red sedan chugs up a slope in the backstreets of Sultanahmet, the tourist quarter, I suspect that this is one of those occasions when a hotel 'tout' has taken me to a seedy establishment where the receptionist will slip him a commission for my custom and I will find out, too late, that I'm stuck in a 'dive'. Instead I'm happily surprised to find that not only is the Albino (odd name, that, but my curiosity is dulled by travel weariness) a new-minted hotel, I am its very first guest. Owner Salim, rubicund and jolly, pours refreshing red tea into a tulip-stemmed glass (this is a fine Turkish tradition, may it never die) and in due course summons staff to raise me up a few steps to the lift.

Calling a stop near the midway point of the journey, at midnight on 26 March, will give me time not only to reflect on the experience but to map out the next few months' itinerary, taking me from Greece right through the Balkans to Central Europe. Until now I hadn't fixed on a place to spend this break but warm praise from a fellow bus passenger for a particular pension on the Mediterranean coast has persuaded me to head south in a couple of days. I will end up spending weeks at Koc Pension, in the fishing village of Ucagiz, so small and secluded no more than one in a thousand Turks has probably heard of it.

DAY 319 (27 MARCH): ISTANBUL
Arrangements are swiftly made for return-flight ticketing to Istanbul. After the hard work of travelling, the transition to a less demanding pace of life promises to be trouble-free.

Checking my travel budget, I find that the voyage thus far (including airfares) has cost US$15 001 or US$47 a day. My estimated spending was US$46 a day, so it gives me some satisfaction that, like a glider pilot, I have achieved a gentle landing after a ride that has had more than its share of turbulence.

DAY 320 (28 MARCH): ISTANBUL
On the way to the airport this morning my only thoughts are of the Mediterranean haven that awaits me. So, when the security officer on the other side of the metal detector at the departure terminal—whose job it is to frisk me—says 'Stand up', my jaw drops.

'I can't,' I say, torn between amusement and indignation.

'Stand up,' he repeats robotically. Hands on tyres, I hoist myself to his chest height, to show that I'll comply with his instructions as far as I am able.

Evidently, the officer regards this as 'a false move'. Urgently he radios for assistance, and while I'm settling back into my seat half a dozen officers appear from nowhere. Quickly surrounding me in a rugby scrum, they force me to move across to a nearby leather bench, away from the lengthening queue of presumably legitimate travellers.

Still in the huddle, I'm now addressed—'barked at' would be a better description—by the officer clearly most senior in rank. 'Your seat has not been inspected,' he bellows, pointing at my cushion.

Taking the hint, I transfer to the bench and offer up my new, mildly expensive Jay cushion. It hadn't occurred to me that this might be a suspicious article but by the way the chief receives it—tentatively, in contrast to his rough command—it would not surprise me if his next step were to call in forensics experts, followed closely by the bomb squad. For a moment I think the chief is going to try ripping off the seat's protective plastic cover, wrecking my investment, exposing me to a recurrence of pressure sores and forcing me to miss my flight (for which I now hear the final boarding call).

'You cannot go,' orders the chief and stalks off, flanked by a couple of his trusties while the others hover menacingly over me, lest I make a 'run' for it. Five anxious minutes later, the chief returns, accompanied by a fluent English-speaking woman who introduces herself as the customer relations officer for Turkish Airlines. Unapologetically she translates the news that my cushion is being returned to me and that I should have stood up when asked. I tell the goons through her that they need retraining but their response is as stony as ever.

Two days later I hear that Istanbul Customs officers have impounded a large quantity of heroin in what they are claiming is the biggest drugs bust of all time, or something to that effect. I begin to think of the incident in a kindlier light.

Drifting purposelessly through the next few weeks, I feel a quiet satisfaction in having ignored those well-meant but essentially hysterical calls to cancel my journey, or head for European pastures, in the aftermath of September 11. In these unsettled times, while taking sensible precautions against clear and present dangers, the best advice

I can think of is to go *against* the media flow. Pack everything you might possibly need or want, but leave your preconceptions behind. The Middle East and Central Asia are surprisingly safe regions of a world that is overwhelmingly friendly. I know: I've been there.

DAY 319 (8 MAY): BACK TO ISTANBUL

As I resume my journey, another drive from the airport in another red taxi delivers me not to my old haunt the Albino but to, lo and behold, the Albion. Only six weeks in business, and already a kindly meant remark by some pedantic foreigner has reduced Salim's individualistically named hotel to one of a uniform bunch. Fortunately, the traditional service of red tea in a tulip-stemmed glass remains unchanged.

This morning at St Sophia I encounter the pleasure of being accorded *Ucretsiz* status. Any time this happens, it makes my day.

Ucretsiz is one of the sweetest-sounding words in the Turkish tongue. It means 'free' and, although it never occurred to me that just being in a wheelchair should entitle me to a discount, I soon find that ticket-sellers in this country are just as likely to wave me through and stamp my pass *Ucretsiz* as they are to make me pay. Even those who charge sometimes insist on giving me a discount. Normally I refuse to be patronised; here I unbend and accept the consideration flowing my way.

Aghia Sofia certainly deserves to be ranked among the Wonders of the World: the only problem would be whether to class it as an ancient or modern wonder. For nigh on sixteen centuries it has struck awe into all who have beheld it, both outside and in. Initially it was the largest Christian house of prayer anywhere on Earth; then, after the Turks took Constantinople in 1453, it became a mosque; and finally, since the 1930s, it has been a museum.

A bare chandelier that appears to be as big as a skating rink underhangs the giant central cupola, inducing giddiness in onlookers, or rather uplookers. When my gaze returns to floor level, I cannot believe what I am seeing. A large celadon vase clearly labelled fifth century AD (yes, even older than the building it now resides in) is being pawed all over by a young woman while a man in her thrall, most probably her boyfriend, looks on indulgently. In a hoarse whisper that seems appropriate for this now secular house of worship, I exhort her,

'You can't do that. Don't touch it, it's an ancient work of art.'

'There's no sign saying you can't touch it,' the lady drawls in a smug American accent.

I fire back, 'Most people don't need to be told' before taking to my wheels.

Where better to take a Turkish bath than in Istanbul? Towelling off and lying down in the steaming tiled hothouse does have a special dimension when, gazing up at the shimmering beehive-shaped ceiling, you reflect that people have been coming here for the same purpose as you every day for the best part of 600 years.

Disrobed and money put in a safe, I wheel through a tunnel just wide enough to admit me to the washroom where plastic dippers await beside hot and cold taps. Filling the dippers, you can proceed to sluice yourself as I do, or hire someone to do the hard work for you.

Soap is supplied, and again the world divides into those who help themselves and those for whom the luxury would become a chore if they didn't have a servant at their beck and call. Massage is an optional extra and, shucking off the hard yards of the long haul, I decide this is no time to stint. Time to splash; time to splurge.

DAY 322 (11 MAY): ISTANBUL

To the Covered Market, one of Istanbul's oldest and most popular and, dare one say it, Byzantine haunts. Over 4000 shops are clustered here, where the kilim carpets and silver lamps of Oriental fancy are an everyday fact.

Mentally rehearsing my wheel-away-in-disgust-and-come-back-in-contrite-hope bargaining technique, I join the crowds bustling their way through the dusky market paths until I come to a corner shop that looks promising. Mum's birthday falls next month and she has expressed a wish for a silver pendant. Fairly specific instructions have been given, and I only hope for the shopkeeper's sake that what he has to offer me will match her stated desire.

We're in luck. I find a suitable pendant, but now it's time to fix on a reasonable price. Because the aforementioned elasticity of the Turkish lira guarantees that this will be in the tens of millions, I have to hesitate and calculate before expressing my displeasure and reluctantly wheeling away.

It's funny but, when I come back, the salesman, Ali Gulec of the Interesting Giftshop, is smiling expectantly. Eventually he agrees to reduce the damage by a few million, using his own calculator, until I think that what we shake hands on must be a good price for a worthy gift. Only when Ali agrees to leave the shop in a colleague's hands and leads me on a bracing march through the bowels of the bazaar to a long-established bistro—where he invites me to take Turkish coffee and sticky baklava cake with him—do I realise he wouldn't be going out of his way if our transaction hadn't been a bargain, for him. After courteous conversation with the bistro owner and me, he melts into the crowd and a hidden hand plants the bill on my table. It is for the equivalent of US$11. Don't talk to me about the grand Istanbul market: twice bitten, forever shy.

DAY 323 (12 MAY): ISTANBUL

Galata Tower, which provides superb panoramic views of the medieval city across the water, poses two great obstacles for me. First, there are steps leading up to its first-floor entrance; second, the lift takes people only as far as the lower observatory where naturally the view isn't quite as superb as up above.

The kindness of strangers comes to my rescue in both cases. After I'm assisted some of the way by Turks from the immediate neighbourhood, a Dutch couple volunteer to lift me up the broad staircase and then, once I've reached the lower observatory, they mount the stairs to get the snaps I couldn't have taken for myself.

A year from now, newly arrived home, I will open the mail and find a superb fivefold set of black-and-white photos that, laid side by side, give a panoramic view of wondrous Istanbul. Even later, I will frame them in remembrance of a magical city and my unsolicited benefactors.

Safely back on *terra firma*, I pedal through a warren of winding lanes seeking an outlet: the thoroughfare Istiqlal Caddesi, known in its glorious European heyday at the end of the 19th century as the Grande Rue de Pera. It is right here, eighteen months after my visit, that one of two bombs will go off, within minutes of each other, shattering for who knows how long Istanbul's charm and reputation as an exotic getaway. Those bombs will wipe Istanbul off the map of the faint-hearted and jittery, but it is a city that has survived the ebb and flow of empires and will bounce back as surely as the Bosporus flows into the Black Sea.

DAYS 326–327 (15–16 MAY): GALLIPOLI AND TROY

From here, the Gallipoli peninsula, the Turks launched the military campaign that captured Constantinople in 1453 and brought the curtain down on Byzantium after a thousand more or less glorious years. The event that may be said to have *raised* the curtain on Western civilisation took place some time previously—about 1200 years before Christ, it is now thought.

The name of that battle is so resonant that, more than 3000 years later, Hollywood drools over the four-letter word that sums it all up: Troy. From Homer's epic *Iliad*, the bulk of all theatre and literature can trace their origins. And even those who have never read that work have heard of the Trojan horse.

This is also, of course, the place that gave rise to the Anzac legend and so I spend two days taking tours of this most warred-over tract of land.

My Gallipoli tour guide, Captain Ali Efe, is a retired Turkish Army man, a walking encyclopaedia on his special subject, who shows due deference to the fighting men of both sides. So when, at the end of our minibus tour, he hands me a small container that opens to reveal a bullet on a tiny bed of red cloth, I don't quite know what to do. Is it one of ours? Theirs? Theirs by right of who fired it, who stopped it or who won the campaign (the Turks) or the war (the Allies)? Though in two minds whether to accept such a present (but I do), I find it quite revealing that bullets from those eight months of hell can still be found lying around nearly a century on.

Apart from the fact that there were no bullets in Trojan times, I muse that at Troy all the mementoes must long since have been spirited away. But my expectation is confounded by reality. I discover that three years ago an American–German team brought to light pottery and other relics older than any excavated before them. These come from a Neolithic culture now dubbed Troy Zero and are dated *circa* 3600 BC.

DAY 332 (21 MAY): BODRUM

Without setting out to do so, I have been lucky over the years to visit the sites of a couple of Wonders of the Ancient World: the site of the

Pharos lighthouse at Alexandria and the Pyramids of Giza. Today I can add the Mausoleum of Halicarnassus to that list.

The tomb of King Mausolus, whose name lives on in death and in all buildings erected to commemorate the late and great, is astonishingly modest. The visitor, however humble, must surely look down from the lofty stone viewing platform and think, 'How time sinks the mighty.'

DAY 333 (22 MAY): BODRUM TO UCAGIZ
Although it will become clear only in retrospect, today marks the mid-point of my epic traverse of the world's largest continent. Fittingly, I spend it travelling—by minibus across south-western Turkey, from the Aegean through cliff-hugging roads down east. Changing buses at Kas (pronounced Cash), the journey takes me into sun-kissed citrus lands and back to my ever-welcoming friends at Ucagiz close by the sparkling Mediterranean.

DAY 339 (28 MAY): DEMRE
In the fourth century AD this southern settlement was known as Myra, a town whose bishop was the father of Christmas as we know it.

Strange as it must sound, the real Santa Claus lived not in Arctic climes but here, by the Mediterranean, in a country now 99 per cent Muslim. Oh, and another thing: his contemporaries tell us he was a jolly thin man.

What else do we know about Nicholas of Lycia, Bishop of Myra? He travelled to Palestine and Egypt in his youth; became the patron saint of Russia, children, prisoners and sailors; and saved Myra from a famine by unloading a large shipment of grain bound for Byzantium. (This last feat sounds less like a miracle when you learn that his parents' wealth derived from cereals.) In a lovely reversal of fortune, I also learn that Nicholas was appointed bishop after leaving Constantine's torture cells just as a divine decree arrived telling the church elders to appoint as bishop the first man to enter the church.

Finding the semi-ruined Church of St Nicholas is not difficult once I'm in Demre. I keep an eye out for a conventionally stout man dressed in red and white, but then I spy a plaque that dashes my hopes of ever seeing the elusive Claus. In 1087, it states, merchants from the Italian town of Bari ransacked the saint's grave.

For those who believe in Santa as a living annual miracle-worker, it is disturbing to clap eyes on an ornately worked marble sarcophagus. But then someone tells me this basilica was erected in the eighth century, 400 years after Nicholas's time. Destiny, it seems, is determined to keep Santa's fate an open question for some time to come. However, as the afternoon bus speeds me back to Ucagiz, I see a sign that hints at where he just might be now:

The love of Myra's bishop
Extended to the whole world.

DAY 345 (3 JUNE): GOREME, CAPPADOCIA

Happy birthday to me, although at 48 there is no time to let the grass grow under one's wheels. This personal new year's day finds me in the most amazing fairyland setting, a valley where volcanic tuff has been fashioned over the ages into shapes known as chimneys, sniggered at by some Westerners as unmistakably phallic although strait-laced Turkish tour pamphlets prefer the term 'mushroom-shaped'.

Today, the town of Goreme is abuzz with football fever, as around lunchtime the nation's heroes take on cup-holders Brazil. In high birthday spirits, I'm enjoying a beer in front of the big screen at the Orient Restaurant when Turkey scores the first goal.

The hundred fans crammed into this enclosed space erupt like Vesuvius. I sit amid deafening screams, flags being waved wildly and red-and-white chests and painted faces leading war whoops. Then, early in the second half, Ronaldo works a miracle and, a few minutes later, Brazil go 2–1 up, before finishing on strongly. The previous hour's joy fizzles into sullen dispiritedness.

DAY 348 (6 JUNE): ANKARA

This is the capital Kemal Ataturk built, far from the dissipations and distractions of Istanbul. Here in the pure air of the central plateau, above it all, the warrior hero and founder of the Turkish Republic lies buried.

The Anitkabir (Ataturk Mausoleum) sits atop a Turkish acropolis, the approach road guarded by army recruits. The guard changes on the hour, every hour in a ceremony evoking a solemnity unlike anything else to be encountered in Turkey. Seeing my predicament as a small seated figure at the foot of a staircase with perhaps two hundred steps from base to crest, two guards are crisply assigned to lifting duties. The first thing I do after dismissing them with an elaborate display of gratitude is to amble across to the raised tomb.

At the opposite end of the concrete plateau, in a tomb on a markedly more human scale, lies Ataturk's loyal deputy, Ismet Inonu, overshadowed by his leader in death as in life.

Tonight I dine with a Turkish diplomat I met at Ucagiz and her husband, a lawyer, at a favourite restaurant of theirs in the suburbs. I am struck by how closely they link Turkey's future greatness to acceptance within the European Union. When I mention some countries' traditional view that Turkey should not be granted access to their rich-country club—being a nation of which only 3 per cent actually lies in Europe and whose 70 million Muslims would significantly alter the character of the union—they seem crestfallen. European status was an ambition harboured by Ataturk himself: is that a muttering I hear from the general direction of his mausoleum? Must be the wind.

Tomorrow, the manager of the hotel I'm staying in here has agreed to set aside a prior engagement to drive me to the bus station, something it would never have occurred to me to ask of him. This is yet another example of the unsolicited kindness that greets me at every turn. I'm humbled.

DAY 350 (8 JUNE): TARSUS

Welcome to Tarsus, birthplace of St Paul. I peer down into two excavated rooms from what is undeniably an ancient dwelling. Whether those rooms, now underground, were indeed where the boy then known as Saul played, long before he grew into the man who spread Christianity to Greece and the Near East, is a matter of ... well, faith.

DAY 351 (9 JUNE): BACK TO ANTAKYA

Biblical Antioch, my first landfall in Turkey, becomes one of my last destinations as I return to it for just one afternoon to visit St Peter's Church (Senpiyer Kilisesi), a fourth-century monument to the man Christ called a Rock and who is revered by Catholics as the first Pope.

St Peter is popularly depicted as holding the keys to heaven. Unfortunately, the ticket-seller at the gate of the church built in Peter's honour three centuries after he passed this way is fiercely possessive of his earthly bunch of keys, refusing admittance through the barred and gated opening in the rock.

Rather than engage in an unholy row, I refrain from entering the cave but take a photograph from the courtyard in front of it and head off down the hill. 'Hill' is something of a euphemism in this case. The 2-kilometre descent is so steep, and the asphalt so burning hot in mid-afternoon, that if I go too fast my palms get scorched but the momentum carries me unstoppably on. Poor preparation, be cursed: gloves and forethought would have spared me this hell.

DAY 358 (16 JUNE): MARMARIS TO RHODES
Friendly Turkey is at its shining summer best as the sleek and crowded hovercraft churns up the waters at Marmaris dock before high-tailing it across the seas to Rhodes. Yet again I am leaving Asia for Europe's shore, saying farewell to a friendly country which soccer success has united in feeling good about itself. The next fortnight will remind me how lucky Turkey is in that regard when division and ill feeling reign not so far over the horizon.

The golden rule of travelling overland or by sea, rather than by air, must be broken once more—though, in my defence, it is for the first time in months and the last time in the journey. The Palestinian uprising, now raging for nearly two years, has led to suspension of the passenger ferry service that used to link Athens to the Israeli port of Haifa via Cyprus. I may be knocking on Europe's door, but still cannot break out of the Middle East's orbit.

CYPRUS: 18 JUNE–2 JULY

When I sub-edited on a Greek newspaper in the mid-1980s, Cyprus was never mentioned apart from the description 'divided island'. When all is said and done, that remains the essential and inescapable truth about the place today. It is hard to see the day when a country that suffered wholesale 'ethnic cleansing' in the 1970s, long before that term came into use, will be reunified: one is tempted to take odds on

Korea getting there first. Without a doubt, Cyprus is one of the world's saddest lands, a blasted heath of downtrodden aspirations. Through all history, this has been a place where different people were forced to live together but no one felt securely at home.

DAY 361 (19 JUNE): LARNACA

Round the corner from the hotel where I've found a room stands the Church of Agios Lazaros. Here, the Greek Orthodox faithful believe the mortal remains of Lazarus lie, the man Jesus raised from the dead (the first time).

When it becomes apparent that the object of veneration is in a crypt, down a particularly awkward set of stairs, I decide to remain on the ground floor, observing the gruesome sight of what is said to have been Lazarus's heart. It now lies like a pensive pink jelly in a glass booth.

It's impossible to forget this island's division for long. A giant Turkish flag is etched into the hillsides of north Nicosia for Greeks in the south of the city to behold and tremble at. Barriers, flags and fortifications are everywhere on both sides, emblems of a morbid fascination with death. But not everyone's opinion runs true to ethnic stereotype.

Andreas M., a Greek Cypriot hotel manager in seafront Limassol, confides, 'Many of the people our side says were killed by the Turks were actually killed by right-wing (pro-Greek) death squads. We Greeks made 99 per cent of the mistakes. Our children are taught in the schools that the Turks as Muslims want all the power in the world, therefore you must expect them to behave atrociously.'

Sheikh Mustafa is imam of Limassol's Grand Mosque. His discourse, rendered eerie by the fact that his Arabic is translated for my benefit by a Palestinian gravedigger, says, 'One country is better than two; I believe it still. They are negotiating so there is hope. When they understand Islam better, a solution can happen in this generation.'

Twenty-something Mustafa Erguven, a merchant marine captain, is canvassing for a municipal election in Kyrenia (which the Turks call Girne). 'We want Turkey to leave the island, for us Turkish Cypriots to govern ourselves.'

Melios, a Greek Cypriot Australian who has returned to his native island but cannot set foot in his hometown of Famagusta, now in the

Turkish-run north, tells me, 'I cannot help hating the Turks. They killed my father, not with their bare hands but ... he could never get over the shock. Too much blood has flowed: memory is too strong. Whenever there can be a solution, there will have to be two states in Cyprus.' Drained of words, Melios bids me goodbye and enters ... a Turkish bathhouse.

Mustafa D., aged 60, gives me a lift from Nicosia's Green Line north to Girne. A successful glassware exporter, he owns factories in the town, a mansion in Famagusta and a summerhouse on the north coast—and he has been diagnosed with terminal cancer. In him, hope tempered by realism outweighs fear. 'One day there will be a union of our communities, I think as one state. But not while the current generation of politicians is in charge.'

Two young soldiers man a checkpoint on the Green Line. Christos, a 20-year-old raised in south London, says, 'The Turks? They're animals. If one of them comes over here, I'll fucking shoot him in the head. Every day they throw stones at us.'

His comrade, Pte Michael, blurts out, 'It's our side which is most to blame. People on our side were killing innocent Turks' (Christos nearly blows a fuse at such loose talk) 'which gave Turkey the excuse to come in and protect their own.'

Susan, wife of a Greek Cypriot diplomat in Ottawa, is visiting her aged father who lives above the *taverna* 20 metres from the UN buffer zone. 'Muslims are fanatics the world over,' she declaims. 'I see no solution. Ever. It will be better as two states, not one.'

In north Nicosia is a remarkable fingerboard. It reads 'To Martyrdom' and one wonders, 'Why would I want to go there?' Go down the street indicated and you come to a neatly tended Turkish Cypriot cemetery. Outside the entrance is this noticeboard: 'The Greeks have destroyed children, young ones, olds, and so many who had no protection'.

In south Nicosia, this sign overhangs a Greek-side checkpoint: 'THERE IS NO GAIN WITHOUT SACRIFICES AND FREEDOM WITHOUT BLOOD'.

Taken all in all, it's enough to make a humanitourist weep. And what do I think of it all? What a false creature is the nation. How can it own an individual soul when it is such a multifarious, five-winged, four-headed, triple-hearted, double-faced thing?

DAY 365 (23 JUNE): NICOSIA

Here's an irony for you. The visitor to Cyprus can move freely from south to north, but with very few exceptions Cypriots themselves are confined to the north or south of their 'common home'. Today is my second crossing this week of the demarcation line that bisects the world's last divided capital, and when I return south of it Greeks are amazed that I haven't been interrogated about why I was so keen to consort with the enemy.

Most of the day is spent on the north coast, in the picturesque once-Greek, now-Turkish port of Girne, where all the goods in the shops have either come from the Turkish mainland or been smuggled here in defiance of UN sanctions. Girne must have the world's only Irish pub that doesn't stock any Guinness: the brewery wasn't willing to run the gauntlet.

Back in north Nicosia at 4 pm, I am confronted with a dilemma. Whether they want to be self-governing or a Turkish colony, the whole half city is agog with anticipation as Turkey—one of the sensations of this World Cup tournament—continue to mow down all opposition in their path (Brazil the only exception). If Turkey win today, the red-and-white boys have made it to the semi-final.

But travellers who go to the north must be back in Greek Nicosia by 5 pm or else they will not be allowed across the line. Do I miss the football and join in the excitement? At 4.40 pm, with a goal in the dying minutes of the match, Turkey win through again, and the celebrations explode. I make it back with minutes to spare.

DAY 367 (25 JUNE): NICOSIA

Only in a country with such a penchant for the tragic would you find a Museum of Barbarism. An ordinary-looking suburban house, its interior is a series of grisly photographs showing what happened to the family of its former occupant—a Turkish Cypriot general—when Greek troops ran amok there on Christmas Eve 1963. One of the milder exhibits is a photo of the general's wife, hacked to death in the bath.

South of the line, a visit to the National Struggle Museum restores the balance of terror. I reach it by pushing down laneways flanked by abandoned houses, now bomb sites, which have been kept as they were, one suspects, purely as visual propaganda. The museum records the battle of pro-Greek forces to escape British rule and become part of Greece. Three hangman's nooses (the very ropes with which the British hanged three 'martyrs') honour the heroic dead.

DAY 368 (26 JUNE): NICOSIA

Turkey's dream run in the soccer World Cup has come to an end. Having witnessed the jubilation in north Nicosia after a win, I'm glad to be in the south tonight.

DAYS 369–373 (27 JUNE–1 JULY): KYKKOS MONASTERY

The Nissan van climbs and curls, clambers and coils around the mountainside, on a corkscrew road with champagne views. We're a happy party of day trippers and pilgrims heading for the mountain peak.

There sits one of the sites most sacred to those of the Orthodox faith, not so much for its pure, calming air and sylvan setting as for its great treasure. The Virgin Mary icon here—kept in a silver-embossed phylactery with a window through which it can be observed—was brought from Constantinople in the 11th century. Miracles, of course, are claimed in its (her) name, mostly miracles of healing, but apart from that the icon is one of the three most venerated paintings Greek Orthodox followers ascribe to St Luke. The evangelist is believed to have received the panel direct from the Archangel Gabriel.

The community of monks here is as old as the icon, a thousand years. But as I am welcomed and shown into one of the empty cells—a guest room which will be my home for four nights—Padre Orthonikos tells me the brethren today number just eleven.

From previous overseas visits in Egypt, Nepal and South Korea, I know that those who are not of the faith (be it Coptic or Buddhist) are welcome to attend the services, observe the routine, of monks. This I promise myself to do by rising early on Sunday, having slept through the five o'clock bell for the first three mornings.

Friday-evening prayers are over. The pilgrims and sightseers have gone, the monastery is closing down. A flight of birds has left raucously for its night refuge. The summer air is almost vibrating, peace is at hand. Yet my thoughts, like fresh waters ever flowing in, are running to secular matters, and a small question of logistics.

Tomorrow Turkey play South Korea for third place in the World Cup, and the day after that is the final itself, in far-off Yokohama.

The monk in charge of guest hospitality has just asked me to stay an extra couple of days if I am enjoying the atmosphere here. I am, and would like to stay longer. My itinerary is not so fixed, but ...

'Padre Orthonikos,' I begin, my voice faltering in hesitation about how to put this, 'on Sunday, in the outside world, there is a certain football match.'

The unworldly-looking figure in the black cassock purses his lips, apparently straining to comprehend.

'This is a big event,' I continue. 'Brazil are playing Germany.'

He pauses. At length, a smile lights up his face. 'No problem,' Orthonikos assures me. 'We will give you a television!'

The good father keeps his word. Early Sunday afternoon, he leads me to the far end of the courtyard, fingering a set of long keys. Finding the one he wants, he turns the lock of a door previously unopened during my time here, and we enter the VIP guest room. Behind lace curtains, I ensconce myself in a large armchair as Padre Orthonikos turns on the large-screen TV and finds the right channel.

Then, before he leaves me to the kick-off at Kykkos, he switches on the airconditioning and wags an admonishing finger in my direction. 'Today is Sunday. Many people come to see the Virgin Mary. I am going to close the door. Please do not open it to anyone.'

I see his point. The cult of the Virgin Mary must not be despoiled by St Ronaldo worshippers. If football fever there must be, it will be quarantined. I promise piously.

The crowd is huge, the audience global. This is not how I had envisaged watching the match (the original scenario had been at a pub on Cyprus' south coast tourist strip), but at least I am not altogether disconnected, being in one community of eleven and another of a billion and a half simultaneously.

Outside again, the late-afternoon sun licks me like a furnace flame. Pilgrims in long leggings walk along the colonnade on their way to see the Virgin Mary.

A husband detaches himself from his wife—he must have seen an earthbound rapture written all over my face—and asks, in a thick German accent, 'Do you know who won?'

Sunday morning, at ten past five, the morning has taken a peep at the night, and will be back a little later. The deep and sonorous chants of monks, intoned in liturgical Greek, soothe and lull me as I sit at the back of the chapel ... I relapse into sleep in my mobile pew at least half a dozen times in the ensuing 90 minutes. These sounds have filled this space, wafted over these mountains, every morning for a thousand years. At my core I am at peace; and I am at the core of a timeless collected serenity.

When the congregation disperses, a new day has dawned. We emerge into the paler light of day possessing a sense of rightness with the world that does not leave me.

Chapter 18

THE GLORY THAT IS GREECE

As for the gods, it seemed to be the same thing whether one worshipped them or not, when one saw the good and the bad dying indiscriminately.

THUCYDIDES *HISTORY OF THE PELOPONNESIAN WAR*

JULY–AUGUST 2002

GREECE: 2 JULY–12 AUGUST

This was my first lengthy visit to Greece since the mid-1980s, when I worked on an English-language paper in Athens for a year, and my first real opportunity to see the country. Even in those days I was struck by how popular politics (*politiki* in Greek) is. Of a Saturday night in a downtown Athens taverna, even football (a sport Greeks are also mad about) has to compete for attention with screenings of parliamentary debates.

But, more than its great contributions to Western civilisation, what charms the visitor today is the Greeks' love of ease and social occasions. The syncopated rhythms of the *bouzouki*; the sinuous *syrtaki* dance; the convivial laughter and inclusive conversation: all are washed down with *retsina*, the gods' own nectar. Greece is essentially a thing of the spirit, the spirit has a name and it is zest. That hasn't changed in the past 3000 years, and I doubt it will in the next.

DAY 375 (3 JULY): RHODES
Seen at its best from the sea, the Old Town of Rhodes possesses a stunning symmetry of fortified walls, broken by crenellations and gaps where motor traffic mocks their medieval impregnability. Once inside, the impression of being in another age is also mocked, this time by the

tourist hordes—and on Rhodes in high summer that cliché comes to life—yet so rich is the town's history that even they cannot entirely spoil the experience.

From the 14th to the 16th centuries, this largest island in the Dodecanese group was a sort of Christian flagship in Muslim waters, run by the Knights of St John. Ippoton, known in English as the Avenue of the Knights, is formidably steep, frighteningly narrow and bone-crushingly cobbled, each stone so resistant that it can take ten minutes to achieve 400 metres of progress. But those 400 metres are worth taking slowly, and not only because you have to.

First, if you don't, you risk up-ending the wheelchair in what would make my little Syrian mishap pale into significance. Second, as you look up, on your left and right are the predominantly Gothic residences of knights from the various countries of Christian Europe, each imposing façade with its own medieval device.

DAY 377–381 (5–9 JULY): KARPATHOS

These are lazy, throwaway days, the first on which I can relax and go at the local pace.

On my leisurely route towards Athens, I was looking for an island that was not so remote it might lack that modern convenience without which I am in real difficulties—the flush toilet—yet not so popular that tourists at this season would swarm there like bees.

Karpathos fits the bill beautifully. As the ferry approaches this long, straggling island, pinpricks of light from villages that lie deep in mountain valleys give me a warm feeling about this retreat even before we reach port.

The port's name, Pigadia, strikes me as rather ugly. But the town itself is not, although there is no opportunity for sightseeing until the morrow. By the time I find a place to stay, the church bell across the square has tolled midnight. Then I discover the lift isn't working in the only easily accessible inn around, so the manager, after some hesitation, allows me to kip until dawn on the sofa in the TV lounge.

Next morning, after breakfasting at one of the many seaside tavernas while gazing out at fishing boats rocking in the harbour, I collect my bags and hire a taxi to deliver me 10 kilometres around the coast at an even more remote and laid-back destination, Ammoopi.

Oddly, it is easier to find a hotel at this tiny resort than it was in Pigadia. For all its remoteness, the Argo has satellite TV in the bar—I spend quite a bit of time watching Wimbledon—and an unbeatable balcony view that makes the prospect of a few days' relaxation particularly inviting. Disbelieve anyone who has been to Ammoopi and says there is nothing to do there: you can sleep, read and eat, or, to vary the routine, eat, read and sleep. But then I haven't seen fit to mention these activities before on this journey, so it might give a more realistic picture of my Karpathos experience if I were simply to summarise the events of a typical day in this backwater. Here goes:

DAY 380 (8 JULY): AMMOOPI
Nothing doing.

DAYS 382–383 (10–11 JULY): KARPATHOS TO CRETE TO SANTORINI
The Caspian crossing may have been a nautical mile or two further but, at nearly 24 hours, this has claims to being the longest sea voyage of my entire trip, and I am impressed by the crew's willingness to go out of their way to make it enjoyable. Hours are spent sunning myself on the viewing deck.

Santorini and I are no strangers. I saw in the New Year of 1986 here, before flying back to Athens in a light plane whose pilot was already tipsy on retsina. Ease is what this place is all about, which makes me feel all the more conspicuous when, among the smart set, I am let down by my usually reliable wheels. For some time now, the tyre on my right wheel has been developing an almost rakish buckle—if the chair could walk, I'd call it Chaplinesque—and it chooses today to come off the wheel rim altogether. Luckily, a young couple from Australia whom I've just met restore the rubber to the wheel, but the chair has signalled clearly enough that I've been pushing it too hard.

Here's a paradox for you. The main town, Fira, is high up on the lip of a giddy drop into a submarine volcano—one of the least hospitable places imaginable for a wheelchair user. Yet it is here that the owner of a pension, by the grandiose name of the Hotel Palladion, insists I stay free of charge, the only occasion in my travelling life where this has happened.

DAY 386 (14 JULY): MYKONOS

We are transported to fabled Mykonos by a touch of luxury in the form of a fast-tracking catamaran, the inter-island transportation favoured by the jet-ski set. 'Discovered' in the 1960s by Jackie Kennedy-becoming-Onassis, this is one of the Mediterranean's gaudiest jewels. It is still a party-goer's dream, but the prices more than live up to the billing. You pay A$8 for a small plastic cup of beer or, like me, you don't.

DAY 388 (16 JULY): ATHENS

Even for someone who knows Athens like the back of his hand, and who lived and worked there for a year, this is a city whose attractions never pall.

As the ferry ramp lowers to reveal a pomegranate moon rising behind the port skyline, a 'tourist police' officer whistles up a taxi and *commands* the driver to take me wherever I want, by the shortest possible route.

We drive up over the rise and down to Zea Marina, a cove lined with thousands of yachts, and around the coastal road towards Paleo Faliron, site of the 2004 Olympics water venues. Unable to remember the name of the hotel where I put up last time, I eventually spot a miniature medieval Greek Orthodox Church I recall having viewed from the hotel balcony. The hotel's name, in lights, reminds me why I couldn't think of it. Cavo d'Oro is Spanish or Portuguese, anything but Greek.

DAY 389 (17 JULY): ATHENS

Nobody wants the old Athens to change, except perhaps a few million of the people who live here, and a perambulation around the Acropolis—no easy thing, now that excavations have begun for a branch line of the underground railway—assures me that in many ways it really hasn't done. The Parthenon, that glorious ruin—or, as I once heard a Liverpool soccer fan describe it to his mates, 'a pile of old rocks'—still occupies the same majestic lookout it has done for the past 2500 years.

One new feature is the underground rail network I just mentioned. In 1985, when I didn't need it, one of the few things Athenians envied their northern European cousins was a Metro. Now that I'm in a wheelchair, the Attiko Metro network is hugely welcome.

DAY 391 (19 JULY): ATHENS
Once in Santorini, and once in Athens, the buckled tyre has come off the wheel, slewing me to an embarrassed and unscheduled stop. In this car-, van- and truck-congested metropolis, the bicycle is a rare bird. But, following a series of comical charades that elicit some bizarre reactions, I eventually find myself in a street containing a bicycle shop.

Extraordinary luck has come my way. Not only is this cycle-shop owner able to see at once that a wheelchair wheel is essentially the same as a bicycle wheel, he actually has a small but thriving sideline in wheelchair repairs. It had been my hope to get a solid, tubeless tyre to match its partner but, this not proving possible, I'm grateful that he at least has one in stock that is the right size for the rim in question.

DAY 392 (20 JULY): ATHENS
The tiny Athens flat I lived in back in the 1980s was about 200 metres from a first-century AD Roman theatre, the Herod Atticus Odeon. In this scene of rapid urban redevelopment, I'm relieved to see it still is. In some trepidation that my old landlady, Helen, might get an unavoidable shock seeing me in a wheelchair, I knock at the old address.

A relative answers the buzzer and, on being persuaded I know Helen, breaks the news that she died in 2000. Her sister, whom I also know, is on holiday in the Peloponnesus. Give her my regards, I say, but don't mention the wheelchair. It's not that I retain any uneasiness about it, just that it seems wrong to pass on news of her long-ago lodger as a paraplegic, wrapped up in a garbled and necessarily alarming second-hand report on the causes of my new status.

This hot summer evening, in the steep bowl of the Odeon, 5000 music lovers have gathered to honour Mikis Theodorakis, at 75 the Grand Old Man of Greek music.

On occasions such as this, being in a wheelchair is a decided advantage: I am given the equivalent of a box seat, just to the right of the stage, and the avuncular, slightly stooped maestro himself is easily persuaded to sign my programme.

DAY 393 (21 JULY): ATHENS

It is disappointing on a visit to the National Archaeological Museum to discover that although the museum boasts a brand new hydraulic lift—especially designed to enable wheelchair users to avoid the forbidding entrance staircase—finding someone who actually knows how it works provokes a near-panic among the curators. Presumably, by the time the Olympics have come and gone, they will have got their act together.

DAY 398 (26 JULY): EPIDAURUS

This World Heritage-listed site, 30 kilometres east of Nafplion, has two claims to fame. The first is that it is where the Temple of Asclepius, an early Greek healer, existed (and the purity of the air at this elevation is explanation enough why the ancient health fiend located his practice here).

Moving from the temple grounds up a spiralling road that leaves me a bit short of puff, I reach Epidaurus' second attraction, the auditorium. Another Hellenic Festival performance, this time of Aristophanes' *The Birds*, often regarded as the first comedy ever performed, is under way and I ponder the probability that audiences around 500 BC would have watched this same play from these same marble seats.

DAY 400 (28 JULY): OLYMPIA

This rural setting is where the Olympics were held for much of their first thousand years. *Bingo! Let's have them here permanently*, I think after hitching my chariot to a small group of fellow travellers staying at my hotel. Of course you would have to limit each country to providing no more than half a dozen competitors, just to keep the village village-sized. There would be no television rights because you wouldn't televise it (that only encourages sponsors and the ugly trappings of greed and other selfish ambitions). The winners would be garlanded with laurel wreaths rather than medals of any colour. And, of course, the merest hint of beach volleyball or synchronised swimming would be punishable by hemlock. The aim would be nothing less than a revival of the amateur spirit.

The saddest ruin of all, given that not a column of it remains standing today, has to be the Temple of Zeus. Here stood another of the Seven Wonders, a statue of the great god himself fashioned by the most eminent sculptor of the ancient world, Phidias.

DAY 402 (30 JULY): KALAVRYTA, PELOPONNESUS

This town—barely more than a village, really—is close by the monastery of Agias Lavras. The old monastery was burnt down by the Nazis, but the monks today welcome visitors to a sturdy-looking replica.

Back in Kalavryta, Dimitri and Nikos, the Greek–Australian brothers who run the best hotel in town, make me feel at home. In their thirties now, the Brisbanites decided a decade ago that, while their family were in Australia, their hearts were in the mountains of southern Greece, so they acted on that sentiment and have never looked back. Downstairs they run the town's premier eatery—sentimentally named Taverna o Australos—and, while I wouldn't have said no to a meat pie and sauce at this point, I must admit even that wouldn't have held a candle to the brothers' *pièce de non-résistance*, goat in lemon sauce.

DAY 404 (1 AUGUST): DELPHI

I have come to consult the Oracle.

But the slopes of Mount Parnassus, home to the gods of yore, are really unsuited to wheelchairs, which is a shame considering the detours I took to get here. Fortunately, the ticket-seller—sparing me the necessity of paying—co-opts a family of Athenian day trippers to consult the Oracle for me.

Half an hour later, having paid their respects at the Sanctuary of Apollo, they return with broad smiles. In faultless English, the husband says, 'We told the Oracle you were an Australian. And she said you will travel far.' Ye gods!

DAY 405 (2 AUGUST): PATRAS

On awakening this morning to the sounds of a busy port, my minds beats back on a sea of remembrance to another 2 August, in Muscat, another coastal city far to the east of here. The brute fact headlining the radio news that morning invaded my life as well as Kuwait. Yet this time also connects to an earlier one: the spring of 1985, when I lived and worked on a boat in the Greek port of Piraeus. The life of this city swept by waves reminds me that this may be 2 August but there was a before as well as an after – and, while some things are lost over time, others are as recurrent as the tides.

So how does one gauge the personal difference between these 'two August' dates? I'm not the person I was then: I know myself better now. In ancient times the Greeks' vision always extended inward as deeply as it did outward. They were interested equally in psychology and geography. The Oracle was right. I have indeed travelled far.

DAY 406 (3 AUGUST): ITHACA

The ferry from Patras drops anchor at the quay of Vathy, deep inside a fjord-like inlet on the northern shores of Ithaca. Ever since Odysseus' ship came in, this fabled island has symbolised the place of rest at the end of a long voyage. Being several thousand kilometres short of my goal, I trust this isn't an omen.

Oppressively hot nights are to be expected at these latitudes in August, along with the tourist throng. We are in the euro zone at high season: it is unrealistic to expect bargains. But my dander is up when, despite his staff telling me there is a room left (at 8 pm), a surly hotel owner refuses to consider reducing the tariff from 60 euro a night (about A$100) to something more in the price range of a long-distance traveller on a budget.

After a brief but artistically controlled tantrum, I repair to the calmer environs of Kantouni, an outdoor restaurant soothed by the lapping waves of the Ionian Sea. So friendly are the restaurant staff, and so hot the night, that I wonder whether this wouldn't be an occasion for calling the hotelier's bluff and sleeping out on a stretcher bed in the courtyard. The waiter consults the patron, and says this should be no problem if I'm willing to wait until the last diners leave at midnight. I've checked out the ablution facilities: no problem there, either.

At 10 pm, on returning to the hotel to collect my bags, I meet the hotel owner in radically changed mood. Fawning over me now, he says, 'Thirty euro. You have 30 euro? Welcome to my hotel.'

After a moment's hesitation, I choose a room in preference to the courtyard but go back to the restaurateur to apologise for changing my plans. He explains the hotel owner's change of mood: the last boat came in an hour ago. Until then, if the hotel honcho thought he could secure a paying guest at 60 euro, he was playing the game for profit.

This is the high season and he is in business, after all.

DAY 410 (7 AUGUST): PREVEZA

Preveza is famous throughout Greece for its delicious sardines. So tonight I enjoy one of the best meals of the journey—sardines and red wine drawn from genuine hogsheads situated in the on-site cellar of Amvrosios restaurant.

The only jarring note is struck by the restaurateur who, on learning that I am heading north to Albania, appears to go into shock. 'You will be robbed!' he warns me. This side of the border it's a familiar refrain. I order another wine and put such remarks down to experience. Theirs, not mine.

DAY 411 (8 AUGUST): PARGA

This will sound morbid, but you would be surprised at the number of people who want to go to the Underworld before their time. Here in western Epirus one leaves the town of Parga by speedboat, heading first along the Ionian Sea and then up the River Acheron to the beach resort of Ammoudi. From here it is a couple of kilometres by road, and 100 metres through tall grass, to a spooky underground vault. This is believed to have been the gateway to Hades, where the dead—and nowadays package tourists—go.

Chapter 19

CURSE OF THE BALKANS

*Each nation demands that its borders revert to where they were
at the exact time when its own empire had reached the zenith of ...
medieval expansion.*

ROBERT D. KAPLAN BALKAN GHOSTS

AUGUST-OCTOBER 2002

When you look at the fractious history of the peoples who have
occupied Europe's south-east down the ages, you realise that,
notwithstanding the wars of Yugoslav disintegration last decade, this
region is actually living through one of its most benign and outward-
looking eras.

Your average Serb may not yet like your average Croat—although
there are plenty of examples of love breaking out across the racial
divide—but the predominant feeling I got, from Macedonia to
Bulgaria, was one of grudging tolerance. You might not entrust your
neighbour with the family silver but you recognised him as someone
with broadly the same aspirations as yourself, someone who in any
event had been here more or less as long as your own folks and was in
no hurry to leave. There are grounds for believing that, as the
European Union extends its proverbial hand to such countries as
Bulgaria and Slovenia, rubbing along with the neighbours will
increasingly be seen as preferable to rubbing them out.

Serbo–Croat is a language that unites peoples often seen as visceral
enemies, even if it is called Serbian in Serbia, Croat in Croatia and
Bosnian in Bosnia. Religion can unite even as it divides – the Muslims
of Albania may have more in common with their co-religionists in

Sarajevo than with their fellow Albanians—but that is a curse not confined to the Balkans (ask anyone in the Middle East).

Of all the countries visited on this odyssey, none came as a more pleasant surprise than Bosnia. Some of the most positive and heart-warming signs of humanity in today's world are to be found on the streets of Sarajevo and Mostar. The winter of their discontents has been a long time thawing, but now is the season of regrowth. There is no better time to visit a place that has been through hell than when it has emerged from the ruins and planted its feet confidently on the road back to normality. It is like seeing a drought-stricken country come to life after the rains. In these days not only is it safer to be in Mostar than, dare one say it, Miami, but the reception you get from the locals will justify your choice several times a day.

Like the gentle rain that droppeth, the mercy of a visit to the Balkans is that it is twice blessed. The visitor will be refreshed to see that not only does life go on after a man-made catastrophe, it goes on getting better. The people are overwhelmingly hospitable. These are people who know how great it is to be alive. As a wheelchair user in the Balkans told me, in one of those statements that turns your customary way of looking at things on its head, 'Those people who think we need their charity to maintain our self-respect are the real disabled ones.'

ALBANIA: 12–25 AUGUST

DAY 416 (13 AUGUST): GJIROKASTRA

A free visa is granted on arrival—let's face it, Albania doesn't have any incentive to put obstacles in the way of people wanting to come here.

Long a byword for inaccessibility, Albania reveals why in the first minute I spend on its soil. At Kakavija, the border with Greece, you know you've entered Albania because here the smooth bitumen hardtop degenerates into a mosaic of rutted tar strips that barely deserve the name of a road at all—and, a few kilometres later, even that is gone and we're on the gravel.

Everything about Albania sets it apart: the people speak Tosk and spend leka. Vying with Moldova as the Continent's poorest country, it is no joke to point out that the country's biggest export is Albanians: they flee by the boatload to Italy whenever possible, and have become

Greece's primary cheap labour force. This is one of two European countries with a majority Muslim population but mosques are few and far between, and churches even more so. Under the 40-year rule of the communist dictator Enver Hoxha, this became the world's only officially atheist state, and open displays of religious devotion are still almost unknown.

In the perpetual pointlessness of a Gjirokastra evening, I fantasise about being an advertising copywriter for a Tirana tourism agency. My biggest poster, just white words on a pitch-black background, would read: 'Visit Albania, the Land of Absence. Whatever you're looking for, it isn't here.'

This town has 28 bar-restaurants (I had plenty of idle time for counting them) but none stays open after 6 pm. In this almost food-free zone, I eventually track down a *souvlaki* (but xenophobia cuts both ways and, rather than call it that, the Albanian shopkeeper insists it is a 'hamburger'). Just as I am handing her a banknote that she indicates is much too large to change, a stranger steps forward and offers to help. Indicating I should wait a little distance away while the souvlaki-burger is prepared, he hails an old friend along the pavement and hurries over to embrace him. By the time my food is ready, the shopkeeper is demanding to be paid, and the 'helpful' stranger is nowhere to be seen. Welcome to Albania. (There is a happy coda to this: ten minutes later, the man is careless enough to be seen with friends at a coffee shop, and sheepishly returns the dosh.)

Outside the police station yesterday evening, I thought I'd stumbled across a scoop, with hundreds of men pushing against the compound gates and rattling them, police glowering from the inside. A popular uprising against government corruption, perhaps? No. A schoolteacher I met in the street who practised his English on me—only after a reflexive look round to see if the coast was clear—explained, 'They are all applying for exit visas. But first they must pass through several stages, and they want to go inside to pay corruption money to the police for another signature (on their forms). This one signature will cost them US$45.'

Assuming that, as a professional man, he might know these things, I asked him what the average monthly salary in Albania was. 'US$45,' he replied without pausing for breath. Unemployment, he continued, was a staggering 90 per cent.

DAY 418 (15 AUGUST): FIER

On the bus trip today to this 250 000-strong town, I was reminded yet again how one can travel to another time by travelling to another place, when I saw an old farmer with a grizzled weather-beaten face using a bullock to plough his land. Not since China many years ago have I seen such a sight.

In some parts of southern Albania, donkeys are still the most common form of road transportation. The communists banned all private ownership (of anything), so hardly anyone has been driving a motor for more than ten years, and it shows.

Women carry a heavy burden, too: some I saw bent double under hayricks two metres tall.

At the hotel where my presence has sullenly been tolerated (the paranoid society that Hoxha cultivated has not reverted to normal nearly 20 years after his death), I am getting used to the restaurant kitchen closing in the middle of the evening mealtime with the announcement that *everything* is off.

DAY 420 (17 AUGUST): FIER

Disaster strikes at one in the afternoon. Crime scene: Fier railway station. Motive: to steal whatever is in my blue backpack. Offence: to snatch said pack from the ground where I have placed it to assist those helping me up into the goods van to get a hand-hold on my chair.

Once on board, I know immediately the bag has been stolen and raise a hue and cry. A policeman on the spot disappears without trace. Heads protrude from every carriage. One passenger reports seeing a young man with a beard fleeing the scene. Quarter of an hour later, the police arrive in force.

The only silver lining to this dark cloud is that just a minute before boarding the train I transferred my passport from the backpack to my sports bag. That's safe and, with the nearest Australian embassies in faraway Athens and Belgrade, its presence halves my woes.

At the police station I'm presented with a form but refuse to make a statement until they get serious enough to find an English-speaker who can explain it to them. A legal interpreter is roused from his Saturday-afternoon slumber.

Then it's back to the Hotel Fieri, where the hard-nosed manager initially says the place is full (a blatant lie, room keys as thick as bedbug colonies cluster on the wall behind reception) but eventually relents under police pressure.

This evening I pass lonely and dejected in my room, not even bothering to go down to the restaurant to see what's off the menu.

DAY 421 (18 AUGUST): FIER

No word from the police for nearly 24 hours, but then the still unfriendly manager informs me upon my return from an hour's stroll in the town that two officers called to see me. Outside the police station, where I have to battle past yet another throng of locals desperate to depopulate the country, a paramilitary-looking type brandishing a sidearm hassles me until my case officer, Detective Sergeant Idris, appears.

In the office he tells me, 'We have good news.' The old heart leaps. 'My bag has been found?' A frown. He takes from his drawer my trusty camera (but seven rolls of film from Greece and southern Albania will never see the light of the darkroom now); my digital watch which prophetically gave up the ghost just a week before the disaster; and a bookmark (but not the book it was marking).

Enter Ilana, a redheaded devotee of the Albanian dream—to live in Italy. She translates while Idris's superior, Commander Aslan, tells me the thief sold the camera illegally, which is how they tracked him down, but apparently failed to recognise my Sony shortwave radio for what it was and so left it in the haversack when he threw it into the toxic local canal.

'Your bag will flow down to the Adriatic,' young Ilana assures me, in the evident belief that somehow this will come as a consolation. Fier being 30 kilometres inland, I nod acceptance that one could not seriously expect scuba divers to recover it.

The small fortune of 3800 leka (A\$50) that the accused found in the bag went on vodka which is why, when the police found him staggering beside the canal, he invited them to take him into custody rather than making a run for it. At this gap in the conversation, Idris and his squad usher in Lawrence Nika, 34, whom 'we have been working with'. Nika has a slight limp, which may be the result of the police 'working with' him, or maybe not.

I know this makes me sound like a bleeding-heart liberal but Nika is a pitiable figure. Criminal since fifteen, without education or friends, he is so pathetic that, while I really would like to feel angry, such a precious emotion would be wasted on him. My brain has seized on something in the way they introduced him, and won't let go. They said he was also known as Niko. I look straight at him and repeat the word. 'Niko.' He grunts his recognition.

'Mama, papa?'

'Athina.' My suspicion is confirmed.

'You will be robbed!' the Ithaca restaurateur had warned me, backed up by a rousing Greek chorus. They were totally right—but what they didn't say was that it would be by someone of Greek parentage.

DAY 422 (19 AUGUST): FIER
My robbery has made today's main Albanian newspaper, delivered fresh from Tirana. In a column featuring a natty graphic design of an artist's impression of handcuffed wrists, my name is spelt right and Fier police are given great credit for what sounds like the rare coup of actually making an arrest.

The police now inform me there is more 'good news': those missing film rolls have been found. But, despite a personal plea to the Procurator's Office—the procurator was on his way to lunch, and waved me aside—they cannot be returned to me until the 'necessary formalities' are observed. (As of the time of writing, they are yet to reach me.)

DAY 424 (21 AUGUST): TIRANA
Europopark, an Austrian-owned hotel, is the height of luxury in a capital conspicuously devoid of it. However, as I find from experience, the toilet-roll holder in the designated conveniences at Europopark repeatedly snaps from the wall and collapses to the floor at the slightest touch, giving a whole new meaning to the term 'disabled toilet'.

Predictably enough, a room at Europopark comes at a cost I'm not prepared to pay, but luckily one of the reception staff recommends I try the Stephen Center, an American-run Christian outreach coffee shop next to the main city market that has been known to rent out rooms. Normally I would be wary of placing myself in the hands of evangelists in a land that already has its own established religious creeds—even if they were suppressed for 20 years—but Albania is not Ithaca, and the thought of sleeping outside here is too ridiculous to contemplate.

DAY 426 (23 AUGUST): TIRANA

Tirana Zoo is the most depressing sight in these fifteen months of getting about Eurasia. This concrete jungle reeks of stale faeces. The first cell 'houses' a mangy grey wolf, the second a mangy grey owl. The dinginess is accentuated by an old drunk who totters along behind me, gibbering. A second mangy grey wolf, this one more like a Tasmanian thylacine, frantically paces back and forth along the four metres of concrete wall at the back of his cell. The pursuit must be as literally maddening for the wolf as it is distressing to the onlooker. He cannot get away, but I'm glad to.

DAY 427 (24 AUGUST): TIRANA

Today is my last chance to see what Albanians have made of Enver Hoxha's legacy. Unlike Brezhnev, this communist dictator didn't fake his wartime exploits but his heroic wartime resistance has long since been submerged in the public memory by his brutal repressiveness for 40 years after the war.

One way to summon up Hoxha's ghost is to visit the Genocide under the Communist Terror room at the National History Museum. The names of 5157 people killed by his regime are etched in stone here: another 30 383 are listed as persecuted.

MACEDONIA: 25 AUGUST–1 SEPTEMBER

DAY 430 (27 AUGUST): OHRID

Ohrid is landlocked Macedonia's apology for a seaside resort, so it gets quite giddy during the summer season when swarms of urban *arrivistes* descend on its tepid shore. Thankfully, I have arrived days too late for that frenzy and days too early for the international poetry festival, so pottering around town really is restful. After Albania, you need 'restful'.

Orthodox churches are dotted around town and on the stone façade of the 11th-century Church of Sveti Sofija I see a strange 'unorthodox' script. This, I later learn, is Glagolitic, the earliest form of Cyrillic.

DAY 431 (28 AUGUST): SVETI NAUM

After visiting the town's churches, many pilgrims continue on around the pine-forested lakeside road to a point near the converging borders of Macedonia, Albania and Greece. Here, on a hill above the lake, they file into the church and monastery of Sveti Naum.

Below the hill a purling stream empties into the lake, spurting jets of froth. The water's pristine clarity, and the fish teeming in it (which are legally protected), are therapy for the soul. Later I learn that Sveti Naum is highly recommended for mentally disturbed people. On hearing this I emit a nervous laugh, but the truth is that my busy days are contented ones so that, physically and psychologically, I've seldom felt better.

Just as I am gazing vacantly across the water at a town on the Albanian shore, my reverie is interrupted by a young roughly dressed man who introduces himself as Hristo. My first thought is that he is going to beg from me, but instead he launches into a tirade against the Albanians, who make up one third of this tiny country's population. They ought to be deported, they are not Macedonians, he tells me with great passion, and then adds, 'But I'm not a nationalist.'

The curse of the Balkans has struck again. If racism is a disease spread by ignorance of our common human nature, Hristo is clearly a troubled man. Perhaps he is here to take the Nature cure. So I hold my tongue, the easier to depart in peace, and hope Sveti Naum can work its magic on him.

DAY 432 (29 AUGUST): OHRID TO SKOPJE

The morning news is full of last night's bus hijack. A band of Albanian militants—'terrorists', the state radio calls them—kidnapped a busload of passengers near Gostivar, south of Tetovo, and police blocked off the road while negotiating for their release.

This news fills me with anxiety: will the bus service be stopped, delaying my onward journey? No, this is Macedonia, where a little local difficulty doesn't get blown out of all proportion. My bus will leave on time but, avoiding the Gostivar road, will go the long way up to the capital.

Much of Skopje was destroyed in an earthquake in 1963, and the rebuilt city is a dreary place. Dusk finds me foraging through its deserted streets for somewhere to stay. At the youth hostel, where I booked ahead, the duty receptionist on seeing the wheelchair announces there are no vacancies. I have grave suspicions about this but, seeing all the rooms are upstairs, I back off. Eventually a taxidriver suggests I try the Hotel Bimex, a homely establishment 'on the wrong side of the tracks' and not mentioned in my guidebook, but the family who run it invite me in as if I were a long-expected guest.

The Bimex's rooms are so small that in Japan this would be classed as a 'love hotel'. In fact, as the night wears on, it becomes obvious that it is not so much a bed-and-breakfast as a brothel. But the 'girls' and customers alike smile shyly as they quit the bar for a good night's unrest.

DAY 433 (30 AUGUST): TETOVO

The hijack is over, with all passengers released safely by their Albanian National Army captors. Radio can now reveal that police shot a hijacker dead after the ambush. An Albanian–Macedonian in Carsija market dismisses the event as an orchestrated election stunt. Whatever it was, the episode's peaceful ending has reopened the road to Tetovo, enabling me to keep faith with my itinerary.

'Micky' is tense. My taxidriver is Slavic–Macedonian and he's driving me into outlaw territory. Tetovo is tense. Just last week two Macedonian police reservists were shot dead in this town of 80 000 of whom 80 per cent are ethnic Albanians. We are 10 kilometres from Kosovo.

Passing down the main street, I see the Albanian flag of the double-headed eagle hanging from every streetlight. When I ask why, Micky forces a smile. 'The government banned it yesterday.'

BULGARIA: 1–15 SEPTEMBER

DAY 436 (2 SEPTEMBER): SOFIA

What a grand capital this is. Wide boulevards, curious byways, bread shops that get up your nose in the nicest way, and public architecture on the monumental scale. The more I travel, the less I find myself photographing people, the more snaps I take of streetscapes, churches and quirky-looking structures, as if something in them expresses the soul of Man too often hidden behind that infuriating mask, the face of Man.

Early this afternoon, and more than a bit peckish, I succumb to an attack of the 'munchies' and take a table outside McDonald's. (I tell myself there will be time enough later for homegrown cuisine.) Keen to relax with a book, I am perhaps a bit off-handed when Vanya, a stylishly groomed woman of 30 or so, invites herself to sit opposite me. Soon, though, we are talking like old friends, and indeed we gradually become just that.

Her English is excellent, and when Vanya tells me she reads avidly in it I need no convincing. So far all I have ordered is a Coke, so she takes the opportunity to suggest we move round the corner to a café that has become *the* place to be seen in Sofia. While we are shooting the breeze, Vanya nudges me. 'Look who's on the next table.' I turn round, affecting a casual air. Ten young people, enjoying themselves. 'I don't know. Who are they?' I whisper. She gushes, 'They are the stars of Bulgaria's biggest TV soap opera.'

In seconds she has rushed up to one of the celebs, introduced her friend 'from Australia' and organised a photo shoot with my camera. The photogenic actors are smiling with the ease of those who own famous physiognomies and to whom this sort of thing must be an everyday occurrence. A couple of them even appear to be mouthing the word 'kangaroo' in acknowledgement of my origins.

When we return to our conversation, Vanya is positively glowing. First meeting a foreigner, now hobnobbing with the famous: this has made her day, and the excitement is catching.

DAY 437 (3 SEPTEMBER): BANSKO

Every bit as charming and rustic as advertised, few possible improvements stand between this provincial town deep in the Rila Mountains and perfection. One might be to replace its wheelchair-hostile backstreets with some terrazzo. But even that is not enough to keep me from dining à la *mehana*, a traditional Bulgarian restaurant whose interior is warm and inviting, like a scene from *Grimm's Fairy Tales*. In one of these, Kasapinova House, tracked down through the directions of my pension host family, I partake of a Bulgarian regional dish, *kapama*—a simmering stew served in a clay pot. May McDonald's never come to Bansko.

DAY 438 (4 SEPTEMBER): DANCING BEAR PARK, ANDRIANOV CHARK

In the right season it is still possible to go bear hunting in Bulgaria, and when planning this part of the trip I thought that might be a mildly interesting diversion from museums, churches and traditional markets. Although this is not the right season, these thickly forested mountain slopes are the natural habitat of the European brown bear, and it would be a pity to come here without seeing any.

Sixties sex symbol and latter-day animal-rights campaigner Brigitte Bardot has become a vocal defender of the rights of these bears not to be taken by Gypsies (the Roma) and turned into circus acts. She and her supporters in groups such as Vier Pfoten (Four Paws) allege that our furry friends are the victims of gross cruelty.

You cannot be long in Bulgaria without seeing brown bears led around by halters held by their Roma handlers. What Bardot has done is sponsor a set of sanctuaries where these bears, removed from Roma custody, are kept under kindly supervision. The Roma are paid compensation. It all sounds like a neat piece of progress, but life (as we know) is not so straightforward. An hour in the ursine presence this morning has convinced me their whole kind would be better off without humans of any description (as they no doubt once were).

At this park—a hectare of grass, hollows and a cave—the six resident specimens of *Ursus arctos* are closed in by a high-wire fence. Leaving them alone may be their new protectors' aim, but that's not exactly how things work out. One of their three keepers, Ibrahim Garaliiski, explains why the growing bears are spayed: 'We don't want to have baby bears because we can't look after them in the forest.'

When nineteen more bears currently living with the Roma end up here, the Dancing Bear Park of Belitsa (a village close by) will be the biggest of its type in Europe, brags Vier Pfoten. But then, when you consider that the Roma have lived off the proceeds of dancing bears for centuries, what will this change mean for them? Tsvetelina Ivanova, Vier Pfoten's publicity director in Sofia, frankly admits, 'Each of these "dancing bears" feeds about 25 persons from their big families.'

The compensation is something, to be sure, but it is hard to imagine happy-go-lucky bear owners of a certain age—many Roma bear-handlers are on the far side of 60—finding new ways of earning their livelihood.

DAY 440 (6 SEPTEMBER): PLOVDIV

Today is 1885 Unification Day, a public holiday for the Bulgarians, who are clearly not ones to let their historical past go unremarked.

The name of Bulgaria's second city sounds ugly to my ears, suggestive of a pudding that failed to rise, but the Old Town quarter is just oozing with character. Nineteenth-century Plovdiv 'baroque' houses with eaves projecting over the cobbled streets account for much of it. But the jewel in Plovdiv's crown is a magnificent example of Orthodox architecture, the onion-domed Church of Constantin and Elena. Dating from 1832, the current structure is the latest of several churches to have occupied this site since very early in the Christian era.

On the cobblestones opposite the church walls, a mustachioed man who looks as if he had stepped out of a sepia photo *circa* 1910 cranks up a Wurlitzer. On the next corner sits another, offering his own finely worked watercolour sketches of the memorable streetscape around us.

After a brief negotiation I hand him the equivalent of US$25 but he detains me for a favour. When I arrive back in my homeland, would I send him a photograph of myself with the sketch in my own home? It is a casual but compelling request and weeks after I return, when more pressing business is out of the way, my promise will be kept.

DAY 442 (8 SEPTEMBER): BURGAS TO SOZOPOL

The overnight train from Plovdiv arrives at the Black Sea coastal town of Burgas bright and early, but my eagerness to seize the day encounters a mechanical setback. Having the compartment to myself, I took the wheels off my chair and rested them on the floor while the rollicking of the carriage across the central Bulgarian plain guaranteed me a restful night. But, on rising, I find that the tyre I bought in Athens is flat. It dawns on me that the source must be a slow leak, the likeliest culprit being those oh-so-charming cobblestones of old Plovdiv.

Fortunately, minibuses to Sozopol, the beach resort just down the coast, depart from directly in front of Burgas station, but the hundred or so metres wheeling down the platform on my lopsided mechanical steed leave me feeling as deflated as the offending tyre.

Once in Sozopol, I again have no alternative but to 'limp' around town until I come to a service station. Ten minutes later, with my wallet a little lighter but looks of appreciation and gratitude all round, I am back on the road again, ready to face the day totally pumped.

This is a good time to be in Sozopol, with the annual Apollonia Arts Festival in full swing. Rolling alongside a beachside park this evening to join the crowd at an open-air concert, I am surprised to run into Vanya. She is in town specifically for the festival, she tells me, and although we don't spend long together here we agree to meet back in Sofia next week.

DAY 445 (11 SEPTEMBER): VARNA

Now is the tail-end of the summer boom. Hundreds of white deckchairs sit unoccupied, looking out to the Black Sea.

An autumnal chill makes me wish I'd put a windcheater on for my stroll along the beachfront boardwalk.

Funny thing, this journey. A week today, it will be a year since I was at the eastern end of the Black Sea: now I'm on its western shore.

At noon I find myself by the south wall of Varna's imposing Assumption Cathedral, whose towering gold onion domes look as if they had been airlifted straight from Kiev.

But what's this I see on the path beside the church? A bear, forepaws down, being led by a halter.

In a flash I have bounded up, eager as a puppy to communicate with the Roma man and his gold-capped-but-otherwise-gap-toothed lady. I need to know: is this bear's contented life as a future inmate of Belitsa going to mean misery for them?

Acting on a brainwave, I rub my fingers together in the universal symbol for money. The Romany wife grins, utters the magic formula, 'Brigitte Bardot', and indicates the money will be rolling in before long.

DAY 446 (12 SEPTEMBER): VARNA

Distance, and the absence of newspapers, help me to see through to the heart of things. Today I tune into Bush's UN speech, where he raises the stakes against Saddam, accusing him of hiding 'weapons of mass destruction'.

What we are witnessing here is pure Greek drama, and the plot boils down to this: Bush's rage against Saddam is the story of one man trying to kill another man who tried to kill his father. The rest is pure posturing.

DAY 449 (15 SEPTEMBER): SOFIA

Back in the Bulgarian capital, I am outside the most famous and beloved building in the entire country: Alexander Nevsky Cathedral. The large public square out front is almost empty, with the only sounds the dying of the church bells' peal and the rustle of Sunday morning flea-market stallholders setting up.

Then, from the far side of the square, the quietness is pierced by a middle-aged woman's shrill voice. She is wagging her finger at a Gypsy couple leading—you guessed it—a bear on a stout leash. She berates the couple so fiercely that their smiles turn to scowls and they skulk off, animal in tow, as if to avoid further public embarrassment.

Witnessing my astonishment, an English-speaking bystander explains, 'The lady was shouting, "You Gypsies blind the bears to make them tame."' One up to Miss Bardot.

This afternoon, Vanya and I meet up in town by prearrangement and hail a taxi bound for Mount Vitosha, just 8 kilometres south of the capital.

The taxi drops us three quarters of the way up its 2200-metre height. The views from here over Sofia are superb enough, but the icing on the cake is a leisurely ride downhill from this point by chairlift.

Tonight, at 9 pm sharp, I board the Balkan Express train half an hour before it pulls out of Sofia central station bound for Yugoslavia (or what's left of it). As we rock'n'roll towards the border, I feel an unexpected warmth towards cheap and cheerful Bulgaria, a country whose best days appear to lie directly ahead of it.

YUGOSLAVIA (SERBIA): 16–19 SEPTEMBER

DAY 450 (16 SEPTEMBER):
SERBO-BULGARIAN BORDER TO BELGRADE

It's midnight as the train rumbles up to the border. Bulgarian formalities are completed in the blink of an eye. On the Yugoslav side of the frontier (the country is still known as Yugoslavia, although in a few months it will officially become Serbia and Montenegro), two unsmiling immigration officers hold my passport one way up and then the other in a manner that clearly spells T-R-O-U-B-L-E.

Until recently, Australians had to get their Yugoslav visas in advance;

now they are obtainable on the border for just US$15, so I was assured by a Belgrade consular official in Sofia. These officers are clearly in intimidating mood. Strangely, I have found that paraplegia can give one courage in such a situation. I cannot escape, so waiting is the only option. It is unlikely that the officers, who know I am entitled to a visa, will actually throw me off the train, I think (although memories of Syria are not entirely forgotten).

Forcing myself to be calm, I sit out a full minute. The younger of the pair finally breaks the silence. 'You must pay US$30 for the visa,' he says. Keeping my voice steady, I reply, 'I was officially informed the price is US$15.'

'You may not be allowed to enter,' says my adversary and turns on his heel, striding decisively down the corridor with my passport in hand.

I continue to sit still—what else can I do?—and try to think of faraway places.

A couple of minutes later, an agitated-looking young man pokes his head into my compartment and begs me breathlessly to give him US$15. He says he is from Sweden and has never been to this part of Europe before. Immigration is about to throw him off the train and he has no cash on him, didn't realise he would need any, has only credit cards and they won't accept plastic.

Quick thinking is required. He might be: (a) a dupe for the immigration officers, sent to ensure I cough up the exorbitant US$30 they're demanding from me; (b) a thief who wants to trick someone else into paying for his visa and has perhaps overheard the officers saying there is a passenger on board in a wheelchair; or (c) a somewhat naïve 20-year-old Swede who genuinely needs my help.

Whether (a), (b) or (c)—and his blond hair does suggest he is genuine in a land of dark-haired people— I decide it's best to give him US$30. I ask him to spend half of it on securing his visa and offer the other half to the officer who has an Australian passport in my name (which I write down for him on a scrap of paper).

Ten minutes later the Swede returns, smiling and grateful, with my newly visaed passport in hand, and without further ado our train pulls out into the southern Serbian night. Upon arriving in Belgrade, the Swede obtains cash and pays me back. This time, placing my bet on honesty has paid off.

A new day in a new city is always invigorating. New to me, that is: Belgrade, at the confluence of the Danube and Sava rivers, is long in the tooth as cities go, having been founded around 300 BC.

Old it may be but the city is in a fever of reconstruction, and the cause is not hard to see. Several tower blocks flanking the street grid have been left with the stuffing of pulverised concrete and twisted girders knocked out of them—the damage done by the NATO bombing campaign of 1999.

Wheeling down one of the city's main arteries, I spot a hawker on the pavement who is selling T-shirts. A face I've seen before is staring out from one of them. What do the words on the Milosevic T-shirt say? I ask him. (The big lettering, 'SLOBO', I can make out for myself. But the subtitle?) 'Please come back. We were only joking!' This I like: its double edge makes it marketable to pro- and anti-Milosevic individuals alike. For wit like this I don't even bother to bargain. Just as I am folding the T-shirt into my rucksack, two other garments he has for sale catch my eye: T-shirts bearing the likenesses of Ratko Mladic and Radovan Karadzic, both indicted for crimes against humanity, in particular the Srebrenica massacre. My conscience twinges and while I don't return my goods I decide that's quite enough clothes-shopping for one day.

DAY 452 (18 SEPTEMBER): BELGRADE

A third secretary at the Australian Embassy, whom I have asked to give me any standard warnings about travel in Bosnia, offers reassurance tempered only by the usual cautions about pickpockets and avoiding political discussions. Upon checking the visa requirements, she says I must get one in advance from the Bosnian Embassy (cost US$30), and even arranges the time for me to pitch up. It's in the suburbs but the taxidriver knows the street and, when we arrive, the consul's secretary is already waiting by the security gate, evidently expecting me.

This has never happened before. Things appear to be proceeding with such dispatch that I ask the driver to wait. Less than ten minutes later, the consul herself comes out, greets me personally and hands me back my passport, with a very impressive big yellow stamp bearing her confident signature.

I return to the CBD and power up the side street to our embassy. The third secretary is called down. 'Wow,' I tell her. 'That's the fastest visa application I've ever been involved with.' She appears unfazed. 'It's not so astonishing when you think about it. The war wounds on both sides are still raw, so Bosnian diplomats here don't have all that much business to attend to.'

DAY 453 (19 SEPTEMBER):
BELGRADE TO MONTENEGRIN BORDER

It's 7 pm at Belgrade central bus station and I'm guarding my bags like a prize Dobermann, while trying to persuade the gruff-looking bus driver that, despite my alien appearance, bus travel is second nature to me and there *should be* no hassles. The bus door swings open. Other passengers crowd in. And now, despite the usual careful preparations, my ticket goes missing. I search my shirt, jeans and jacket pockets, passport wallet, sports bag and suitcase. Still no ticket.

The driver barks at me, flicks his hand dismissively. A concerned passenger calls a ticket vendor over. She says, 'No ticket, no ride.' '*Manifest, manifest,*' I shout, hoping this is something like the Serbian word for 'passenger list' and that a glance at it will confirm I'm a paying passenger in distress.

After five minutes of chaos, and the driver actually pulling the bus out with me waving frantically from the deep-drop kerb, the vendor corroborates my story just as I spy a scrap of paper sticking out from my passport. Yes, the ticket! I wave it triumphantly for the driver to see. (I had put it in my passport because, as everyone knows, that's a safe place where it won't get lost.) Scowling, the driver creeps back to the kerb and, with the worst of ill grace, allows me to board. I slink into my seat, and hope things will get quieter.

They don't. My bus ride through hell is marred by the attitude of the young co-driver, clearly buttering up the Gruff One, as he demands to see my now crumpled ticket once more. He holds it up to the ceiling light like an immigration officer corruptly out to make a few bucks.

Intent on averting an argument, I parry his disguised demand by rubbing my thumb and finger (money symbol) and pointing to the ticket. (Paid for!) Insults are much easier to take when uttered in a language you can't understand so, after several minutes of invective he loses interest, until we roll in to the border post where Serbia, Montenegro and Bosnia–Herzegovina meet in the midnight darkness.

DAY 454 (20 SEPTEMBER): MONTENEGRIN BORDER TO PODGORICA TO CETINJE

A referendum, to be held by 2006, will decide whether Montenegro regains full independence after 90 years as a Serbian satellite state. Already it 'runs its own show' in the legal, banking and educational spheres. This autonomous territory of ever-shrinking Yugoslavia has already adopted the European 'single currency' as its own.

And it already has its own immigration service. Two blue-coated officers climb aboard the bus, whereupon the co-driver—still seething with hostility—points his index finger in my face and snarls accusingly, '*Americanski*!'

Ah, so this explains my rough ride. They think I'm a spy, or at least suspect that I represent the country that unleashed the dogs of war on theirs.

'Not American. Australian,' I tell one of the officers, handing him my passport. What a pity it's the same colour as an American passport, the first time I've ever noticed this fact. The officer peruses it page by page, scepticism scrawled all over his face.

Hoping that no one here will know that the Howard Government supported the NATO bombing, I wait with bated breath. The officer is in a spot: he turns to the passenger behind me and asks (as the passenger next to me translates), 'Has this person been causing trouble on the bus?'

'*Ne.*' Lucky breaks require no translation.

Brusquely, the officer returns my passport. 'Stay on the bus. And (finger to lips) Ssh!'

DAY 456 (22 SEPTEMBER): KOTOR

After an ear-popping descent to the coast, I find myself in one of Europe's most beautiful towns. Situated on the shore of a deep blue fjord (a rarity outside ice-bound latitudes), this medieval walled city has deservedly made it onto the World Heritage List. However, what I will best remember is the genuine hospitality experienced here, so refreshing after the tension in the Serbian air.

First a couple of shy, giggling teenage girls approach me outside the tourist office and hand me a postcard they have bought and signed, hoping I will remember their town and country 'with pleasure'. Then there is Maria, or 'the black widow' as I think of her. Kotor is not known for its hotels; staying as a private guest is recommended here, so I ask the tourist office if it can point me in the right direction. After a quick telephone call I am introduced to Maria, dressed from head to toe in her black weeds and smiling toothily. Airily I wave away any concern about the fact that she lives in a first-floor apartment without any lift service.

As rain begins to tumble down, I come out of the small cobbled square into the dark recess of a stairwell and, launching myself onto the first step, haul myself up. Catching my cue, the black widow co-opts her grandson into lifting my empty chair up after me.

How do we pass the time without speaking the same language? Beautifully. She begins to prepare asparagus soup and a mouth-watering stew and, while they are simmering, brings out a photo album in which her late husband—an army captain, if I recall—and sons now living in Germany stare out from alternate pages. The memories are so poignant, her heart so full, that we weep together as though it were the most natural thing in the world. Perhaps it is.

CROATIA: 23 SEPTEMBER–14 OCTOBER

DAY 457 (23 SEPTEMBER): DUBROVNIK

Three weeks ago I had to find a dependable address in Dubrovnik for delivery of the next consignment of post and other essential items from home in Melbourne, and in this part of the world a hotel is more reliable than poste restante. The way I look at it, I owe the Hotel P a favour, so I plan to stay there for a fortnight's layover.

With a bit of good-natured haggling, I manage to get a reasonable discount. The Hotel P's reservations manager, Josip, and I agree on a tariff of 15 euro a night *excluding breakfast* but he warns me of a three-day period during my stay when the hotel will be booked solid so I will have to leave for the interim. At the same time he tells me, 'Don't worry, something will be done', and his boss, Ivan (a double for Boris Yeltsin), even offers to put me up in his own home if all the package-tour guests turn up for those three days and I cannot find anywhere else to stay. That is a distinct possibility, as Dubrovnik with its steep hills is the most forbidding place for the wheelchair user I have seen on the entire journey.

But for now I relax. Access may be via the hotel workers' corridor and service lift, but nowhere else in Dubrovnik is remotely as good. If not for the Hotel P, I tell myself before retiring for the night, I don't know where I would have stayed.

DAY 458 (24 SEPTEMBER): DUBROVNIK

This is the jewel in Croatia's tourist crown, and—whatever else I may come to think of Dubrovnik—it scintillates. Sunlight dances off the Adriatic as I roll along the clifftop towards another World Heritage-Listed precinct, the Old Town which came under direct fire during the 1991 war.

I am trundling nearer and nearer to the walled town's great portcullis entrance when I spot a giant kangaroo. To be more precise, it is a giant kangaroo with a glass of beer. Welcome, he beckons with his free paw in a thumbs-up gesture, to Billabong, 'Croatia's first Aussie bar'.

Well, fry me barbecued 'roo, Blue. You could have knocked me down with an emu's tail feather.

DAYS 459–469 (25 SEPTEMBER–5 OCTOBER): DUBROVNIK

My two-week layover is cut in half, and the cause leaves a sour taste in my mouth. With perspective I can see that what happened here could have happened anywhere, and, as happens so often in life, a bad experience can be the stepping-stone to a better one—though one cannot see how at the time.

Everything seemed normal until Sunday, 29 September, when the hotel's director, Marko, studiously ignored my greetings of 'Bon appétit' while dining with his family on the first-floor terrace. This should have rung alarm bells but the hotel staff were treating me cordially, and I was not looking for an argument.

Later in the piece I would admit to not being blameless in the build-up to our explosive falling out. Urged by the waiters and waitresses to partake of the morning buffet, I ignored the fine print of our bargain (price to exclude breakfast), and hoped the management would either not notice or turn a blind eye.

As mentioned, Dubrovnik is almost bereft of wheelchair-friendly accommodation, and it was only on the eve of moving out for my supposedly temporary absence that I managed to find one private room available. Just as the staff were arranging the storage of my heavy luggage, the receptionist said in a low tone, 'It is not sure you will be able to come back and stay here from Sunday, Mr Haley.'

My nostrils instantly smelt rat. 'I'm a paying guest,' I said. 'You can't treat me like this.' Behind the receptionist's head I caught a glimpse of Marko disappearing into his office. As he locked himself inside, another staff member told me he was busy and couldn't be reached.

Others in Dubrovnik and elsewhere later informed me that Direktor Marko has only one focus: milking maximum profits from the Hotel P, a landmark that his family bought at a bargain-basement US$3 million just after the war for Croatian independence. At the end of October a guesthouse owner in Slovenia will spit on the floor at the mention of his name: her family recently cancelled a booking at the P, she told me, when Marko indulged in flagrant overcharging.

From what Josip told me through clenched teeth, Marko jacked up on learning that I had been offered a better rate than he could have got by overbooking tour groups. So, he broke a cardinal rule of good hotel-keeping: honour your reservations, especially when they are prepaid.

Next his loyal lieutenant Ivan went on the attack. 'You cannot stay here,' he bellowed. 'You are a liar. You promised to pay for breakfast, and the kitchen staff tell me you have been eating too much.'

That afternoon, from the safety of my private room, I wrote a letter apologising for having taken four unpaid breakfasts. Correct payment accompanied the letter, but both were returned without explanation.

The next day, when I returned to the hotel to take lunch, I paid in advance and had nearly finished my meal when the waiter tried, at Ivan's behest, to return my money for that meal too. Ivan himself then came over and said, 'If the director finds you here, he will throw you off the balcony.' I completed my meal and left.

This is the first time I have actually been kicked out of a hotel and to say it rankles is a gross understatement.

Staff at Dubrovnik's tourist information office tried to assist, but one of them later quoted her director as having said she could do nothing because 'Ivan is an old friend of mine'. At the police station, though, I thought my luck had finally turned when Domagoj, a young reporter for the local newspaper *Dubrovcka List*, arrived on his daily visit to check the latest news. The police promised to talk to the hotel management, and Domagoj agreed to meet me next morning for an interview.

That evening the receptionist turned up at the room I had taken and told me he was bringing a personal apology from Velimir, a cousin of Marko's (and, I gathered, co-proprietor of the P) with whom he had spoken by mobile phone to Bosnia.

An apology is one thing, but nothing if unaccompanied by action to annul the offence. When I asked if the cancellation of my room booking would be reversed, he promised to pass the message on. But next day management denied all knowledge of any apology.

The interview with Domagoj went well. A week later when I phoned him he said the article had come up well and his editor had assured him 'he will publish it in the edition after next'.

The next week he sounded less confident. He believed (but couldn't prove) that Ivan had phoned the editor. A month after that, the article had still not run. To the best of my knowledge, it never did.

On 5 October, with a heavy heart and even heavier baggage, I set sail for the Dalmatian island of Korcula. With no prior booking, I was directed by the tourist agency around the bay and up the hill to the Hotel Marko Polo, where the management—in stark contrast to the inhospitality experienced in Dubrovnik—welcomed me as if I were the island's favourite son returning home from China.

DAY 475 (11 OCTOBER): KORCULA ISLAND

Yes, Marko Polo (to adopt the Serbo–Croat spelling) was born here in 1254, exactly 700 years before the birth of your own humble scribe—although Korcula's claim is contested by Venice.

This morning I follow the road around to the street leading up to his supposed birthplace. But, when I see that the house must have been at the top end of a very steep street that begins at the water's edge, my curiosity fizzles out. I settle for paying respects from afar to my distinguished globetrotting predecessor, and proceed on my own set course.

DAY 476 (12 OCTOBER): KORCULA TO SPLIT

For most of the day I steam through the enchanted Dalmatian islands on a large and luxurious ferry before docking at dusk in the ancient port of Split.

Here I would have undertaken my usual dogged quest for lodgings had a stroke of good luck not spared me the effort. Maya Petríc, the manager of a trading company who is at the dock awaiting a shipment of goods, sees me pushing away from the ferry towards the place where I hope taxis will be standing. Stopping me with a word, she says I should stay at a place she just knows will be perfect for me. When she says 'a place' rather than 'a hotel', I grow a tad suspicious but her evident goodwill soon dispels all qualms. After a few kilometres' drive down the coast we come to it: not a hotel, but a senior citizens' home which keeps spare rooms.

The oddity of this choice of traveller's accommodation appeals at once to me. In a long journey, after all, there should be variety in shelters as there is in cuisines sampled, music heard and cultures observed. And, as a good proportion of the residents here are wheelchair users themselves, no one seems put out by the relatively young addition to their number. It hardly needs to be added that Maya Petríc refuses any payment for her good deed.

Old folks go to bed early. Come 9 pm, there is no one in the TV room so I amble in and switch on the set. Good news: we have satellite TV. Tragic news: bombs have exploded in nightclubs on Bali, and well over 100 people are feared dead, most of them ... my people. Thoughts mutate into questions faster than they can be formed. *There is more than one Bali: how will this affect Hindus in the villages? Who did it? Islamic extremists, no doubt, but al-Qa'eda? Possibly. Soft target. Why didn't people see this coming? Then, what could they have done to stop it, on an island that thrives on tourism?*

And look here: I am maybe five times as far from Bali as Tasmania is, yet because of the time difference—it must be 6 am Sunday eastern Australian time now— I am hearing about this bloodbath before most Australians. How weird is that?

DAY 477 (13 OCTOBER): SPLIT

I sit with a breakfast tray in the TV room. The morning news is still dominated by yesterday's horror. John Howard stands firm, but these deeds, though indefensible, are not mindless. The Axis of Evil keeps spinning faster and faster, but violence is the constant at its hub.

BOSNIA–HERZEGOVINA: 14–21 OCTOBER

DAY 478 (14 OCTOBER): SPLIT TO SARAJEVO

Even before our bus rolls up to the border posts, the conductor is puzzled by my visa stamp instead of impressed as I had rather hoped he would be. Checking with the driver that he is choosing the right English words, he tells me slowly, 'Not ne-ce-ssary.' When the seemingly carefree border guards give us a warm welcome and echo the conductor's surprise that I have gone to the trouble of obtaining a visa in advance when they are given out at the border *for free*, the only sensible response is a self-mocking laugh.

Evening brings us into Sarajevo, capital of the Muslim–Croat Federation of Bosnia–Herzegovina, one of the two entities established under the 1995 Dayton Accord that concluded the bloodiest conflict in Europe since World War II.

The very name of Sarajevo tugs at the heartstrings of this generation because it's not every day a bomb goes off in a bread queue or the residents of a city have to run the gauntlet of snipers whenever they venture outside. But Sarajevo's most poignant moment came in 1914, when a Bosnian Serb shot dead the Austrian Archduke Franz Ferdinand on one of its street corners, lighting the fuse to World War I.

For a city so closely associated with violence, what can possibly account for its reputation as a place that everyone—resident and visitor alike—instantly falls in love with? I hope to discover the answer for myself before too long.

DAY 479 (15 OCTOBER): SARAJEVO

Quite late last night I found a hotel willing and able to accommodate me. Judging from the stares in the foyer, you would think Bosnians had never seen a wheelchair before. Unlikely, I think, given the severity of war casualties, but, oddly, I see no other wheelchair users on the streets.

Sarajevo's hilly topography makes it postcard-picturesque. Directly opposite the breakfast terrace of my hotel, the Saraj, quaint houses poke up from the hillside as if a sketch in some well-thumbed missal had sprung to life. While much of the city's historic heritage was blasted to rubble by Bosnian Serbs in the 1992–5 war, a surprising amount remains. The UN troop presence is much in evidence, and the fact that you hear of hardly any outbreaks of violence directed against them suggests that their presence is broadly welcomed.

DAY 481 (17 OCTOBER): SARAJEVO

Where the road forks in the centre of town, an eternal flame burns in a brazier. The first reaction on seeing young scamps darting up to hold their hands over it for as long as they can bear the pain is to scold them for irreverence. But I sit back and see that older Sarajevans indulge them. That there are children at all, given the recent horrors, is surely more important than solemnity. This resilience, enabling a love of life to prevail over a powerful death wish, has also inspired the city fathers to 'implant' rubber splotches in the pavement: shaped like hands. Each of these indentations, known as Sarajevo roses, marks the spot where a shell exploded during the 1990s siege in which 60 000 inhabitants were killed or wounded.

On a gentle rise opposite here, a well-shaded public park lies beneath a brown-and-yellow carpet of autumn leaves. What can possibly account for Sarajevo's reputation as a place that everyone falls in love with? I have enough answers now. Thank you.

Armed men keep their own vigil in the square outside the Catholic cathedral and, more discreetly, on the street in front of the city's one active synagogue. But church bells ring and muezzins cry. Sarajevo's bruised spirit is healing.

Tonight I take an outside table at what until recently was the To Be or Not To Be restaurant. In front of me is a confronting photograph of a cellist sitting in the gutted interior of the National Library, over the subtitle 'Urbicide '92'. But Enis Selimovic, the restaurateur who created the poster in his other incarnation of graphic designer, has decided that his eatery's name was too equivocal, so he recently renamed it, in the cause of affirmative action, To Be, To Be. No Question.

Despite autumn's chill, this feels like the springtime of hope. If you want to see the world on a confident new morning, now is the best time to be in Sarajevo.

DAY 484 (20 OCTOBER): SARAJEVO TO MOSTAR

In the cool of morning, this long train snakes through misty valleys whose scenery is perhaps the most evocative of the entire journey so far. At 9 am we reach Mostar. The stationmaster carries my bags into his office, happy to let me take as long as necessary to find a room in the town. Following an extensive search in which I cover several kilometres, I find what I am looking for directly opposite the station.

The family renting out this spare room of their house are Serbs, whose very presence in a town run by Muslims and Croats means that they are often treated as symbols of a despised minority. But they are decent people, and their presence here tells me there must be times when the most heroic thing you can do is try to live a 'normal' life.

Its very geography divides Mostar. North of the Neretva River is the Croat quarter, south of it live the Muslims (and a handful of Serb families, of whom my hosts are one). When Stari Most (Mostar Bridge), the six-century-old brick-arched span that was this city's symbol, was blown up in 1993, it represented the collapse of more than a key transport link. Early in 2004 it will reopen amid jubilant scenes on both banks of the Neretva. All you can see today is scaffolding high above the rapids, but that alone is reason to take heart.

DAY 485 (21 OCTOBER): MOSTAR

Hope also resides in a three-storey neoclassical building on what is still known, perhaps wistfully, as Marshal Tito Street. This is home to a remarkable centre dedicated to using music as a way back to normality for children traumatised by the recent war.

The core purpose of the centre, bankrolled by Luciano Pavarotti, is to transform Mostar children's perception of life as a catalogue of horrors. Under the direction of Amela Sarić, a mother of two and dynamo of energy in her early forties, between 70 and 80 children receive weekly tuition at the centre. The goal is to repair the ravages of years of combat cacophony by regular exposure to more pleasant sounds. 'Our aim,' explains Sarić, 'is not for the children to be taught to play or compose music but, by following the rhythm and melodies made by a xylophone, flute or some other instrument, to bring out the sense of harmony.'

SLOVENIA: 25 OCTOBER–4 NOVEMBER

DAY 490 (26 OCTOBER): LJUBLJANA

The smallest country in Eastern Europe, Slovenia achieved the closest thing to a 'velvet revolution' of any state to emerge from the shadow of Yugoslavia. Its ten-day war of 1991 had the least bloodshed of all. It was a firm act of will, almost a civil uprising, that saw off the Serbs. From a nation of two million people, that's as gutsy a performance as anything since David got within a stone's throw of Goliath.

The placid Slovenes—not for them the excitable passion of the Serb or Bosnian—inhabit the westernmost of all ex-Yugoslav countries, not only in their geography, but with a capital W in their democratic instincts. That they have been accepted in the new wave of European Union expansion is proof that this pro-Western outlook is recognised by the West itself.

The capital, Ljubljana, is a picture-book idyll of how every European town might look if it could be built to human scale. Friendly and engaging, its small ambit (population 280 000) makes it the most accessible of destinations and all the central sights lie within ten minutes of one another by foot or wheel.

DAY 493 (29 OCTOBER): PIRAN

Slovenia owns just a sliver of real estate on the Adriatic, a mere 20 kilometres of the Istrian Peninsula coast wedged between Italy and Croatia, but it certainly makes the most of that. Built around a lazy fishing harbour, the town of Piran could be transplanted across the water to any point south of Venice and only the accents of the inhabitants would tell you it wasn't Italian.

This afternoon I take the minibus south along the coast to Portoroz, another beach resort, but one with a difference. Here the Hotel Palace offers its guests a full range of thermal baths. Three months in the Balkans have primed me for this novel form of relaxation, but first I must ask whether a paying non-guest (as opposed to a non-paying guest) may sample this little luxury for himself.

The manager, a pleasant-faced chap who gives me his card—Fredi Fontanot, Esquire—tells me that I am welcome to take a free bath at the management's expense, because he has always liked 'the idea of Australia'.

Offhand, no other European country comes to mind where one can see three distinct environments—city, beach and mountain range—in such close proximity. Of the seven nations I have traversed since quitting balmy Greece, this is the Balkan land least cursed—or, rather, most blessed.

Chapter 20

WALTZING BY THE DANUBE

My friend ... Welcome to the Carpathians. I am anxiously expecting you. Sleep well tonight ... I trust that your journey ... has been a happy one, and that you will enjoy your stay in my beautiful land.

BRAM STOKER Dracula

NOVEMBER 2002-JANUARY 2003

The Danube and the Carpathians are the two dominant geographical features of the next four lands on my journey, taking me from the Balkans back to the Black Sea and then looping back into the heart of central Europe. Along with Poland, Hungary spearheaded the overthrow of communism in Eastern Europe in that year of miracles, 1989. Romania, by contrast, never really got round to throwing out the communists until the December 2004 elections removed their socialist heirs from power, even if it showed a particularly bloodthirsty zeal for getting rid of the dictator Nicolae Ceausescu. Moldova is a land torn between allegiance to Romania and Russia, its sense of nationhood stunted at birth. And in many ways – when I was in the country and indeed until its own elections of December '04 changed everything – Ukraine was the most disappointing of the four: still in the thrall of a communist leader, Leonid Kuchma, who baulked at all economic reforms and rules in a way that the old Kremlin hardliners would have applauded.

Call them what you want—the Wild East, the badlands—their history of rough and ready justice makes exploring this quartet an adventure within an adventure. Yet to judge even Romania as a superstition-ridden territory full of Gothic grotesquerie is a distortion that can blind us to the everyday struggles of ordinary people—town dwellers and peasants—whose concerns would be instantly recognisable to their counterparts in any country.

The blue Danube, which flows from central Europe down to the Black Sea, broadening as it goes, and the green mountain chain give these lands one type of unity; their experience of communist ideology, another. But in several other ways, starting with their size, the differences outweigh the similarities.

The area of Ukraine, the largest country in Europe (if one discounts Russia as a hybrid, most of it being in Asia), is eighteen times that of Moldova. Ethnically the Ukrainians are Slavs; the Moldovans a mixture of Slavs and Romanians; the Romanians mostly descended from Roman settlers (as the country's name implies); and the Hungarians are a race unlike any other.

HUNGARY: 4 NOVEMBER–3 DECEMBER

For eleven centuries, ever since their ancestors rode west from Central Asia, the people who call themselves Magyar (rhyming with 'rajah') have been keenly aware that they are like no other. What sets the clannish Hungarians apart is also what makes their culture most interesting to the outsider: its food and folk traditions being but two examples. Apart they may be; individualists they are not. In fact, their strong sense of collective identity explains why communism took root here and also why the forces that uprooted it in the end acted as one. Virtually all of Hungarian history and art can be seen as an unending struggle to be left alone.

DAY 500 (5 NOVEMBER): KESZTHELY, LAKE BALATON

They're not struggling tonight, but nor are they alone. Music dominated by accordion and violin, of a type associated in my mind with fairground rides, pervades the Hungaria Gosser, a restaurant reputed to serve the best goulash in this lakeside town, and some say in all of Hungary. The *specialité de maison* arrives steaming in a sort of Hungarian wok, a silver bowl suspended over a low flame.

DAY 501 (6 NOVEMBER): KESZTHELY

Even when Keszthely is not enveloped in fog, its atmosphere is gloomy and thick, and getting around is like wheeling through a short story by Poe. The three-storey houses with their acute-angled gables and eyebrow embrasures frown on the passer-by. It's all pleasantly spooky.

DAY 508 (13 NOVEMBER): BALATONFURED TO BUDAPEST

It is not that Hungarians are unfriendly, I tell myself, just—well, perhaps—a little stand-offish, or perhaps it is better to say they are unusually respectful of others' space. I suppose that might come from having been invaded over and over again.

Working out how to get myself, with my luggage, up to the virtually inaccessible railway platform is a puzzle worthy of the nation that gave us Rubik and his cube, and I 'crack' it (with assistance) just in time.

And then one is left alone to contemplate the pastoral charms of the pancake-flat Great Plain all the way to the outskirts of Budapest, Hungary's greatest pride and joy.

Hours are taken up with finding 'digs' for a fortnight's layover, long enough to soak up the city's atmosphere and plot an itinerary covering the final few months of my route through to northern Scandinavia. Partly for architectural reasons—central Budapest dates from the 19th century, when staircases seem to have been *de rigueur*—and partly out of hoteliers' reluctance to offer discounts for a longer stay, I am almost out of options when a taxidriver suggests we try Nepstadion.

It's not listed in my guidebook but the driver is quietly insistent that this will be the place for me. When we roll up to the building, I wonder if he has lost his mind. This is where Budapest would probably hold the Olympics if it ever won the right to host them: a 100 000-seat national stadium used principally for soccer matches and athletics meets.

However, a special discount rate of US$10, a real bargain, is struck without fuss; and I repair to a modest-sized but clean room in that part of the stadium designated the Hotel Pilon.

Later I discover that Nepstadion is the home of Hungary's sports academy and the hotel exists to put up sportsmen and sportswomen from all over the country, and even overseas, who come here for training.

DAY 510 (15 NOVEMBER): BUDAPEST

Today is short on relaxation, long on business: the getting of visas (Moldova done, the Ukrainians a work in progress); the collection of mail, and the sending of mail (a more complex matter, taking up to two hours). Sometimes I look on travelling as the hardest unpaid work I'll ever do.

DAY 513 (18 NOVEMBER): BUDAPEST

We've only just become acquainted but Budapest—with its magical blend of history, elegance and dynamism—is already up there with Isfahan and Istanbul among my favourite cities.

The best way to savour the capital's special ambience is to head straight up, or down, its version of the Champs Elysées or Fifth Avenue: Andrassy Boulevard. This morning I do both, beginning at Vajdahunyad Castle, an 1890s specimen of kitsch designed to reflect architectural styles from all over Hungary. From the castle to Heroes' Square, where Andrassy begins its long straight run to the Danube, is a mere 200 metres, but to reach it you must make a slight detour around what is a magnificent sight: an open-air skating rink where the mass movement of people, counterclockwise, resembles a painting come to life. Then it's across the street and along Andrassy, 3 kilometres of never-failing interest all the way down to the river.

Once there, it is impossible to resist ambling onto one of the stately bridges that span the mighty Danube and link the half of the city I've just come from—Pest (pronounced Pesht)—with Buda. Originally Buda was the preserve of royalty, Pest where the commoners lived. I leave it to your good sense to work out which quarter was built on the higher bank; which on the lower, more flood-prone tract of land.

DAY 515 (20 NOVEMBER): BUDAPEST

Authority and I have never hit it off. That said, it is no fun being led away in handcuffs from the precincts of a national parliament—especially when it's not even your nation, there is no great principle at stake, and the parliament belongs to an 'emerging democracy'.

On approaching the neo-Gothic parliament building, I could not help noticing a powerful dose of regimentation. A dozen police, some in paramilitary gear, were holding back dozens of tourists behind a chain-link fence and it must be added (though this may be just my imagination) that the atmosphere was somewhat menacing.

The previous day, the parliamentary tours office had told me to arrive 20 minutes early for one of the tours, which commence on the hour. But now I wasn't allowed to 'overstep' the line so I couldn't even make it to the office to buy a ticket.

After ten minutes of this, with a growing risk of missing out on the tour, I observed aloud that the uniformed squad preventing me from buying a ticket was more what one would expect of a fascist state than a parliamentary democracy. This is a provocatively rash thing to say, given that the word 'fascist' is bound to touch a raw nerve in a country that was part of a pretty evil Axis before George W. Bush was even a twinkle in Barbara's eye.

The chief of the parliamentary guards didn't exactly have smoke coming out of his ears but was clearly having no truck with such talk. 'This is police territory,' he warned me, unconsciously confirming my point.

By this time Elizabeth, the parliamentary officer in charge of foreigners' tours, had arrived and pleaded in vain for me to be allowed to join the noonday group. Further pleading by her elicited grudging approval for me to come back later that afternoon and try again.

As I began to move off, with the thought of spending a couple of hours in the city 'killing time', I found my way blocked by a rookie from the Fifth Police District. While he had removed his name tag he had forgotten to take off his serial-number tag, so he can confidently be identified as Officer 18246. It was 18246 who whipped out the handcuffs and took gleeful delight in tying my wrists behind the back bar of my chair before leading me off to the police station three blocks away.

Major Tibor Varga, 18246's boss, listened with what appeared to be thinly veiled impatience as his zealous young gun outlined the case against me. The major then demanded to see my passport. On this of all days, with no visa to collect or money to change, I had left it behind at the stadium hotel. At last, Varga agreed to let me join the tour of parliament provided I produced my passport ID (which I did next day).

At 2 pm I was back behind the parliamentary lines and finally, with Elizabeth leading the way, shown over the colossal edifice which took seventeen years to build—democracy takes even longer—and would swallow the MCG whole, if such a thing were possible.

DAY 518 (23 NOVEMBER): BUDAPEST

Every Saturday night the city backstreets resound to the vibe of Hungarian folk dancing. Tonight, I sit goggle-eyed in a corner while zithers and fiddles get the joint jumping.

Early in the proceedings, the floorboards of this rather shabby but undeniably authentic venue audibly creak. Later, when the crowd swells to a round hundred, they groan. But the Transylvanian zithers are galloping ahead at full twang and the revellers, dressed as if attending an 18th-century folk festival in the heart of Europe, are clearly lapping it up.

They leave the best till last. Just after 10 pm an 80-year-old violinist with the energy of someone a quarter his age takes centre stage. All the way from Romanian-ruled Transylvania, the celebrated Sanyi Bacsi saws that virtuoso fiddle fit to bring the house down.

DAY 520 (25 NOVEMBER) BUDAPEST

This evening I visit a planetarium with a difference. Calling itself the Laser Theatre, this 'sky show' incorporates musical arrangements by pop singers and groups including Madonna, Pink Floyd and Queen. Graphic designers have tailored their creativity to the music of the spheres. Tonight's 'star turn' is Jean-Michel Jarré, the 'godfather' of such spectacles.

Naturally enough, it is impossible to describe a light show in words, but that doesn't stop the official brochure from trying. With an obvious fondness for the word 'light', the first two sentences set the tone:

> Cobwebs woven of emerald laser light are spun into transparent veils by ruby flashes of light where pulsating polygons dance madly amid thousands of vivid light waves. Suddenly, fireless fireworks explode in the midst of a cavorting vortex of light to crown this enrapturing celebration.

DAY 521 (26 NOVEMBER): BUDAPEST

The neoclassical State Opera House is one of the most impressive buildings on Andrassy Boulevard, which is saying something. Tonight I have my own personal conductor (a man in a bow-tie leading me on a detour through the building so that I can reach my seat without being obstructed by stairs).

Being no ballet enthusiast, I cannot say whether this 'Don Quijote' (Hungarian spelling) is better than any 'Don Quixote' staged elsewhere in recent years, but it is what occurs after the show that makes me think everyone should go to the theatre in a wheelchair. Immediately the final bouquet is tossed on stage, the personal conductor appears at my side, ready to escort me through the labyrinth to the building's exit. But, as that way takes us near the dressing rooms and we have to wait a minute for the lift that will take us down, I am treated to the sight of the prima ballerina, a Brazilian with the delightful name of Pollyanna Ribeiro. She struggles not to drop any of eight bouquets while curtsying and being kissed on both cheeks by an obviously overwhelmed Brazilian ambassador to Hungary. Graciously, the pair let me take a more formal photo of them, much to the annoyance of my personal conductor who is itching to get into the lift and away.

DAYS 524–525 (29–30 NOVEMBER): EGER

Eger's charm resides in its winding streets and fine examples of Zopf architecture—an elegant hybrid of the classical and baroque, the formal and the fantastic, peculiar to central Europe.

Irina, a typically open-hearted Egri who met me by chance while I was registering at a local hotel, has *adopted* me (I can think of no better word for it) by offering to show me over the castle, and then acting as my escort to the town's nationally famous Gárdonyi Theatre. Given that I was never going to understand a word being uttered on stage, my initial regret was that this Friday night I couldn't have seen a homegrown theatrical product. However, after the performance I could appreciate what a lucky coincidence it was that my visit fell on the same night as a local version of playwright Arthur Miller's *Death of a Salesman* (*Az ügynök halála* in Magyar). After all, every market economy has its Willy Lomans, and the scourge of alcoholism is not unknown in Eastern Europe either.

DAY 527 (2 DECEMBER): SZEGED

My last stop in Hungary brings me within reach of Transylvania.

Szeged is a large town, laid out according to an interesting pattern of concentric boulevards. I buy roasted chestnuts from a stall in the sunken cobblestone square, which has been converted into a Christmas market.

With the temperature perhaps 5°C above zero, I eat them huddled at the ideal distance of two metres from one of the mini-bonfires lit by order of the civic authorities. Much closer and I would share the chestnuts' fate.

ROMANIA: 3–14 DECEMBER

DAY 528 (3 DECEMBER): ARAD

On a rainy day like this, Arad railway station must be one of the most dispiriting places on Earth. People who are obviously dirt-poor, in ragged clothes and many of them wandering round in an alcoholic stupor at ten in the morning, would inspire pity if they didn't make me so concerned for the security of my bags. The contrast with self-possessed, self-confident Hungary couldn't be more marked.

DAY 530 (5 DECEMBER): SIBIU

In this history-punctured neck of the Transylvanian woods, the dread of Dracula cannot be entirely avoided so the best policy is to confront it during daylight hours.

For seven centuries, the Gothic pile now christened the Evangelical Church has been this town's most prominent landmark. Iacob-Lucian Marginean, a young tour guide steeped in its lore, ushers me through a door that is usually padlocked and points to a row of medieval tombstones normally off limits to visitors. Lo and behold, there is the coffin lid that once covered the mortal remains of Dracula's (Vlad Tepes's) son, Prince Mihnea the Bad.

When we get talking and I mention that the lifestyle of the Gypsies (Roma) in today's Romania actually interests me more than tales of vampires past, Lucian offers to introduce me to one of their two contending rulers, both of whom live in this central Romanian town. The Gypsy king (or, if you prefer, Romany emperor) he has in mind is Iulian Radulescu, a distinctly unwell-looking monarch who weighs a staggering 164 kilograms and lives in a mock-Italianate mansion in one of Sibiu's poorer districts. Lucian warns me that Radulescu is seldom home, but we hop into a taxi hailed on the street and trust to luck. When Lucian discovers that King Iulian is not only at home but willing to grant us an audience, he is bug-eyed with amazement.

Surrounded by a rather dishevelled band of courtiers, his majesty dispenses with protocol and chattily informs us that he has visited 220 countries. Both aware that this is a score more nations than actually exist, Lucian and I exchange glances but hold our peace. After all, the pronouncements of a king are above contradiction.

Jolly and beaming, Radulescu spreads further enlightenment by assuring us that since the solar eclipse of August 1999 the Roma have cast aside their old reputation for laziness and become 'spiritually mature and not frightened or terrified of any work'.

Our deferential smiles appear to incite even freer speech. Recently, the monarch tells us, he wrote to all (220?) world leaders, asking them to lend his people sums of money, repayment guaranteed after 100 years. Next he divulges a secret of high state that has Lucian and me struggling to contain our astonishment. 'Bill Clinton is really a Gypsy but he refused to admit it because if he did he was afraid they would make him leave the presidency.'

As you see, King Iulian is an easy figure to ridicule, but over the years he has attended international conferences on indigenous peoples and he speaks affectingly of the need to educate young Roma about their cultural history. The Romany in Romania is still the butt of widespread daily discrimination. In Bucharest back in the mid-'80s I saw one of their number thrown headlong through the plate-glass door of a café (a sight not easily forgotten). In the capital today, of course, things have progressed: now they are thrown bodily out of McDonald's.

As Iulian is keenly aware of his people's low status in the land of their birth, it is hard to remain non-judgmental about his pet project of building a full-scale replica of the Taj Mahal at a cost of A$50 million. I get Lucian to ask him where the money will be coming from.

'We have fifteen tonnes of gold to pay for it, but that has been confiscated by the Romanian state,' says Radulescu.

Still, he looks very confident about his chances of getting the lucre released. Why? Because the ruling president, Ion Iliescu, is (keep this a secret, won't you?) a Roma himself.

DAY 532 (7 DECEMBER): PITESTI
Last night I sat in my hotel foyer captivated by the first decent snowfall of the entire crossing. It was dumping down so heavily that after an

hour my wheels could barely move through the white crush on the hotel doorstep.

For the first time I realise that over the final stages of this transcontinental trek the intense cold is going to be my greatest handicap. Paralysis has not left me without feeling in my lower extremities and now I discover that, if the temperature outside is 0°C, my feet—where the circulation is sluggish at best—feel 10 or 20 degrees colder. Extra socks and fur-lined boots are clearly not going to be enough to save me.

DAY 535 (10 DECEMBER): BUCHAREST

Once before I passed this way—in 1985, at the height of Ceausescu's reign, when he was busy ripping the heart out of old Bucharest. My most vivid memory of that visit is the razor-wire coils in so-called Liberty Park. Today the people have their political liberty, but most find that their economic chains still chafe.

The most durable physical reminder of Ceausescu's days is the gargantuan House of the People, said to be the biggest building in the world after the Pentagon. Seven thousand homes, not to mention seventeen religious buildings of considerable cultural significance, were destroyed by one man's megalomania. I feel no need to visit. Just to know it exists is enough—too much, rather.

Instead, I head to a highly recommended market. My aim: to secure some material protection against the beastly cold. I bargain for a scarf (not a problem).

Fur-lined footwear is a little harder to track down, but I eventually get that also. What I thought would be the easiest purchase of all, though—a genuine Russian-style rabbit-fur hat with earflaps—cannot be had for love or money.

A cold head can lead to a head cold, so I scurry back to the warmth of the youth hostel where I'm staying as quickly as my wheels will carry me. A numb-induced headache and feet you would put in a refrigerator to warm up are my punishments for venturing out onto the streets of Bucharest in December.

Come morning, my body temperature is normal again, but I am well aware that the road ahead, with winter's worst blasts still to come, is going to be no picnic.

DAY 538 (13 DECEMBER): IASI

How appropriate that I should arrive in this former capital of Moldavia province just as a blood-red sun is setting over the land of Drac.

The university town of Iasi is not over-endowed with tourist sights, but one I make a point of checking out is the simple wooden memorial to the Iasi students who were killed protesting against Ceausescu's rule thirteen years ago tomorrow.

Another tragic monument can be found in Copou Park. The park was frequented by Romania's most cherished poet, Mihai Eminescu, who wrote many of his verses beneath a spreading linden tree that flourishes still. Among a dozen marble busts resting on oblong plinths are those of Eminescu and his sweetheart, Veronica Micle. Eminescu died in 1889, aged 39. Grief-stricken, Micle killed herself a fortnight later—and now the lovers are face to face forever.

MOLDOVA: 14–21 DECEMBER

DAY 540 (15 DECEMBER): CHISINAU

The smallest republic in the old Soviet Union, Moldova is a country principally by default. Hardly anyone you meet actually wants it to be a self-governing state, and it continues to fly its own flag because no one can agree whether it should scurry back under Mother Russia's skirts or attach itself to Romania.

Crossing into Moldova yesterday was special, for two reasons. Passing over the gurgling River Prut on the Romanian frontier at Sculeni, I entered the hundredth foreign country visited in my life—or, more exactly, in the 22 years since first leaving Australia at the end of 1980.

The manner of my crossing the border also represented a rare victory for the individual over blind bureaucracy. As the driver indicated we would be stuck there for an hour or so while everyone's paperwork was processed, all the passengers got down from the bus to stretch their legs. Conscious that my hundredth international crossing called for a little ceremony, I asked whether it would be OK to push myself across the bridge to Moldova and clamber back on the coach over there. My motivation was to make this entry 'under my own steam' after so many occasions of being ferried across a border together with dozens of fellow passengers as if we were so many cattle.

At first the Romanian and Moldovan immigration officers were adamant this was out of the question as the law requires people to make the crossing in wheeled vehicles. Well, I told them, *this* is a wheeled vehicle, isn't it? They scratched their heads but then, to their credit, radioed their superior officers for special permission. After an awkward pause, back came the word that, while it mightn't be a 'wheeled vehicle' within the meaning of their respective immigration acts, it would be safe to let me make my own border crossing just this once, albeit under supervision.

Today I have more pressing concerns than nationalism or bureaucracy, namely keeping my head from turning into an iceberg, and reminding long-distant family and friends that I haven't overlooked what time of year is coming on.

Teeth chattering, I bustle my way through the crowded central market, practising my city-street slalom technique. First hat off the rack is that vital piece of rabbit fur, and it takes less than a minute here to find what a laborious search in the Bucharest market couldn't turn up. Before long, startled shoppers are looking at me as if I were a midget-sized Boris Karloff going through a mid-life crisis.

DAY 544 (19 DECEMBER): CHISINAU

Lunch, and the hour after it, are spent at the Chisinau McDonald's. It looks just like all the others if you can disregard the shifty-eyed soldiers at the front door with rifles slung over their shoulders, not all that casually.

DAY 545 (20 DECEMBER): CHISINAU

The Soviet-era Hotel Chisinau has not exactly moved with the times. I stay there only because it has a lift. But the foyer security officers who operate as pimps—and one suspects fulfil even seedier roles—make you feel you are under constant surveillance, even as a paying guest.

That, at least, remains the status quo in the foyer. Four floors up, there has been a definite post-Soviet shift. Sergei Mifodovski is the type of no-holds-barred capitalist who would thrive in today's Moscow. Here he struggles against conservative local opinion but is confident that interest in his privatised dating agency will pick up once word of it gets about.

Romance, Love and Marriage, as he calls the business, started up just three months ago in Room 440, which he is renting by the month. An English translator with a personal computer and loads of initiative, 30-year-old Mifodovski is anxious to persuade me his business is a legitimate operation.

What does he offer the girls whose charms he has posted on the Internet? Why, romance, love, perhaps even marriage and, if all goes right, the chance to make a new life abroad—which may be the most powerful lure of all in dirt-poor Moldova, where the average monthly wage is less than A$100.

Most of the women he has signed up are Russians, which makes sense, given that thousands of Russian men have left the country in recent years. Mifodovski, himself divorced, explains how his business works. 'When a man responds to one of my girls—say, Vikki here—I write on the Net that this girl was placed by the Moldovan [my] marriage agency. In that case, he must be willing to sign a marriage contract. The fee for that contract is about US$500. The man must provide appropriate medical papers because the girls are afraid of venereal illness. For my part, I also guarantee the girls are healthy, they don't have AIDS and they are not married.'

How can he be certain of any of that?

'Our Moldovan passports are provided with special stamps so we can be sure about marital status,' he replies. And he makes sure the district hospital gives each woman a clean bill of sexual health.

Vikki, a 28-year-old natural blonde, is in no obvious need of an agency to land herself a man. But she tells me a tale of ill use and corruption that is all too credible, this being Moldova. As a qualified gynaecologist, she says, 'I am well able to work as a doctor, and I want to, but I can't work in a hospital here without giving a good bribe to the director. And I refuse to do that.'

How much?

'[US] $5000.'

Plus, Vikki is a divorcée with one child, and the stigma for a deserted wife and single mother in this society is hard to shake off.

Vikki appears to regard Mifodovski as a great benefactor, but now she finds herself in a terrible new fix. As he translates, she tells me through brimming tears that she cannot choose between two of the agency's clients. One, a Swiss man, has been emailing her every day for weeks; the other, an American, keeps her in nail-biting suspense. Clearly, she fancies the idea of life in America far more than going to Switzerland—hence the tussle between head and heart.

Without prompting, she says, 'Our men are of very bad quality. They are only interested in appearance, not in the inner qualities.'

Mifodovski, while striving to retain his professional impartiality, cannot resist a little matchmaking as Vikki digs herself in deeper. He breaks off translating to tell me that Vikki speaks French, the language of her Swiss paramour, who, he adds, has embarked on a crash course in Russian.

While telling me all this, Mifodovski moves about the room to make space for a telephone technician who has arrived to install a second line, for incoming international calls. It is on this line that I leave Vikki, perched on the edge of the couch, still awaiting that long-delayed call from the States.

UKRAINE: 21 DECEMBER–3 JANUARY

DAY 546 (21 DECEMBER): ODESSA

Ukraine recovered its independence upon the collapse of the Soviet empire, but has retained the worst aspects of that demoralised entity—rampant corruption in public services rotten to the core; and a ruthless disregard for personal dignity—without inheriting any of its supposed strengths.

In general, the further east you go in this land the more Russified are the people, many of them of Russian settler stock who feel 'stateless' in the new Ukraine. It was from their ranks that mutterings of secession were heard after the disputed first round of elections in 2004 threatened to catapult Viktor Yushchenko, no friend of Moscow, to power (which duly happened after the second round).

Odessa's glory days are long past but eight decades of pallid classlessness have not succeeded in removing the last trace of rouge from the cheeks of this civic *grande dame*. My introduction to the Black Sea port is not auspicious, however. At this time of year, the tourist almost merits classification as an endangered species (*Homo touristicus*). Add a wheelchair, and jaws drop. The concept of a guest in a wheelchair travelling solo is just so alien here that I am denied admittance to one of the few accessible and affordable hotels, with no reason given. When I disprove the receptionist's assertion that it will be impossible for me to stay there because the lift isn't working—by actually going over to it, pushing the button and watching it rise three levels—and ask why she has lied to me, she drawls, 'I lie because I like to.'

This city has an attitude problem. Even the Hotel Arkadia, way out of town, where at 10 pm I finally find lodgings, is reluctant to open one of the double doors at the entrance so that I can actually come inside.

DAY 547 (22 DECEMBER): ODESSA

Talk about 'back in the USSR'. Taking breakfast here is like going on wartime rations. The hotel's not-so-largesse consists of two slices of Russian 'black bread' and a cup of scalding hot tea straight from the samovar. After much pleading I also receive a single hard-boiled egg. Over the tea, I have what passes for an optimistic thought: today is the 'shortest day' of the year. Mercy be.

The streets of Odessa are not merely potholed but cratered. Of all the cities I've passed through on this voyage, none has the capacity to do so much damage to my wheels. Evidently, Odessa City Council is not receiving taxes or not spending them on road improvements. A local resident tells me, with a shake of the head, that the truth is a bit of both. Every dollar not going on road repairs, he confides, is a dollar slipped into some bureaucrat's deep pocket.

This evening I take my seat to the 1880s opera house for a performance of the two-act ballet *Giselle*. Sadly, my weariness is no contest for the spectacle, and I 'experience' the performance as two acts of hypnosis interrupted by the odd wakeful moment. After a glissade of curtain-closing applause sweeps me back into consciousness, I make my own exit.

DAY 549 (24 DECEMBER): ODESSA

High life and low coexist in marvellous juxtaposition on Odessa's city streets, to a larger degree than almost anywhere else. But those streets have a way of banishing lofty thought, as I discover while the tank-like Volga taxi driven by Igor catapults us towards Primorsky Boulevard.

When a crater in the roadway gives the mechanical beast a jolt violent enough to have dismembered a lesser make, Igor shakes his head in despair.

In sympathy I mutter 'Corruption', but now Igor stares at me in mock dismay.

'There is no corruption in Odessa,' he assures me and then, unable to sustain the pretence any longer, his impassive face is swamped by a wave of laughter.

Igor drops me near the statue of Richelieu, the French noble whose support for the Russians at the time of Napoleon's invasion earned him the gift of Odessa itself from a grateful tsar. I notice Primorsky Boulevard is exceptionally crowded this morning and a massive greystone block overlooking Richelieu's right shoulder is hidden behind a virtual hedgerow of very large wreaths. The road is bumper to bumper with Black Marias and silver BMWs with tinted windows. On the opposite pavement a sombrely clad group of perhaps 200 'solid citizen' types has assembled.

Desperately in need of explanations, I turn round to find a couple of Ukrainians from out of town are also watching the scene. Luckily, one of them speaks enough English to unravel its meaning for me.

These people, he says, are waiting to view the open coffin of the director of a prosperous driftnet-fishing company—'Look,' he interrupts himself excitedly, 'there is the limousine of the deputy mayor!'—who was gunned down last night while parking his car in the family garage. 'Didn't you know?'

I shake my head.

'It was all over the TV news.'

Two considerations restrain me from queueing to view the corpse myself. Not only am I reluctant to affect grief for a man I hadn't heard of until just this minute, but his body is lying up there on the second floor so there are practical objections too. My attitude is not universally shared, it appears. Five minutes later, a couple of less reticent German visitors almost skip across the street in the first flush of excitement at having seen a Mafia boss in the all-too-waxen flesh.

'He was so well dressed,' exclaims one of them. 'Can you imagine it? We've been in Odessa one day, and already we've seen a dead body!'

Journalists are meant to be hard-bitten, but I will admit this comment floors me. 'Perhaps if you stay a week you'll see a thousand,' I return sardonically. Now it is her turn to look shocked.

DAY 550 (25 DECEMBER): ODESSA

Amid all the bleakness of an Odessan winter, I have made a friend. She is Janna Belousova, a doughty businesswoman whose Eugenia Travel Agency occupies a two-storey downtown address. In the upstairs apartment she lives with her husband; downstairs is graced by a piano and a tall fir that seems to have spent all its life growing indoors and is already festooned with gold-wrapped boxes and bunting almost a fortnight before Orthodox Yuletide.

When I arrive in search of a timetable for buses to the interior, I find myself being treated like a member of the family. First, Belousova, who appears to sense that I will be missing the festivities back home, dispatches a worker to the local bakery from which he returns armed with Odessa's famous seasonal bread, *medovik*, studded with poppy seeds and dripping with honey. Next, she tells me something of her own family background: how her father disappeared in the Great Purge of 1937 and was never seen again. Her mother died in 1960 believing the official story that he had been kept in prison exile until his death in 1948. Only later did Janna discover that her father never saw the inside of a Gulag camp but was shot by Stalin's men on the day of his arrest.

Her story would make a moving film, and by flashing forward Hollywood could have its obligatory happy ending. Today three generations of Belousovas work for the family firm: Janna, her adult daughter, and *her* seventeen-year-old daughter.

Janna Belousova is one of those people who have time for everyone, and to retain such an outlook in Odessa seems to me a triumph of the human spirit little short of a miracle. When she lets me use her office computer to send one of my articles home and check my emails, I feel as if all my Christmases have come at once.

DAYS 553-556 (28-31 DECEMBER): KAMYANETS-PODILSKY

This is the story of the Great Suitcase Robbery of Kamyanets-Podilsky.

It probably had its genesis in the resentment of the bus's assistant driver at my occupying the seat he normally gave to a woman from out of town (not his wife). The bus was full, and I had a ticket, but something had to give—and that turned out to be his temper. However, there was no way I was going to sit on the floor (his second preference, his first being that I get off the bus), so I just sat tight and kept my mouth shut. The night was interminable and frosty, with scarcely any sleep in the posture I was forced to adopt—face 'resting' against the cold windowpane under a starry sky.

When the old rattler pulled in to Kamyanets-Podilsky at 5.30 on Saturday morning, the bus park was still shrouded in darkness. The still tetchy assistant driver hovered out of sight around the baggage hold, while the principal driver, Pyotr, deposited my bags on the cracked concrete apron and pointed out their number: four.

As I can never move the heavy suitcase on my own it seemed harmless to leave it behind me while I wheeled all of ten metres into the bus station to phone the hotel at which I had made a reservation. Just as I headed off, a youth who appeared to be saying goodbye to his mother shook me by the hand and started chatting to me in what must have been Ukrainian. Annoyingly, he persisted in doing so for a full half minute even though it should have been obvious that I didn't understand a word he was saying.

Inside the bus terminal, the public phone wasn't working and I was trying to get the drowsy ticketing official to use her receiver to persuade someone from the hotel to pick me up when all of a sudden I felt what I suppose you could call a pang of panic. I rushed out of the double doors to check that my suitcase was still there. It wasn't.

I raised a holler. The bus that had brought me here was reversing slowly, and I'm sure to this day that the driver was looking in my direction and would have stopped to see what the matter was unless he actually knew. However, the only people who could hear my anguished cries were a couple of passengers who had disembarked with me (they were innocent bystanders, I feel sure of that) and the ticket official who had seemed to be in a daze all along.

The report I made out later in the day for Kamyanets-Podilsky's overburdened police force conveys the scale of my loss adequately enough. 'The suitcase weighs about 15–20 kilograms and would not be easy to remove for a robber on foot. It contained about 25 plastic urinals, 40 packets of polythene gloves, fifteen 60ml syringes, twenty

10ml syringes, 400 plastic bags, 60 tubes of lubricating gel and more than 100 catheters, all of them urological and medical necessities for me.

'It also contains nineteen American Express traveller's cheques each worth US$100 [numbers supplied]. Of course they are useless to the thief also, but without that US$1900 my journey must be cut short.

'Also in the suitcase … are several books, including my travel plan for the next four months. This is a personal catastrophe for me. Please help recover my belongings.'

Remembering Albania, I knew in my frigid bones that to have any stolen goods returned in such circumstances would be almost as unlikely a prospect as winning the lottery. So my initial response was not to call the police.

'*Taksi, taksi, taksi*,' I roared at the bemused knot of passengers, until eventually one of them must have talked the ticket official into letting him call from the office phone. After ten minutes that seemed an eternity, a taxidriver bearing a disturbing facial resemblance to Aleksandr Solzhenitsyn turned up. He must have sensed it was an emergency because he began demanding twice what I could calculate a reasonable fare to be for the 160-kilometre round trip from K-P to the Romanian border town of Chernivtsi and back. But this was no time to argue, so I scrambled aboard with my three surviving bags and stated my destination, '*Aftobus.*'

By the time we pulled into Chernivtsi bus park, the sun had risen, inasmuch as it ever rises at this time of year. On seeing the bus there I was mildly surprised, and my heart skipped a hopeful beat. With the broken-English assistance of one of the small crowd of interested observers who gathered by the bus, Pyotr and his deputy were quickly apprised of the gravity of my situation. I recall using the term '*urologica*' and pointing imaginary catheters at my lap in the hope that this would convey the urgency of the matter, but the driving duo seemed resolutely unmoved.

Pyotr jumped down from the bus and, gesturing to the empty hold, was evidently telling the translator how he had shown me all my bags assembled together. No, he replied to a translated query of mine, no one could possibly have put the suitcase back in the hold or it would have been noticed upon arrival.

A picture of the youth who had diverted my attention for that critical half minute flashed across my mind, leaving me uneasy and unconvinced—but of course I could prove nothing. I glanced up to the bus driver's seat. His arms draped over the huge steering wheel, Pyotr's No. 2 was seated there, his face set in a broad grin. So far as the police are concerned, the Great Suitcase Robbery of Kamyanets-Podilsky remains an unsolved crime; so far as I am concerned, it's open and shut.

Back in Kamyanets-Podilsky, I filed the police report mentioned above. The police visited me at the hotel and, sick at stomach, I answered their queries that struck me as strange and embarrassingly personal, such as, 'Why do you carry plastic urinals?' and 'Can you walk?'

Of course these questions had to be translated from Ukrainian into English, and I remain grateful to Natasha, the local schoolteacher whom the police had the good sense to call in. After a couple of days, when she felt it would not be too upsetting to do so, Natasha urged me not to place too much faith in police assurances that the goods would be found.

After making out my statement and answering their questions, the need to resupply the urological kit was uppermost in my mind, as I now had only one of each essential item left. That afternoon I posed a difficult bureaucratic challenge for Dr Dimitri Boiko, the chief surgeon at K-P's City Hospital. But, once he understood the implications of my plight he swung into action, and it is not his fault that it took two hours to complete the paperwork for releasing just two catheters to his Australian outpatient. He suggested making a few telephone inquiries to other hospitals across Ukraine, but the logistical nightmare of accumulating them all was just too much for me to contemplate.

Needless to say, I spent a troubled night. Unless the missing goods were recovered, I could think of no alternative to abandoning my journey. By New Year's Eve it seemed unlikely anything would be returned to me. The detective who had sounded most optimistic in the first 24 hours now told Natasha that my personal items had most likely found their way out of Chernivtsi to be used for the relief of inmates in Romanian orphanages.

On the Sunday morning, having reached rock bottom the day before, I had a brainwave and began to reappraise my plight. While it was ridiculous to think of re-stocking my supplies in impoverished Ukraine, why not make an unplanned detour to the West? And what would the nearest Western country be? Germany. Whom did I know there? Lotti Villinger, a pharmacist I met during my African travels back in the 1980s and with whom I still correspond regularly. Who better than a pharmacist to know where I could get what I needed? Amex there should also be able to replace the traveller's cheques.

My hotel offered the use of its phone to ring Germany. Luck was in: Lotti was there (two weeks later and she would be off on a holiday break to the Canary Islands). More phone and fax calls yielded Amex's assurance that a sheaf of brand new cheques would be waiting for me in Mannheim.

At last I breathed easier. After a nine-day break in Germany, the journey would continue.

DAY 557 (1 JANUARY): KAMYANETS-PODILSKY

This bright, crisp New Year's morning, Andrei from the hotel's business centre drives me to the bus park (yes, *that* bus park) and, with a cautionary word to the driver that could mean 'Take care of him, he's had a rough time'; or perhaps 'Take care of him, he's trouble-prone', he wishes me 'Good road.' God knows, Ukraine could do with a few.

DAY 559 (3 JANUARY): LVIV TO KRAKOW

This morning finds me heading west, on a bus bound for Krakow, Poland's cultural capital and the Pope's hometown, before taking a long-distance coach to Germany.

Now I am being honest with myself, the break couldn't have come at a better time, with the depletion of energy in this snow-blasted winter testing my stamina to the limit. Still, circumstances forced me to take the long view once before, in Ward 13 a dozen years ago. This expedition may have been blown off course but, whatever boundaries there are to my stamina, they mark out personal territory on which time's imprint will never fade.

Chapter 21

A BAD CASE OF MUSCOVITIS

The struggle of man against power is the struggle of memory against forgetting.

MILAN KUNDERA THE BOOK OF LAUGHTER AND FORGETTING

JANUARY-MARCH 2003

My nine-day wander in and around Mannheim need not detain us here. I bought new catheters, urinals, polythene bags and sundry other urological items, as well as a smart new suitcase to put them in. I also bought a pair of expensive German-designed ski boots, with the brand name of Fesswarmers, which should enable me to hotfoot it to the Arctic Circle in comfort.

My friend Lotti, whom I hadn't seen for nearly fourteen years, had her own problems but seeing me evidently raised her spirits. We took a couple of out-of-town trips in her car, Max, after she had managed to disencumber it of a metre-deep drift of fresh snow in what was fast developing into the harshest winter Europe had experienced in two decades.

After Eastern Europe it took time to adjust to the smug materialism of the West and, by the time I just about had, the nine days were up and Lotti was waving me goodbye on the Eurolines coach to Krakow.

For most of Poland's existence it has been played like a concertina – squeezed by Germany on the one hand and Russia on the other. The relationship between its slightly melancholic, self-regarding national character and an intellectual quality—the combination of feeling

261

deeply and thinking deeply—makes it a rather intense country, perhaps too much so for the liking of many outsiders.

And then, of course, this is the most Catholic of countries: to be a Pole one does not have to be Catholic, but it helps. Over 1000 years, just to keep their place in Europe, Poles have driven off Mongols, Turks and communists—all enemies of their faith—with a steely determination.

Behind this insistence on faith lies a harsh historical lesson, learnt at least once every hundred years since the Middle Ages: unless Poles stand up for their beliefs, the ground under their feet tends to disappear.

POLAND: 14–26 JANUARY

Having plotted a course that would take me from southern Poland into the lands of the former Czechoslovakia and then back into Poland, I had asked for a multiple-entry visa—the only one on the whole journey except for Uzbekistan. The Polish consul in Ljubljana, having informed me over the phone that this would cost US$90, then needed two reminders that from a US$100 note he owed me US$10 to complete the transaction.

DAY 561 (14 JANUARY): KRAKOW

Winter is turning in its sleep. Instead of the white carpet that Romania, Moldova and Ukraine laid out for December's visitor, above-zero temperatures have loosed a constant drizzle on southern Poland in mid-January.

Wet underfoot it may be, but only one foot at a time. To get the full benefit from my Fesswarmers, I have to charge two batteries overnight and then clip them to the top of my boots—which, with the battery flex dangling down to the insoles, cannot be worn in comfort. One of the boots is just bearable, the other almost unwearable: it pinches my toes with a pain as acute as that which prompted me to buy these cure-alls in the first place.

When I first hit the street, the temperature of my right foot is perhaps 10°C while the left feels like a pincushion with sensation.

Krakow is a city for all seasons, a showpiece of medieval Europe in the modern world. This rainy night the Bistro Rozowy Slon (Pink Elephant), situated just inside the Old Town precinct, is kept busy satisfying students' palates.

I arrive just on closing time. Next door, quite unexpectedly, another restaurant has just opened up, and what have we here? It's the Golden Kangaroo, which bills itself without much fear of contradiction as Poland's only Australian restaurant. Steak is big, in both senses, but the clientele is small (ahem, it's just me actually) and the beers are Polish.

DAY 564 (17 JANUARY): ZAMOSC

The night train from Krakow cuts a jagged line east by north through wooded Malopolska, depositing me in this small but significant town at the break of another damp day.

On the way here I have struck up a good conversation with Radek Brodaczewski, a university student returning from the scholastic fray. We arrange to meet again later in the day for a personal tour of his hometown.

Zamosc was founded at the height of the Renaissance as a bulwark against the uncivilised Cossack and Tartar hordes out east. In 1992, with its period feel intact, the town was added to the World Heritage List, but even in fair weather it is not a potent tourist magnet.

The collegiate church, built in the last decade of the 16th century, commemorates Wladyslaw Zamoyski, the Polish premier who founded the town and after whom it is named.

Here, in an alcove where you would normally expect to see a more conventional religious diorama or relic, stands a silver suit of armour that, from metal toecaps to visored helmet, could have walked straight out of a book on the Crusades.

John Paul II, when he was Bishop Karol Wojtyla of Krakow, may not have exchanged his vestments for the battledress of a knight, but his tactics against the atheists who ruled his country were militant in their own way—and Poles are not shy about telling you so. Zamosc's role in the defence of Christian Poland is a cause of national pride (pacifism is on shaky ground here), so it is no surprise that in the churchyard stands a statue of the late Polish Pope, marking a visit of his here in 1987.

DAY 566 (19 JANUARY): LUBLIN

From time to time I have stayed in monasteries but never before have I attained guest status at a nunnery. The sisters at Dom Rekolekcyjny offer hospitality as part of their vocation but are not in the business of seeking out 'clients'. Still, in a city where the hotels are all kilometres away from the sights I have come to see and the convent is cheek by jowl with them, the sensible course is to go and ask.

The Mother Superior looks at me with hooded eyes and, for just a moment, I expect to be told this is an impossible request. Instead she asks me to wait and, fifteen minutes later, instructs one of the sisters to show me to her, now my, room. What impresses most is its simplicity—the light, the bedside table, the icon of the Virgin Mary—as well as the no-fuss arrangements for dinner. Few words are exchanged but the sense of acceptance is profound.

On Grodzka, the main street of the medieval quarter, houses that still bear the scars of wartime ravage remain empty all these years on. On one or two façades you can still make out a faded Star of David. Suddenly I feel an outbreak of goose pimples that winter's chill alone cannot account for.

DAY 567 (20 JANUARY): CZESTOCHOWA

No site is more sacred to Polish Catholics than Jasna Gora monastery. Overlooking the town of Czestochowa, Jasna Gora has been a rallying point of tremendous significance in Poland's recent history. On his first tour as Pope, John Paul came here to proclaim 'solidarity' with the workers' movement of that name which was challenging the communists' right to rule. A million Poles stood shoulder to shoulder below the forbidding ramparts, and the scaffolding for the platform from which the new Pope addressed them remains in place today, now a landmark in its own right.

Every August half a million pilgrims come to Jasna Gora on foot, and even on this cold, wet Monday morning in January the monastery's pathways and chapels could hardly be called deserted.

Lech Walesa, the Solidarity leader and one-time president, donated his 1983 Nobel Peace Prize to Jasna Gora's main museum where it takes pride of place.

In the Chapel of the Black Madonna, home to the Poles' most

venerated icon, serenity reigns supreme. The faithful believe that this icon has saved the country itself more than once, and just before descending a ramp into the chapel I am told that this is a special destination of pilgrimage for the disabled. I am rather unsettled on gazing up at a side wall to see wheelchair parts and crutches hanging there, but later it is explained that these have been donated by people cured of their disabilities through the Virgin's intercession.

DAY 569 (22 JANUARY): AUSCHWITZ

The morning train from Krakow judders to a stop at Oswiecim, the Polish version of the 20th century's most infamous place name.

The grim geometry of Auschwitz–Birkenau death camp will be etched into the consciousness of anyone who has viewed *Schindler's List*. Yet, as I pause in the bookshop and later at the ticket counter, the thought occurs: *What is wrong with me that I cannot take in what happened here?* While the question, and the numb detachment, contain their own logic, the fact is that anyone who *could* take in what happened here would go screaming through all the exhibit halls tortured by the psychic force of a million agonies.

Quarter of an hour spent watching the black-and-white official film in a theatrette only numbs me further: before my eyes is a true document of horror, but where is the horror itself? Even now, I remonstrate with myself, I am incapable of imagining a fraction of what happened here.

My chair takes a diagonal path across a field of grass to that sinister sign, 'ARBEIT MACHT FREI' ('Work makes you free'), at the entrance to the camp. Plaques in English, Polish and Hebrew are dotted throughout. The one here directs my gaze to the right. On that patch of ground, every day for years, stragglers from the exhausting work routine were shot down and left to lie in their own blood as a disincentive to others. Barbed wire still overhangs the perimeter fence, even if the Alsatians that once guarded it are long gone.

Recognising that many of my fellow visitors ('tourists' seems an obscenity in this context) will be preoccupied with the fate of family members, I shy away from asking anyone for help up the steps of the camp's perfectly preserved brick buildings.

But there is one exception: Block 27, specifically dedicated to the

Jewish victims of Auschwitz–Birkenau. Here, I can imagine better now, while peering down a hallway whose walls from the height of my shoulders all the way up to the ceiling are studded with ID photos. It is a grim gallery that leaves no space blank. Each face now takes up a few square centimetres; once they filled a continent. These thousands, Jewish through their mother's line, were kidnapped from their homes all over Europe. The numbness has gone. Yes, now I can imagine vividly, and wish I couldn't.

Following the stony paths that separate the prison blocks, a few minutes' pushing brings me to a low-roofed structure unlike all the rest. Protruding from the roof is a chimney that points at a lowering sky. I wheel silently into the darkness. A guide whispers in Polish to a small knot of adults and points to the grey-fronted industrial oven, which is connected to the flue and the chimney now invisible.

Genocide. Holocaust. We have arrived at a point beyond words.

DAY 571 (24 JANUARY): KRAKOW

If Jasna Gora is the spiritual heart of Poland, the seat of its temporal power can be found high above Krakow at Wawel Castle. Not even Athens has an acropolis as commanding as this. Around the year AD 1000 the church and kingly courts occupied these heights, from where the country was governed continuously until the 17th century. Here today lie a hundred kings and queens, and it is here, seven months from now, that President Bush will be brought to see the glory of a state whose leadership gave active support to his Iraq campaign.

DAY 573 (26 JANUARY): POLISH–SLOVAK BORDER

This Sunday morning is sharp as a pin. The solar glint on the metal surface of our cable-car mirrors that of the snow-encrusted rock which we feel we could reach out and touch only because it's sliding past us two metres away and dropping out of sight.

The terminus is Mount Kasprowy Wierch, almost 2000 metres above sea level. Here the white glare is fierce; staying outside for more than a few minutes without proper body cover will earn you a degree in masochism. Where others have come to ski, throwing themselves into cable-drawn chairlifts with split-second accuracy before being whizzed off into Slovakia, I satisfy myself with a hearty breakfast in the cafeteria.

SLOVAKIA: 26 JANUARY–4 FEBRUARY

From 1918 until 1993 Slovakia was the latter half of that country with the longer name. Both it and the Czech Republic under President Vaclav Havel deserve the credit they received for ending that 75-year marriage with such civility (in the so-called velvet divorce). But it is sad that Slovaks felt so overshadowed by the more urbane and affluent Czechs that they went their own way at all, because now Slovakia's struggle for power must focus on forgetting its economic disadvantages and making the most of its few assets.

Tourism is obviously at the forefront here and, among those assets, the High Tatra mountains and the national capital, Bratislava, are the blue chips. I plan to visit both.

DAYS 573–578 (26–31 JANUARY): POPRAD

Mountain scenery at these altitudes in midwinter never fails to enchant. But it was asking for trouble to go round clad in a jacket with only the thinnest of linings.

By evening, after hours of exposure to temperatures that must have been at least 10 degrees below zero, the first symptom, a front-of-head ache, came on. I had no appetite for dinner, and went to bed early. By midnight the headache had worsened into a fever.

Shivering my way to the toilet, I soon noticed (how could I not?) that my urine was the colour of blood. And, while I knew that this must be related to a shortage of bodily anti-freeze, just how serious an impact it was going to have on my travels was a worry that I would have to wait for the morning to resolve.

The hotel's sympathetic director called in a doctor friend who quickly diagnosed pneumonia and ordered me to stay inside, avoid all exertion, take the tablets he prescribed and rest, rest, rest.

As a result of time lost to the Great Suitcase Robbery, I had already decided to abandon any idea of spending half of April pushing my way north from St Petersburg to Murmansk.

Now I dropped eastern Slovakia from the itinerary too, contenting myself with a brief look at Poprad and a little extra time in the capital. By month's end I was ready to hit the road again, taking the direct bus to Bratislava.

DAY 580 (2 FEBRUARY): BRATISLAVA

Unlike the Moldovan capital, Chisinau, this is not some provincial backwater thrust into the limelight but a long-civilised place with its own genuine charm. Overshadowed for 70 years by Prague, it is free to stand tall at last.

As a city that radiates Central European elegance and precision, it would be hard to beat 1100-year-old Bratislava. The Old Town is a photographer's delight, and even an amateur such as I can hardly stow his camera away without having to reach for it a minute later to snap another 'must-see' sight.

All the preceding centuries cannot keep the present one at bay for long, even in an historic quarter. Flanking the street just off the town square, the US Embassy is flying its flag at half mast, in honour of the Columbia space-shuttle crew who perished on re-entry yesterday.

CZECH REPUBLIC: 4–17 FEBRUARY

Just as President Bush's campaign to oust Saddam Hussein shifts up a gear, I find a phenomenon rolling across Europe: public opposition to invading Iraq is clashing head on with strong support among governments for doing so.

It is a wonder of the age how democratic governments can take such a grave decision in defiance of such widespread public sentiment. (Polls at this point show more than 80 per cent of Europeans against the use of force.)

Like their northern neighbours, the Czechs of Moravia and Bohemia adopted Christianity a thousand years ago, yet today the Czechs have a noticeably more flexible attitude to faith than the Poles. For a nation of just 10 million, they have excelled in the creative arts, revealing a genius for writing, and a sense of the dramatic, that have inspired the rest of the world. The names of Kafka, Havel, Hacek (*The Good Soldier Svejk*) and Kundera attest to this.

DAY 583 (5 FEBRUARY): BRNO

The medieval state of Moravia is history, but then it is the reminders of history that make its capital so proud and leave visitors to it so awestruck.

The site of the city's original castle is now occupied by the Cathedral of Saints Peter and Paul. The delightful story is told that in 1645, when a Swedish general was besieging the town and its citizens were defending it tooth and nail, the general declared that he would abandon the assault if his troops hadn't captured Brno by 11 am next day. Came the hour, came the ingenious bell-ringer who sounded the tocsin twelve times. Ever since, so we are told, the cathedral bells have rung noon at 11 am.

I puff my way to the cathedral up forbiddingly steep Petrov Way. Arriving at 10.50, I take a few minutes to catch my breath and hear this extraordinary piece of value-added timekeeping with my own ears. Gong-like, the pealing begins. I count. One, two, three, four faint peals are followed by eleven more, distinct and strong. I scratch my head: it's either 15 o'clock or somebody's just made a clangour. Off down the hill I go, sorely disappointed. These days you can't even depend on things to go wrong right.

DAY 584 (6 FEBRUARY): BRNO

I have Mrs Stumbris, our Form 2 (Year 8) science teacher, to thank for everything I knew before today about Johann Gregor Mendel, the father of genetics. I'm sure Mrs S. wouldn't mind my having gone to the source to build on that foundation laid all those years ago: she was forever instilling into us the importance of empirical checking.

Empiricism was the very basis of Mendel's work. A friar at the Augustinian Abbey of St Thomas, Mendel spent several decades, from the 1840s onwards, carrying out thousands of experiments on peas in the monastery grounds.

Methodically, scientifically, cautiously and cumulatively, he discovered how we humans inherit our looks and other characteristics from generation to generation, all but naming the agents (genes) through which the mechanism works.

His is a poignant story of credit denied until it is of no use to the creditworthy. Mendel presented his findings to the Natural History Society of Brno in 1865, and published them in a scientific paper the following year, but their significance went unrecognised till after his death. Today, in the abbey grounds, an up-to-the-moment museum christened the Mendelianum acquaints visitors with his pioneering work.

A week after the fall of the Berlin Wall, in November 1989, hundreds of thousands of Czechs packed Wenceslas Square to insist on the exit of the communists who had ruled their land for 40 years. They were ordinary everyday people doing an extraordinary every-century thing. Led by the jailed playwright Vaclav Havel, they kicked out their 'masters' in an act of firm and peaceful resolve that could have descended into mass slaughter at any moment if armed men had been issued an order one word long.

Until today I had a seriously wrong idea of what it meant for hundreds of thousands of people to cram into Wenceslas Square, having always visualised it as a space something like Sydney's Martin Place or Melbourne's City Square. Named after the good Bohemian king of Christmas-carol fame, Wenceslas Square (Vaclavske nam) is a boulevard that rolls down a gentle slope for 700 metres and is probably ten times as long as it is wide. The tide of humanity gathered there night after night would have been awesome and, in the end, irresistible.

The 'square' today looks stately yet exuberant. Grand hotels, bustling shops and finance houses are among the edifices eight storeys high that flank its broad central concourse. The traffic streaming between its median strip and the crowded pavements moves with a relentless purpose more familiar in London or Paris than the capital of a Slavic land.

My first settled day here is spent familiarising myself with the inner-city districts of Stare Mesto and Nove Mesto, the hub of Prague's artistic life. There is great contentment to be found in just wandering around a town that has been inhabited for a thousand years. This is the real-life Bohemian rhapsody, and its harmony lulls the senses in a way that needs no explaining to those Australians who have been to Europe. It goes without saying that those who stay at home don't know what they are missing.

At a helpful Internet café, today brings a heart-lightening email that contains a welcome surprise. It's from Stephanie, the friend and journalist whose hospitality I rather abused by dropping from that fourth-floor window a lifetime ago. She wonders how I would feel if she and a close friend of hers, Stephen, hooked up to my European caravan for a few days in Estonia this April. After this long on the road, there is not a world of difference between a lone traveller and a lonely traveller, so I don't have to waste a moment's thought before replying, 'You bet.'

DAY 590 (12 FEBRUARY): PRAGUE

Prague is one of the rare cities where I can use the underground railway. Two stops south of Metro central, I alight at Vysehrad station and take the lift up to a terrace from which there is a superb view to be had, looking back at the city.

Slavin Cemetery is literally in the shade of Vysehrad's twin-towered neo-Gothic church. What I've come to see is Antonín Dvořák's tomb. Just as I expected, he's surrounded by angels.

DAY 592 (14 FEBRUARY): MARIANSKE LAZNE

This is as far west as I go. The Germans knew it as Marienbad (and for some of those who come here today I suspect it always will be), this resort that was once the most famous spa in the world.

Across the countryside the snow lies metres thick, but that has not weakened the determination of the sick and infirm to 'take the cure'. Cup in hand, they lean against the façade of the Holy Cross Spring, absorbing the warmth of the winter sun, what there is of it. Inside the building these cups are filled from any of several taps, each connected to a subterranean mineral spring with specific medicinal properties advertised on printed sheets. These sheets are perused with the grave attentiveness reserved elsewhere for racing form guides. So sedate and, well, 19th-century, is the pace of life here that even bicycles are banned: top speed is achieved by a pair of noble chestnuts drawing a trap.

'Good health' is the conventional toast, and here they really mean it. With the Carolina Spring coming highly recommended for those at above-average risk of bladder infection (which spinal patients always are), I drink litres of the pure fluid until a sense of bloatedness puts an end to my sampling. It takes a decent draught of Czech beer at sundown to restore my fluid balance to normal.

Victoriana still reigns here, with the hotels Empire, Excelsior and their ilk still in business, even if nowadays they fail to attract quite the class of guest that frequented the spa a century or two back. Those whose need for peace of mind was greatest found it idyllic. King Edward VII, when he was only the Prince of Wales; the younger Johann Strauss; Mark Twain, Rudyard Kipling, J.W. van Goethe, Russian writers and German composers: all summered here in their time.

DAY 594 (16 FEBRUARY): PRAGUE

Late on Sunday morning I'm parked under the huge round dial of the 15th-century astronomical 'clock' that is one of Prague's best-known landmarks. A jazz band is bringing New Orleans to Staremestske nam, the Old Town Square.

At noon I cross the square to the pick-up point for a city tour, of the 'packaged' variety I normally shun. But Prague has so many magical sights that the prospect of missing too many of them, in the limited time I have left here, has forced me to relent. Waiting for the tour to begin, I get talking to a jaunty couple from the English Midlands, and the wife tells me the first joke I've heard for ages. 'What's the difference between God and Tony Blair?'

I don't know.

'God doesn't think he's Tony Blair.'

After an hour we cross the Vltava and head up to Prague Castle, in hilltop Hradcany district, where the householder was none other than Vaclav Havel himself until he stepped down just two weeks ago. So absorbing are the sights here that I leave the tour at this point and find my own way back to town, at a more leisurely pace.

Eventually I reach the much-loved Charles IV Bridge (Karluv Most). No other I've ever been on is quite like it. A stone road over the water, it has spanned the Vltava for 650 years, a crossing enlivened by eighteen statues of figures from Czech history.

Tired at the close of a full day's urban exploration, I let Prague's music flow all over me, like a warm bath on this wintry night. A female soprano, accompanied by viola, fills the St Martin-in-the-Wall Church with the sublimity of Vivaldi, Bach, Handel, Verdi and (how could it be otherwise in the Czech heartland?) Dvorák.

POLAND REVISITED: 17 FEBRUARY–1 MARCH

DAY 596 (18 FEBRUARY): WROCLAW

The morning bus from Prague has returned me to Poland—the west of the country this time. The city once known as Breslau is a grim, dark and sooty place, where the liveliest sight is a paddling of ducks.

Tonight in the warm haven of the Bar Smak (where on earth do they come up with these names?) the beer is flowing nicely but, up there on the screen, what's the evening entertainment? Tank formations are on the move, the Luftwaffe flies again. It's *Blitzkrieg* on the Discovery channel. Hey, I feel like shouting, this is Poland, guys. They don't need reminding!

DAY 598 (20 FEBRUARY): POZNAN

Too much seriousness can be bad for you. Luckily, Poznan has the perfect antidote, and it is administered daily in the Old Town Square. Crane your neck and you can just make out two mechanical goats above the clock on the Renaissance town hall (built 1555, restored 1999). As the clock strikes noon, the goats butt their heads together twelve times (yes, everyone counts).

So entranced are the 200 schoolchildren gawping at the sight that, when the goats retreat into their loft for 24 hours' well-earned hibernation, they wave wildly and shout a gleeful farewell.

DAY 600 (22 FEBRUARY): TORUN

'TERRAE MOTOR SOLIS CAELIQUE STATOR.' 'The Earth moves, the Sun stands still.'

With these words, Nicolaus Copernicus turned the universe of astronomy upside down and gave it a thorough shake. The words are inscribed on a plinth beneath a statue of the young Copernicus who holds a framework globe with astrological symbols girdling the Equator.

This is the astronomer's hometown, and children have laid fresh bouquets wrapped in the Polish flag at his feet. It was Nick's birthday three days ago. He was 530, but the statue makes him look 500 years younger.

DAY 602 (24 FEBRUARY): GDANSK AND WESTERPLATTE

Crossing overland from the Black Sea to the Baltic has taken me just under two months. This is where the last leg begins and the first signs emerge that winter's grimness lies behind. It will be just as cold ahead, but sunny. Today in Gdansk it is a brilliantly warm 5°C, but since this is the birthplace of Daniel Fahrenheit, a great man by any measure, I should perhaps amend that to 41°F.

Seven kilometres by taxi out of town, and of course the same back by bus, my first sighting of the Baltic is at Westerplatte. In Hong Kong I once met Clare Hollingworth, the *Daily Telegraph* correspondent whose most famous scoop was Kim Philby's defection to Moscow. By rights, though, it should have been 'breaking' the onset of World War II—a fairly big story by anyone's standards.

Hollingworth was here on 1 September 1939, when a German battleship shelled the Polish defensive positions—the charred pillboxes you still see here today. Simultaneously, Panzer tank divisions rolled across the frontier, striking at Gdansk and other Polish cities. Back in London, Hollingworth's sceptical editors refused to print the story without corroboration, which Neville Chamberlain duly provided later.

Today a single Panzer tank rests on a slight incline within earshot of the Baltic surf. The scene is rightly windswept and blasted. The official memorial is beyond my reach, but I think the sign beneath it says everything satisfactorily enough: NIGOY WIECEJ WOJNY (NEVER MORE TO WAR).

DAY 603 (25 FEBRUARY): HEL

At long last I have taken the advice my friends have been offering me for years and gone to Hel—but I came back!

Hel, I can now say from experience, is a Polish seaside resort visited in winter. But right now it is perfect weather for Baltic seals, which may be why the only tourist attraction open at this time of year is the *fokarium*.

Foka means 'seal' in Polish and the refuge is dedicated to protecting this endangered species, of which six adult specimens live here in saltwater pools. My English-speaking guide, Magda, looks a little startled to have a visitor from overseas at the tail-end of February, as if I had come up out of the water myself. But, for a change, my timing is fortuitous because just yesterday Unda Marina, one of the two female grey seals, gave birth.

Her cub, resembling an orange muff with teardrop eyes, is unnamed as yet. A staff photographer wants to record the first feed, but Unda Marina emits a piteous whinnying sound, perhaps unable to distinguish his videocamera from her *foka* memory of a harpoon. Although she gobbles a fish whole, leaving nothing for her newborn, Unda Marina's maternal instinct is not entirely dormant, as she wildly slaps her shiny skin with one flipper while shielding her cub with the other.

DAY 606 (28 FEBRUARY): WARSAW

The Polish capital was comprehensively flattened in World War II, and I have no time for re-creations of Warsaw 'as it was'. Mindful of the civic authorities' eagerness to give Warsaw's residents a sense of continuity, it just sticks in the craw to kid oneself that castles dating all the way back to the 1950s are really from the 1590s.

The places I will remember Warsaw for are ones stumbled across while getting to know the city, like the starkly simple memorial on Jerusalem Street where the plaque reads, '102 Poles were executed here by the Nazis (*"Hitlerowcy"*) on 28 January 1944.' The remarkable thing to dwell on here is not the commemorative stone itself but the commemorative flowers in front of it. They are fresh.

BELARUS: 1–10 MARCH

At the turn of the millennium, the authoritarian president of Belarus, Alexander Lukashenko, actually asked his Russian counterpart, Vladimir Putin, to take his country (whose name means White Russia) back into an enlarged Russian Federation. No fool, Putin spurned that request, but in the context of regional history it was not so odd. Belarus has never been fully independent for long—at one stage it was virtually a Polish colony; at another, Lithuanian—and had only just emerged from 200 years under Russia's wing.

Under Lukashenko, human rights are suppressed, the media are his mouthpieces and the door to the West, in the form of the European

Union, is closed, locked and bolted. To visit Belarus now, it is often said, is like visiting the Soviet Union 20 years ago. In 1985, travelling across the USSR, I caught a glimpse of what it was like to live under Brezhnev's heirs, and now I brace myself for a fortnight of petty complications. But the end of the road is not far off and I tell myself that most of the lessons lying in wait on this one-man roadshow have already been inflicted.

So this is the month when Iraq will be invaded, everyone feels it in his bones. Bush is rattling the dice and about to cast them. In the Europe I have left behind, feelings are crystallising against military action. But this is Europe in the geographic sense only. Military adventures are old news here: 1918 was just yesterday and a quarter of all Belarussians died in World War II (what a staggering fact). Life goes on as normal.

DAY 607 (1 MARCH): WARSAW TO BREST

On the bus from Warsaw I strike up a conversation with a family of three (father, mother and teenage son) returning home to Belarus after they have cleared the last diplomatic hurdle in readiness for their emigration to Canada at the end of the year.

The father, Oleg, speaks English, and invites me to visit the family at their home in Globukoye, a small provincial town not on my intended route but not so far off it either. Taking his number down, I promise to think about it. One nagging worry stops me saying yes right away: if I agree to stay and then find they don't have a Western-style toilet, well, I won't be able to stay. But this would be a rude response to such a generous request.

DAY 611 (5 MARCH): MINSK

Stalin died 50 years ago today, so how odd it is that I should arrive right now in one of the few places where he would feel right at home if (perish the thought) he were to come back. To mark the occasion, Minsk turns on a blizzard.

In common with many other ex-Soviet republics, Belarus has retained the 'visa support' system that I last encountered in Central Asia, with the state's own tourism agency, Belarus Intourist, issuing the visa invitations.

It is time to meet and greet Tatyana, my visa-supporting agent at what trendy Belarussians like to shorten to Belintourist.

A dark-haired beauty, Tatyana is in her early to mid-twenties, I estimate, as we shake hands in Belintourist's downstairs office on the corner of Lenin Street and Prospekt Masherava. With a relaxing chat in mind, I suggest we adjourn to a hotel, but Tatyana pleads such urgent pressure of business that we end up going next door to a coffee shop.

How foolish and unimaginative of me not to have guessed this earlier: her dream is to travel. Working dutifully for a tourist agency, travel has always been beyond her means—therein lies the irony—and from what she says I gather that the barrier to getting a passport is still set formidably high and the costs are extortionate (for which read 'corruption'). Tatyana is staring through a window to the West but has no way to open it.

I have decided what to do about Oleg's invitation to stay with his family in the country. As going to Globukoye entails only a minor detour on my way back to Minsk this Sunday, perhaps I could convert it into a lunch invitation and spend a few hours there, between train arrival and bus departure. I ring Oleg: he consults his wife and comes back on line, 'Yes, that will be fantastic. Your train will arrive at 12 noon, and there will be a bus leaving for Minsk at three o'clock.' He seems to have known what my answer would be before I myself did.

DAY 613 (7 MARCH): VITEBSK

My coach to the country's far north-east has precisely two people on it: driver Anatoly, and me. We have little to say to each other on the 400-kilometre journey—Anatoly speaks no English—but we get on superbly.

If someone's behaviour exceeds what is acceptable, people say it is 'beyond the pale', a term stemming from the tsarist setting of a boundary to Jewish settlement. Vitebsk was 'within the Pale', and in their isolation that community produced one family, the Chagalls, who produced one son, Marc, whose name will forever be linked with this town.

Now you might think that Vitebsk's city authorities would make the most of the fact that Marc Chagall, world-famous surrealist and postmodernist artist, hailed from here. But this is Belarus, where no one in power is in a hurry to escape the past, and to glorify an individualist who set his own stamp on modern art would be, well, beyond the pale.

There is, however, a modest museum dedicated to the artist. Julia, the museum's curator, who obviously knows her subject, tells me that well into his 98th year Chagall died between the second and third floors while in a Paris lift. Ascending.

DAY 615 (9 MARCH): GLOBUKOYE

The sylvan scenes of dense forest and snow-covered clearings witnessed from my window seat on the train to Globukoye are like something out of Tolstoy. Catching a glimpse of a horse-drawn sled at a halfway halt, I grab my camera but the sled isn't nearly close enough to get the picture I want.

Primed for my descent to the platform, I am greeted by Oleg and his family right on time. Ten minutes later I doff my jacket in the family's apartment, on the first floor of a 1970s housing block. His wife, Marina, has prepared a traditional thick stew, which I consume with an appetite sharpened by my having gone without breakfast.

As soon as Marina goes off to the kitchen to prepare the tea, Oleg hands me a gift for the road. It is a silver fob watch with an inscription on the back—something so unexpected and obviously valuable that I shrink from presenting my own humble token of appreciation.

It really *is* nothing, compared to the watch, but from my rucksack I sheepishly produce it anyway: a box of Belgian chocolates bought at the Soviet-style department store in Vitebsk two days ago.

'My wife doesn't like chocolates,' blue-eyed Oleg tells me in a neutral voice.

Honesty must be a virtue even more highly regarded here than at home, where such a response might be considered a trifle brusque.

Stumped for anything to say, I can only manage, 'Well, I hope you enjoy eating them for her.'

DAY 616 (10 MARCH): MINSK

This morning the BBC radio news continues to chronicle the slide to war.

Near Victory Square I pause to buy radio batteries at a kiosk before trying to pinpoint the precise apartment block where Lee Harvey Oswald, alleged assassin of President Kennedy, lived with his Belarussian girlfriend back in the early 1960s.

Suddenly a voice over my shoulder announces, 'It's not here at all; it's on the next street down.'

Looking up, I meet the smiling gaze of a buxom woman of 50 with a fox-fur wrap that would get her lynched in London these days. My stunned look seems only to inspire her efforts at enlightening me. 'You are looking for Lee Harvey Oswald's apartment, aren't you?'

'Yes,' I stammer. (*Is it so obvious?*)

'Well, it's not here. The original one was, but ...'

'What other one is there? Oswald hasn't been back, has he?' I say, deadpan.

'No, of course not, but in 1985 my good friend Alexei made a film for television here in Belarus and they used an apartment at 4 Vulitsa Communistinay, which is the next street down. Come, I will show it to you.'

Pausing long enough to get a photo of Oswald's real-life domicile, I then accompany the mystery woman (strangely, I never ask her name and she doesn't volunteer it) to the chosen apartment block one street down. It fascinates me that this has greater resonance for her than the actual historical site, simply because of her good friend Alexei.

Negotiating Minsk station is an experience I'm not keen to repeat. Parties hauling me downstairs to the platform for country trains are amazed to hear that I want the international train, yes, the one to Vilnius. Then comes the exhausting challenge of trying to get to the right platform during rush hour—arguing with super-suspicious security goons at every turn—but a semblance of order is finally restored when I am lifted on board the correct train with half an hour to spare.

We churn through the frosty night towards the Lithuanian border.

Unlike their Belarussian counterparts, the border guards who come to stamp me into Lithuania see nothing unusual in my end-of-the-carriage location, necessitated by the narrow corridor: to them I'm just another passenger. Taking my passport, handed up with a smile, they open it to the page featuring my mug shot and process me without question. Turning Kundera on his head, I conclude that the struggle of Power against Man must be to forget everything else and memorise our faces.

Chapter 22

THE USUAL DELINQUENCIES

The Head of the State and the Ministers can be brought to trial for the usual delinquencies according to the decision of the State Assembly …

ALBERT PULLERITS (ED.) THE ESTONIAN YEARBOOK 1927

MARCH-APRIL 2003

Though grouped together as the Baltic States, the three mini-nations on the eastern seaboard of that pond of the same name are subtly different. Take the word for 'street': in Vilnius it's *gatve*; in Riga *iela*; in Tallinn *tanav*.

Their religious beliefs, economies and 'national character' also underscore how each state differs from its neighbours.

But, given their common experience of having been annexed by the Soviet Union, the Russian influence remains a common denominator for all three. Each has sizeable, but increasingly discontented, Russian minorities and Russian remains a lingua franca that will get you by in any of them.

LITHUANIA: 10-25 MARCH

DAY 617 (11 MARCH): VILNIUS

Unlike Riga, which is the biggest city in the Baltics, Vilnius is graced by winding streets that give it the ambience of a friendly town on a human scale. Here, if you meet a familiar face in the crowd, both of you are likely to forget any prior plans and chat in the street, or adjourn to a coffee shop, rather than limit yourselves to nodding acquaintance and hurrying on.

By severe contrast with Minsk, everyone is technologically up to the minute here, with no shortage of mobile phones. As for keeping in touch with home, that is no problem once I stumble upon a customer-friendly Internet café in a downtown arcade. The manager, a young man in a wheelchair, offers me a free coffee and a brochure featuring a city map on which Vilnius Old Town appears next to the 'Uzupio Republic'.

'What is this?' I ask him. A suburb of the capital that has declared itself a self-governing state, he tells me. What an excellent jest it sounds, and I make a note to check it out.

DAY 621 (15 MARCH): VILNIUS

On Gedimino Prospektas, Vilnius's most fashionable address, behind a cairn dedicated to the victims of the 50-year Soviet occupation, stands the old stone KGB building. With the assistance of donations from Lithuanians living in the United States, the names of those who died within its hidden recesses are now carved into the stonework. While its counterparts in Belarus are still following the old order's orders, this KGB 'house of terror' stands as a memorial to its victims.

In 1992, after the structure was renamed the Museum of the Genocide of the Lithuanian People, former KGB prisoners were employed as tour guides. At first it seems a little disappointing that they have now been replaced by younger 'professionals' such as Livijus, although I soon learn of his close personal connection with the place.

Officially, 1037 people were executed somewhere under our feet, intones Livijus, but the real toll is known to be much greater. Twelve were executed on one occasion, he tells me, and then, obviously struggling to maintain his professional objectivity, he adds softly, 'My grandfather was among them.'

By 1947, KGB prisoners in this building (originally and ironically named the Palace of Justice) occupied 50 'ordinary' cells and two set aside for solitary confinement. Nocturnal interrogations continued for weeks on end; 'active interrogation' was code for physical torture. Most notorious of all the torture chambers was the 'cold pool room' where a swimming pool was covered in a thick sheet of ice. Prisoners were ordered to stand on a plank extending out over the pool, and when they eventually dozed off they would fall from it. Succinctly, one ex-prisoner described their fate thus, 'Eventually they would end up on the bloodstained ice floor.'

DAY 622 (16 MARCH): VILNIUS

It would have to happen on a Sunday. At the youth hostel where I am staying, a short ride from the Gates of Dawn, I am stuck fast. Thick ice wedged in both axles has 'glued' my wheels to the mainframe, and the two principal antidotes—force and anti-freeze—are equally ineffective.

The YHA's English warden calls on the services of a Russian-speaking handyman she employs for sundry emergencies. A combination of uncommon sense and judicious application of anti-freeze eventually detaches the wheels from the chair's iron grip, and a grateful guest goes on his way.

Before independence the square in front of Vilnius Cathedral was a well-known rallying point for opponents of Soviet rule and, as I cross it in the evening twilight, I see about two dozen young people (university students, it turns out) holding a candlelight vigil there. 'Iraq?' I probe, almost intuitively. They nod silently, not knowing if the armed might they oppose is being unleashed even as they gather.

DAY 623 (17 MARCH): VILNIUS

A signpost beside Vilnia rivulet announces that you are about to enter the Republic of Uzupio, which is really an artists' colony in one of the capital's pleasantest parishes. These Uzupians have discovered that one of the surest routes to publicity is to keep yourself apart.

The joke is now six years old and still drawing them in. Billing itself as the Baltic answer to Paris's Montmartre, the trendy quarter has become a haven for eccentrics, anarchists and *bons vivants* of all descriptions. Of course, its founders do have to pretend to be governing the place, but the choice of Uzupio Café, a pub-restaurant nestled by the stream in the shadow of a 13th-century Orthodox church, must at least enhance the likelihood of its Cabinet meetings drowning in consensus.

Every year Uzupio marks its independence on April Fool's Day, and on 1 May it holds a World Championship of Fools in which the competition is inevitably keen.

While at the Uzupio Café, I am introduced to Alois Lekivicius, who is described as Lithuania's leading exponent of slow pipe-smoking. This, I openly admit, is a new sport to me. Lekivicius takes this as a cue to produce from an attaché case his prized collection of pipe-smoking competition photos. With impressive sincerity he informs me that he has smoked a pipe in one hour 45 minutes, but that the European slothful-puffing record is three hours 15 minutes. Shifting in my seat, I scramble for an exit line. It's been a pleasant evening, but I must have an early night.

For me, the jury is no longer out on Lithuanians' reputation for eccentricity, even if they do have a habit of calling themselves Uzupians instead.

DAY 626 (20 MARCH): VILNIUS

The invasion of Iraq has begun.

Shock and awe may be on my menu, but they are off that of the newly opened New York-style diner in the centre of town. It is filling up with an early-evening crowd, none of whom is paying any attention to the MTV music rocking away on the large television screen at one end of the room.

A waitress saunters over. 'May I help you, sir?' 'Yes,' I reply, 'I will be ordering a meal. But first, I was wondering, do you have CNN or BBC on your television? I particularly wanted to watch it tonight.'

A look of extreme consternation blots out her smile. 'I'm sorry but you cannot watch that,' she coos. 'They have a war on, didn't you hear?'

'Actually I did,' I say, meeting her steady gaze. 'That's what I wanted to look at.'

This obviously strikes her as an odd request. She crosses the room and, after an intense consultation with her boss, some invisible hand flicks a remote-control and Eminem disappears, to be replaced by a stranger percussion still—that of the aerial cannonade bombing and battering Baghdad.

By the time my meal arrives fifteen minutes later, the whole room is transfixed by the pyrotechnics on the screen. Flashes of light and the rumbling thunder of heavy ordnance hold us mesmerised. There is nothing wrong with the meal, but I will never remember what I had.

DAY 628 (22 MARCH): KAUNAS

What Kaunas has to offer the visitor is reassurance that the quirkily eccentric national character is not confined to the capital. Two of the most offbeat museum collections so far encountered on this overland ramble are to be found right here. At No. 106 on the main drag of Laisves aleja (Freedom Avenue) stands the Zoological Museum, the result of one man's lifelong obsession with taxidermy. Inside are some 13 000 stuffed animals (I'm perfectly willing to accept the museum's word on that). Among this menagerie of the inert are a great anteater from South America, a tigress with her cubs from the Russo-Chinese borderlands, and a dingo (from you know where).

DAY 629 (23 MARCH): KAUNAS

This morning I am ready to tackle another of Kaunas's unique contributions to world culture. Christianity was a latecomer to Lithuania, but still, to find a permanent exhibition devoted to (art)works of the Devil is enough to raise eyebrows even in one who thought that by now he had seen everything.

Antanas Zmuidzinavicius (1876–1966) kicked off his miscellany of satanic images with thirteen Lithuanian examples. In Lithuania, as in the West, 13 attracts a horde of superstitions, but it did not turn out to be at all unlucky for Kaunas's leading devil-worshipper.

As the years wore on, the diabolist broadened his assortment of artworks, until he had 260 of them by the time of his death. Again, death was a good career move for the Kaunas monomaniac: today the number of exhibits stands at 2000 plus.

DAY 630 (24 MARCH): SIAULIAI

Amazingly enough, even Kaunas must yield to Siauliai when it comes to collections of the unusual and downright weird. This morning I spent an hour in utter thraldom at the town's Water Supply and Wastewater Enterprise Museum, a monument to sewerage that deserves better treatment than I can give it here. On top of this, the town's Cat Museum is said to be the world's best of its type—which is entirely plausible—and only my pressing schedule prevents my writing expertly on the Anti-fire Protection Museum, the Bicycle Museum and the Zaliukiai Windmill Institute. This last-mentioned establishment illustrates the 'long history of the windmill' by reference to a local specimen that 'no longer operates'.

LATVIA: 25 MARCH–3 APRIL

DAY 633 (27 MARCH): RIGA

Item in the *Baltic Times*:

> The war in Iraq is not deterring people who plan to travel to Riga for the Eurovision Song Contest 2003, according to tour operators in Latvia's capital.

If the Latvian capital is somewhat behind the times (punk is big in the Riga fashion world right now), its quaintness is bound to attract backpackers in years to come, I am sure, after Europe's more flamboyant attractions have palled.

For reasons that escape me and probably always will, Riga has one of the world's best collections of Art Nouveau architecture. At exactly 100 years of age, a bank on Baron Street serves as a classic example, while prime specimens of *Jugendstil*, Art Nouveau German-style combining classicism and flair in stunning façades, are seen to best advantage on Alberta iela (street) in the newer suburbs.

DAY 634 (28 MARCH): RIGA

Exhibits in the Museum of the Occupation of Latvia (1940–1991) deal systematically with Latvia's domination by two great powers.

In June 1940, two days after Paris fell to the Nazis, the Russians marched into Riga. Mass deportations, which began instantly and accelerated in 1941—that period labelled the Year of Horror by the Red Cross—are commemorated in a re-created Gulag barracks.

In August 1991, when Mikhail Gorbachev was held captive at his Black Sea dacha and the fortunes of the Soviet Union reached a turning point, I followed those dramatic events on TV in the rehabilitation ward of the Austin Hospital.

For Latvia, and the other two Baltic republics, the same events provided the opportunity to reassert their long-lost independence. So weakened was Moscow by the drift of events out of its control, and the ultimate defeat of the attempted coup, that on 24 August the USSR itself recognised the independence of all three states.

Strange to say, the museum's exhibits add up to an indictment of most Latvians for supporting either the Nazis or the Soviets—and that seems to be the historical truth of the matter. Yet it is hard to voice confidence that any society as geographically vulnerable would have acted more nobly.

Latvians pride themselves on their hearty, even gutsy, approach to the business of eating. On Caka iela just along from the Hotel Viktorija is Staburags, an all-you-can-eat restaurant.

Here the speciality of the day, every day, is roast pig leg, washed down with excellent Latvian beer. Actually, all-you-can-eat is a bit of a misnomer: more-than-you-could-possibly-eat-if-you-stayed-here-all-day-and-half-of-the-night is more like it. Burp.

DAY 636 (30 MARCH): RIGA

On the outskirts of the capital, housed in an ugly steel-and-glass building that could easily be mistaken for a tyre warehouse, is the Riga Motormuseum, whose assemblage of antique, veteran and downright classy automobiles is guaranteed to have car lovers salivating.

One suspects wry intent behind the caption for the 1914 Hansa torpedo race-car, one of the many fascinating exhibits, when it says, 'In 1914 German racers made a journey from Berlin to Moscow. It was supposed to be the first stage of a journey round the world. Unfortunately the World War I spoiled this activity.' How thoughtless of the Kaiser.

The most remarkable exhibit of all is a Rolls-Royce Silver Shadow with a wax dummy of ex-Soviet leader Leonid Brezhnev at the wheel. Brezhnev was a keen driver, we are assured: it was just that his passion for cars outran his capacity to drive them safely.

'In 1980 on one of his drives near Moscow, Brezhnev himself at the wheel, the car met with an accident—collided with a truck. Luckily Brezhnev was not injured.'

Many Latvians must swallow hard when they come to that 'luckily', but what makes the exhibit so memorable is that 'Brezhnev' is sitting up with a bloody gash over one eyebrow and looking suitably concussed.

ESTONIA: 3-11 APRIL

DAY 640 (3 APRIL): PARNU

Snow lies over the parklands and on the public buildings. It keeps me off the footpaths and makes me skid all over the roads. Worst of all, it gums up my chair's works and doubles the effort involved in pushing myself round.

Most of the town's best-loved buildings date from the 17th century, when those peace-loving characters, the Swedes, came rampaging and pillaging hereabouts. Needless to say, these are the buildings that visitors to the place drool over and marvel at. Your Parnu parvenu prefers to live in modernistic Scandinavian-style houses composed of vast glass sheets, acres of Baltic pine forest and acute-angled snow-friendly roofs.

DAY 642 (5 APRIL): KURESSAARE, SAAREMAA

Estonia's western islands—exposed to the full force of Nature out in the Baltic—are renowned for experiencing more extreme weather than the mainland. Yet nothing could adequately prepare me for the journey from Parnu to the island of Saaremaa yesterday, undertaken just as a 'severe weather event' was bearing down from the Arctic.

So uncertain were bus schedules that I elected to take the service to Virtsu, a nondescript speck where the ferry leaves for Muhu, a small island leeward of Saaremaa, rather than wait for the direct bus to Saaremaa (which stood a higher chance of being cancelled). After half an hour spent trying to keep myself on the high side of hypothermia at Virtsu, a luxury coach full of geriatric Finnish fun-seekers pulled up and agreed to give me a lift to the big island.

DAY 643 (6 APRIL): KURESSAARE TO TALLINN

Still the snowflakes sweep and swirl, driven furiously to earth from a steel-grey sky. This morning I arrive at the bus station in good time but filled with disbelief. I am certain they will announce all today's services are cancelled due to the snowstorm.

The announcement never comes, instead the bus does. And so begins a nine-hour slog all the way to Tallinn, a trip that normally takes four hours. We battle the whole way through fields of late-lying snow and, halfway through the ordeal, the driver shakes his head in amazement and curses this weather as the worst he has ever come across 'at this time of year'. Apparently this is the sort of tempest you can expect once every decade or so—in January, not in April.

DAY 645 (8 APRIL): TALLINN
Last night Stephanie Bunbury—the friend who was first on the scene after my descent from the windowsill in East Melbourne—joined me in the Estonian capital for a few days together in this icy outpost of civilisation. These days will be just as cold, but brighter now.

Along for the occasion is a close friend of hers I hadn't met before. Stephen Dalton writes television reviews for the *Times* in London, the city where Stephanie has been working as a journalist for years. Stephen and I strike up an immediate rapport, and I just know that the days to come—though filled with memories we'll all look back upon fondly—will pass much, much too quickly.

This morning, while Stephanie and Stephen are taking a late breakfast at their hotel, I am on the opposite side of town impersonating a snow plough. As I take a visible breather on one of the city's street corners, and try to get my bearings, a two-man hit squad from Tallinn's leading morning daily approaches me and asks what I am doing. I explain that I am near the end of a long journey in the wheelchair and just looking round Estonia.

Since they are braving the elements to do a round-up of all weather-related news for tomorrow's issue, I find myself thrust into the media spotlight. Next day a photo of me appears on page 9 of their esteemed rag ... at least, it must be me beneath that snow-encrusted rabbit-fur hat, because my name (spelt correctly!) is in the caption.

DAY 646 (9 APRIL): TALLINN
Their interest piqued by what I have told them about Navitrolla, a famous cartoonist here who is a sort of Estonian Leunig, Stephanie, Stephen and I nip inside the artist's studio high on Toompea hill which doubles as a shop selling a remarkable variety of merchandise. This incorporates creative work of his, ranging from boxed T-shirts and postcards to framed prints.

Navitrolla (real name Heiki Troll) reminds Estonians of their national character, not only through his artworks but also by his very name. Navi and Trolla are two long-established towns (his mother hails from Navi, his father from Trolla). A one-man tourist attraction and household name across Estonia, Navitrolla remains at 32 a 'country boy' who prefers to spend time on the family farm outside Tartu, Estonia's second city, and come to Tallinn only when business (or the odd Australian interview) beckons.

Fame has certainly not given him airs. Asked does he remember how old he was when he first drew something and what it was, he gives an involuntary laugh. 'My mother tells me, I'm sure it's true, that when I was a very small kid I took off my pants and painted a whole wall of our house in shit, and my mother says she said, "Maybe my son will be an artist." '

Like Michael Leunig, his guiding spirit is the quicksilver element of whimsy, and any attempt to define his work is courteously but firmly resisted. The closest he comes to giving it a label is 'Zen painting'—a definition by anti-definition. When I ask does his art contain an underlying message, he smiles and nods vigorously. 'Many ... but the most important is: open your eyes. The world is full of things to see and, of course, you will never understand it all but if you try you will be happier.'

Before leaving the studio, I buy a little happiness in the form of a T-shirt that reflects his philosophy well. Over a black background a shaggy-haired animal which Navitrolla dubs the Sorrow is powering its way across the sky. Beneath it, a wry tag is printed in Estonian and English: 'The Sorrow Flies Away'.

DAY 647 (10 APRIL): TALLINN
At the mint-new youth hostel on Uus tanav, where I am lodging directly opposite the Lithuanian Embassy, Stephanie and Stephen arrive just in time to see the dramatic pictures from Baghdad of Saddam's statue being toppled. 'They won't know when to get out,' predicts Stephen.

On this our last night in Tallinn before the two S's head west for a few weeks in Berlin and I continue north to the end of my circuitous line, we are on the lookout for an authentically Estonian dining experience. After a while we happen upon a dimly lit establishment that looks like a student hangout, a place specialising in beer that reluctantly serves food as well. This will have to do, we concur, with looks that stop a fair way short of out-and-out enthusiasm.

On our way to an empty table on the far side of the room, I see a lonely-looking piano. Flipping its lid, and to warm up my fingers as much as anything, I riff off 16 bars of *Memphis Tennessee* (don't ask me why) before gliding across to our chosen table. Before we reach it, a round of applause breaks out from the student crowd at the bar, and I bow low.

Chuffed though I am at this burst of appreciation, I notice it is not followed by any special effort at instituting table service or subsequent reductions in the cost of food or drink. But our attitude tonight is devil-take-the-hindmost and, as soon as Stephen returns to the table, drinks clutched in his hands, we offer up toasts and get on with enjoying the evening.

Had anyone back in Ward 13 prophesied that a dozen years into my blank future I would be spending an evening in the warm company of friends old and new at an Estonian bistro, I might have paraphrased the Eurythmics' Annie Lennox and shot back: 'Sweet dreams are *not* made of this.' But, having travelled the world and the seven seas, here am I to disagree.

Chapter 23

HERE BEGINNETH THE AFTERLIFE

(To every thing there is … a time …)
to break down, and a time to build up;

Ecclesiastes 3:3

1991-2001

To relate the story of life as a paraplegic from the early days of my hospital stay up to the time of my Eurasian expedition is like chronicling a second life. It is certainly one so dramatically different in its externals that people who have come into my life since then have been known to wonder what I must have been like before. The answer to that, say those who knew me then, is … very much the same except taller.

After those first months, when the shock wore off and the circulatory system stabilised, all the hurdles on the track to recovery were mental. The first barrier to get over was the thought *My life has been ruined.*

Surmounting that obstacle gave me much needed confidence. I was back in the race. Learning old skills anew and fresh ones, too, reminded me that this period was not just recovering from a life-threatening trauma but preparing for the something (just what I couldn't begin to imagine) that would be my future life.

These days, when some immigration form is shoved in front of me that demands to know my height, I'm always tempted to jot down '142 centimetres'. But that is only the most obvious change between my first and second incarnations. It takes several months to adapt to the whole caboodle of physical reconfigurations (but, note, what matters is the adaptation, not the changes themselves: in the end, mind—its strength and singleness—is all).

How did the crisis leave me physically? First, those stainless steel metal rods they implanted in my spinal column back in 1991 are still there and will remain there, if only because it is good to avoid unnecessary pain. A scar runs down my back, also from the operation. My feet are still red raw, the toes clawed and ingrown. I suffer from increased flatulence; and unless I do a lot of pushing about—another reason that travel is good for my health—a 'wheelie's paunch' develops, marring my naturally athletic film-star looks.

Occasionally I surprise people by moving my legs, but this is no party trick: the doctors at the Austin told me that on average I had 3 per cent of the motor power necessary to walk. (The strength in my right leg is slightly greater than that in my left.) The only use of being able to move a limb to this modest degree is that it keeps me in my place, not tempted into the forbidden paths of bipedal perambulation by having an out-of-chair experience.

I can't wiggle my toes any more, but then how much time do *you* spend doing that? As for keeping in time to music, I find tapping my fingers just as satisfying.

Self-image remains as important as ever, but in the end what difference has the great descent caused to my physical envelope? After all that has been done, and said, it's just a change of posture. Make that two changes of posture. In the daytime the change is there for all to see, but my slumbering form is also different.

In an earlier chapter I remarked that in hospital the spinally injured return to babyhood. Toilet training begins all over again—this time involving quite inventive ways of doing the basic functions, which most of us think we've left behind when we celebrate that birthday with three candles on the cake. The lifters and turners even teach you how to protect yourself while sleeping. They counsel you on the importance of sleeping on your side (because to spend the whole night, or even hours, on your back is to risk exactly the problem, bedsores or pressure sores, that plagued me during my wanderings through the Caucasus and Iran).

My initial reaction when told I must learn how to turn myself, without waking up, was to scoff. I shot back at the messengers, 'We don't wake up when we toss and turn in our sleep, so how am I ever going to get a good night's sleep again?' Their reply was along the lines of, 'Forget tossing your body about, but by levering yourself onto your opposite hip you can easily go from lying on your right to lying on your left and within seconds you'll be back in the Land of Nod.'

All my scepticism was unfounded, I am happy to say. The turners knew exactly what they were talking about, and the technique has now become second nature: you might say I could do it in my sleep.

But the best coping mechanisms for a particular spinal patient always depend on how much physical function has returned, and there are limits to that. Unless there has been a sea change in understanding of the condition since I was at the Austin more than a decade ago, those limits are usually reached (or, rather, whatever regrowth is ever going to occur does so) within a month of the event that has inflicted the injury.

Psychically, though—the way your brain makes sense of your life and its potentials—healing seems not to begin until there is no prospect of further physical regrowth. It is as if the mind cannot accept your 'new body' and what must be until what is becomes truly unalterable.

Hospitals are not ideal seedbeds for rehabilitation. The sights and sounds, and sometimes even smells, of suffering tend to depress the hardiest spirit—and a ward full of people whose vitality is reeling from a heavy blow is a ward full of fragile spirits. And yet, if it is true that there is always someone worse off than yourself, a hospital is likely to be where you two will meet up.

The patient who had the biggest effect on my outlook was my next-bed neighbour Paul. He was nineteen when, one Friday night while his parents were out, a mate came round to his place and suggested they go for a drive (in the mate's car). Seeing his friend was drunk, Paul tried to talk him out of the idea, instead suggesting that they order a pizza and eat in. But the mate was deaf to persuasion so Paul went along for the ride. When his friend drove the car up a tree, Paul suffered upper-spinal lesions which left him a quadriplegic, unable to feed himself or even move his head without causing further, and possibly fatal, injury.

The mate escaped from the wreck without a scratch and never once visited him in the ensuing months. With the wisdom of hindsight, it is possible to see that the distress wasn't all on Paul's side, and I can only hope they reconciled in later years, for both their sakes.

But Paul's hospital life made mine feel like the equivalent of a hiccup. He was in constant pain, which he bore manfully. His head was gripped in a type of vice called tongs, preventing all movement, and whenever they were adjusted he was subjected to teeth-grinding agony. Still in pain, he had to deal with police visits designed to prosecute his 'mate'. And every day he was confronted with the sight of his distraught parents and other relatives struggling to cope with the impact of his tragedy on their lives.

Without meaning to do so, Paul taught me how much of a relief it is to have no one else to blame. It's a strange blessing to realise that, having survived an attempt to take your own life, you will never have to bear the burden of blaming someone else for the way you now are.

Thinking about Paul, and how I at least had no one to blame for being where I found myself, led naturally to the next mental stepping-stone in my recovery, the thought *So why blame yourself either?* Loath though I am to pretend to any 'expertise' on suicide, I did come to the considered view that only a few cases of self-annihilation are heroic, and only a few are acts of cowardice. Most are deeds born of desperation, by no means acts of free choice.

They are the result of decisions taken under enormous mental and emotional pressure that make them seem the only possible 'choice' but are in fact the opposite of what choice signifies: selecting one course among a range of alternatives.

When I tried to end it all, I was mad—as I have since come to accept. People thrown off mental balance are not held by the law to be responsible for their actions; and I cannot respect any moral law that would make them so. Another thing that those who are quick to condemn their fellow human beings' weakness do not seem to appreciate is that suicide attempts are not entirely due to an emotional impulse. The mind in pain provides its own rationales, and they appear as compelling and real as debt on your credit card (and sometimes more logical). To a mind under siege, ending the endless onslaught of pain can appear a thoroughly rational response to an apparently uncaring world. Our self-image is renewed by what others tell us about ourselves: if they say only bad things or nothing at all, eventually we will turn in on ourselves. It bears repeating: humans, like other creatures, will instinctively seek out the least painful course.

That is why, as every jailer knows, prolonged isolation will break almost anyone's spirit, and why even people who go into jail protesting their innocence can be so disheartened that they take their own lives. I am thinking now of the Aboriginal teenagers whose deaths in custody sparked a Royal Commission more than a decade ago.

Over the years such a surprising number of people have told me of their suicidal thoughts—people whom I would never have suspected of these dark stabs of self-reproach and self-belittlement—that I have come to believe everybody has a greater or lesser breaking point. I am not saying that everyone thinks of rejecting the gift of life, but that at some point we each feel that life has been diminished or devalued, and that some of us will see no point to the stretch of existence immediately ahead of us. Many of us will bide our time waiting for the point to emerge; but a few cannot, that is all.

Having come through my ordeal, I am not about to trivialise the feelings of those few by saying, 'Wait around and things will sooner or later change for the better.' Maybe they won't. Where words run out, no advice can be as effective as a touch of compassion.

To try talking someone out of suicide would be hypocritical, after what I have done. But, for those readers going through their own hell, I would put one picture in front of you that was unimagined by me then. If your 'death wish' is really a cry for attention and affection, and not a response to acute fear as mine was, picture the faces of your closest loved ones (in my case, my parents) bending over you and contorted with grief. No words of mine can alter the depth of your despair, I'm not that presumptuous, but be prepared to know that when you damage your tired unwanted self you will not only be evoking pity but horrifying those you care for most.

And then, if you must go ahead, know that others you care for (without ever admitting it to yourself) may misunderstand and feel cut off from you. When you've attempted suicide and 'failed', you don't really want visitors. And it was odd how the topic itself was sensitively avoided on several occasions at the Austin when I was visited by my uncle and an old family friend. At times such as those, looks of sympathy count for more than words anyway.

But a brother of mine never visited, and the reason he didn't was out of religious conviction. Influenced by his wife, he had converted to Catholicism during my absence and felt it necessary to disapprove of my courting mortal sin by staying away. Thirteen years after the event, I am still struggling to see his absence as nothing blameworthy but an act of fidelity to his creed—doing what he understood to be the right thing by his faith. We have never yet spoken about it.

Once the first—and necessary—stage of self-pity has passed, the mind is like a child ready to enter upon a new stage in its physical growth: incredibly receptive to stimuli. In my case, the lifter's timely observation that 95 per cent of spinally injured patients go on to enjoy productive lives spurred just such a revolution in my own thoughts.

In my first few months at the Austin it never occurred to me that I had a future—I couldn't picture what that might look like—and the mere mention by a casual visitor of life in the future tense would plunge me into a depressive state that could last for hours. In those days my unhappiness manifested itself in bleak meditation. Normally, people can't stop me talking (it's my besetting fault, just ask my former friends) but in those days I uttered hardly a word. My personality had been turned inside out. The post-traumatic stress and re-traumatising outcome of my suicide attempt so shattered my oneness that the months-long battle to become whole again was fought in intense silence (and, while that is a battle no one else can fight for you, it does help to have allies).

And then out of the blue, one May morning a simple thought washed up in my mind, *I'm alive, so what am I going to do about it?*

The initial answer—and I recognised the humour in it instantaneously—was, *Well, I could always do nothing.* And so, in theory, I could have. This was Australia, after all, a pioneer of the welfare state. Laziness has always appealed to me as a way of life. In practice, the problem with doing nothing is that it's so incredibly hard to sustain over time. (Believe me, I've tried.)

Of course, my mind turned to the 5 per cent of patients who, according to that inspired lifter, go on to become vegetables. Thinking of them, death once again seemed preferable to a meaningless life.

A word at the right time changed everything or, more precisely, the way I looked at everything. It fell from Dr Ungar's lips when he cited

Montesquieu's oft-quoted observation about seeing life as a glass half full or half empty. Whether the wise doctor shrewdly chose his moment to impart this wisdom, or said it without knowing I was ready to be nourished by it, is now beyond recall. But this one remark did inspire me to concentrate on what I had rather than what I no longer had, and my thinking grew more positive in the ensuing weeks.

Ungar also took time to reintroduce me to the outside world. Only now did news that the Gulf War had ended come to my notice, without the news having any repercussions on me. A television above my bed would be turned on in the evening, and I began to follow events at home and abroad.

During childhood music lessons, I was always fascinated by the tick-tock of the metronome that sat on my teacher's piano lid. If you could imagine a metronome synchronised with the vibrations of grief, as I now could, it would spasm ever less frequently as the distance from the grief-inducing event receded.

There can be no forced marches on the long road back, whatever we have lost, whether it be something tangible or intangible—our parents, our limbs or the person closest to our heart. At the point of no return the mind and spirit adjust themselves, not callously but protectively, to going without the lost element (and going *on* without it, what's more). Spirit and mind cherish the missing element and absorb its nourishing ingredients, making us stronger, more whole and sometimes better human beings than we were before.

A few people become withdrawn and self-absorbed and remain that way; most others, as the lifter told me, end up using the past as a building block for the future rather than rejecting it as so much worthless rubble. A warped sense of humour helps. Considering the statistical certainty that the way we live is going to produce some spinally injured people every year—given society's stunning array of disablers, including cars, heavy machinery, diving pools and mosh pits—the thought arises, *What is the ideal age at which to break your backbone?* My answer would be, *About 36.* Why? Because you're old enough to have lived one life, yet young enough to embark on another. Those who know me best will wince and refer to that warped sense of humour but, as with all humour, its deployment can have serious benefits, and the benefit here lies in 'owning' the new reality, accustoming your mind to the unalterable fact.

Positive thoughts now found an hospitable dwelling in my recharged brain, where for months the sole residents had been foreboding and negativity. The strongest chain of thinking began with the recollection that, during my travelling life while still totally able-bodied, I had climbed five mountains as well as the pyramids of Meroë, Sudan.

These ascents I accomplished not with ski poles and crampons but by good old-fashioned step-after-step trudging. *Millions of others, who could do the same, haven't,* I reminded myself, *so what if I never do that again*? Pele will never again play international soccer; Dennis Lillee never bowl for Australia again; Muhammad Ali's boxing days are behind him. But their lives do not become worthless: they move on (to use that excruciating phrase). A fully accomplished life means you're dead already. Other fields remain to be conquered.

That said, my life is not a template for anyone else's (the decisions and directions in it are not even ones I would necessarily take again if I had my druthers). But I don't regret the episode that changed my life that warm March night in 1991. What is done is done. While I didn't want to be alive when I came to, and to see my parents' faces made me feel that they couldn't have been more grief-stricken if I had 'succeeded', now I see things differently. Regret is as futile as blame. Along with a Lamborghini in the drive and a jacuzzi in the bathroom, it is a luxury I cannot afford.

Survivors will know that, every time in our lives when the emotional scales have become so unbalanced that we feel things can never be normal again, time has recalibrated them and put things right. Despair is the darkest hour in the long night of the soul. If we endure it, no matter how gloomy the void, everything will resume its proper shape and colour in time. New hope always dawns. If we can wait long enough, the first rays of daylight will reach us, but, if we cannot, the night-time never ends.

Just when the relentless tide of ill fortune would finally ebb away was only one of the uncertainties I had to deal with—but that was another lesson I needed to learn: how to handle uncertainty. Recalling that my troubles first surfaced in the form of a panic attack, I could now see that in future I must welcome uncertainty as a stimulating challenge to do better, not treat it as a threat.

Early in my reporting career, I had viewed 'creative tension' as essential to converting an ordinary job performance into one of which I could be proud. Somehow, as the years wore on, I sought more certainty (perhaps that's what people are really talking about when they refer to getting more conservative with age). With experience, I can now distinguish between hope and expectation. Part of the reason that the invasion of Kuwait hit me so hard was that I had a fixed expectation that work in Bahrain would pan out in a certain satisfying way (which it did not), and that the region would remain stable enough for daily routines to become a source of reassurance (which they did not).

Maybe I was unlucky. But what should I learn from that? Only that Sod's Law is no respecter of frontiers. Shit happens. As a good friend has recently reminded me, an inflexible attachment to plans is the royal road to disappointment and discouragement, if not worse. Travelling Eurasia, I savoured its delights in advance by plotting out a detailed itinerary, but then I would recall the lesson that facts change and plans must be flexible enough to fit the most up to date of them. The catastrophe of September 11 served to reinforce the lesson but, by then, my war on terror would be won.

Words make a universe of sense all by themselves. It was inevitable that wheelchair sports such as rugby would be rechristened 'murderball' to accommodate the Australian penchant for exaggeration. And, given the equally Australian penchant for the diminutive term, wheelchair users sound much more approachable as 'wheelies'. But, to the best of my knowledge, it was one of my contemporaries on Ward 13 who came up with the brilliant idea of putting non-wheelies in their place by calling them 'uprights'. It makes bipeds sound like stick-in-the-muds. If a silence lasted too long, and he sensed people's thoughts getting to them, this cheery soul would call out, 'Hey, out in the corridor, there goes an upright.' The upright would never get the joke, of course, which was one more reason to laugh.

By separating them from us at that stage, my fellow inmate helped buttress *our* sense of community, which was a great service to everyone there on the way to eventual reintegration into the wider community. Calling them uprights and us wheelies entrenched in my mind, at least, the naturalness of our method of getting about. They walk; I roll.

Only much later, when living in the wider community, would it occur to me that in some ways we who move about on wheels are the lucky ones. Imagine spending your life on a bicycle: it would have its drawbacks (negotiating staircases being the most obvious): but on the flat we can actually move faster than most of you uprights, whereas downhill we just speed away, you really can't keep up. Uphill, of course, is a different kettle of eels but, if we are prepared to wait long enough, someone will always, eventually, come along and give us a push.

What I went through in the Mideast and afterwards inoculated me against fear—not in all its guises or when it comes to the dread of personal rejection—but physical fear, certainly, and it took away some of the fear of dying. No one can say how the approach of that ultimately inescapable event will find me. But I feel that, so long as the physical pain associated with dying isn't prolonged, I will face it with more equanimity than would have been the case if this crisis hadn't thrust my head inside the lion's jaw once already.

For the most part, we shrink instinctively from the idea that death is part of life. Our society does everything to keep the day at bay, as if it were alien to the process of life rather than its culmination. Seen properly, though, being aware of death should sharpen our sense of purpose in living. Coming anywhere near to forsaking the gift of life is bound to make you treasure it more.

But I have no taste for morbidity. The Taoist philosophy of neither approaching too close to danger nor giving it too wide a berth is one I find appealing. The key to successful travel in the post-September 11 world is a realistic appraisal of danger. Avoid countries at war or degenerating into anarchy, but don't stay at home in the belief that the ceiling won't cave in.

Crisis certainly creates two kinds of opportunity: the opportunity to act, and the opportunity to reflect about life at a deeper and more rewarding level. What did I learn from my horror stretch of 1990–91? To accept that, however happy and content you are today, rough patches *do* lie ahead. We are born in crisis; we die in crisis. So it should come as no surprise if we have to undergo a few crises during the bit in between.

One clue to contentment as a non-walker is to stop chasing a cure. From long-ago lectures at teacher's college I recall that one definition of good health is being well adapted to your environment.

In the West hardly anyone needs convincing that those of us in wheelchairs are not sick. But if you're not sick, and regard your new life as one in which walking just plays no part, then the notion of a 'cure' is downright illogical. My mother is not reconciled to this: she has occasionally said, and obviously clings to the hope, that one day I'll walk again. With all due respect, I couldn't give a tinker's cuss whether I do or not. Perhaps I cannot afford to waste the emotional energy necessary to invest it in a hope that may prove fruitless.

This viewpoint is one I don't extend to people who are clearly at odds with their environment, and in that sense unhealthy. If I had HIV I would be hoping, praying and agitating for an AIDS cure. But these days paraplegia probably won't kill you, provided you survive the trigger event. So wanting to walk as desperately as the late Superman Christopher Reeve did only strikes me as detracting from the enjoyment of life as wheelies find it now, and as it will quite possibly continue to be for decades.

This is not to wish failure on any of those people working towards a 'cure'. For all I know, my attitude is a minority one, and anyway to restore full bodily function to the disabled is surely a creditable goal.

In mid-June I was transferred to the rehabilitation ward. This was progress but, as with all moves, it took some time to settle in. Our days were busier now: there was a physical workout at ten in the morning, followed by toileting (training the bowel, how to avoid 'emergencies' through proper nutrition) and manual rehab in what I disdainfully called 'the sheltered workshop'.

I was lumbered with two hours a day of woodwork classes in the carpentry room. In vain did I tell the German immigrant pensioner who marvelled at the refusal of timber to be moulded once it was in my hands that none of this was news to me.

Long ago, at high school, an even more long-suffering woodwork teacher, Mr Eversham, gave me a mark of 49 in the subject. I recall him telling me that he could have justified giving me 51 but that might have encouraged me to think I showed some promise in the subject, and he didn't want to give me false hope.

This well-meant effort to build meaningful structure into our day was generally but not entirely pointless. Computer lessons at the Austin developed skills that have been of considerable benefit in the afterlife.

Sport was not neglected: the rehab centre had its own tennis court, and I nearly kept fit adapting my serviceable old game to the new conditions. Back in the gym, team games and developing upper-arm strength on pommel horses and a click-counter device took me all the way back to secondary school again.

The physiotherapists, whom I had first come to know early in the piece when they would spend an hour at a time 'ranging' my arm to ensure that muscle tone wasn't lost for good, now focused on my possible aptitude for non-wheelchair movement. After fitting calipers and hanging me bat-like from beams, they had their answer: aptitude for NWM, 'none'.

Rehabilitation was to Ward 13 as senior high is to junior: the giver of greater latitude and responsibility prior to being jettisoned into the real world 'out there'. Now, for the first time, an attempt was made to build fun into our routine. One Friday night, two of the more personable female nurses (and I believe they had been chosen for just this quality) arrived in dark sunglasses, dressed up as the Blues Brothers, and screened the original cult movie, transforming the normal boring round with scenes of unbridled hilarity.

Occasionally the rehab unit would venture out en masse—once, I recall, to a steakhouse in the neighbouring suburb of Ivanhoe. While our exploration of this alien terrain called the outside world offered us joys unknown to the Rover on Mars, I did feel typecast, vaguely sensing that if things continued in this direction the rest of my life was going to be spent exclusively among wheelies. This, I think, was the first stirring of that healthy impulse to rejoin the larger community.

In glorious late September, seven months after admission to the Austin, the long-awaited day of discharge arrived. Initially it was great to be 'home', under my parents' roof way out of town in tranquil seaside Corinella.

Although I had been adjudged too well to stay in hospital, this was still a perilous stage of my recovery. I remained on tablets to keep my moods stable, as the transition to life outside after months in an institution can be as unsettling for a hospital outpatient as it notoriously is for ex-prisoners.

October and November were months of quiet and steady recovery, but early in December the pills I was taking—added to the lack of varied and stimulating activity in my life—took their toll. Over a few days, I had a reaction to the haloperidol capsules. Supposed to keep me calm, they had precisely the opposite effect. I would threaten violence and eventually an ambulance arrived at the doorstep to return me to the Austin, accompanied by a police escort.

The drug reaction had been characterised by uncontrollable jitters, my hands and body shaking as my brain was seized by wild and sometimes hallucinatory fears. This was worse in its way than the breakdown itself, certainly more frightening for Mum and Dad to be around me. I spent a couple of weeks back on Ward 13. Sadly, it was on this second visit to the Austin that Dr Ungar, to whom I owe so much, collapsed while on his rounds one day and was moved in a coma to Ward 24, where he died just before Christmas. His glass had emptied; mine was gradually refilling.

Early in 1992, as my parents and I recognised that sepulchral Corinella was not an ideal place for someone my age to recuperate and move forward, we heard about a nursing home exclusively for residents with broken spines.

St Jude's, in the south-eastern Melbourne suburb of Chadstone, was home to men and women from age 20 to 70, ranging from the very active ones—who were free to head off to Chadstone shopping centre unaccompanied—to a couple of elderly inmates with advanced dementia. For some reason, at that juncture the prospect of living in a nursing home, especially one dedicated to the patron saint of lost causes, tickled my funnybone no end.

The actual experience wasn't nearly so amusing. The regimentation was more inflexible than life at the Austin. Breakfast was standard fare issued at a standard time, without privacy. If you were lucky, toast and tea and tepid soup were served at 5 pm: if you were detained somewhere else for fifteen minutes, the humiliating threat of going to bed hungry was held over you—and occasionally made good. What else can I say? At my age, one soon tires of bingo.

Three months at St Jude's had what I call a positively negative effect, giving me all the incentive I needed to move into the community earlier than anyone had foreseen.

The problems of finding a suitable place in which to live independently as a wheelchair user are complicated by the general practice among real estate agents of not identifying which properties are accessible. They also send staff out to meet you who haven't a clue whether there is a step at the threshold and, if there is, what it will take to surmount it.

There is no point in arranging a 'view' of a flat that has a step of 60 centimetres' depth (a sheer drop) with no ramp. Much less than that and I can grab both the walls and lever myself into the apartment, provided the floor is level from there on in, with no ghastly dips and perilous obstructions to negotiate.

On occasion a flummoxed agent would try to retrieve the situation by offering to supply a ramp, under terms to be agreed, but sometimes the angle at which such a ramp would have to be placed could not have avoided obstructing the driveway. Too steep, and it would be of no practical use. 'If I can't get inside, then I can't live here.' I remember drilling this basic fact of life into more than one head seemingly unable to wrap itself around this, to me, bleeding obvious reality.

After a couple of weeks spent scouring the suburbs, I found my perfect flat in the suburb of Carnegie. Of course, like most house- or flat-dwellers, I just knew it was the one. I was elated to find somewhere I could call my own—even if I was renting—and this, along with my new work situation, made a vast difference to my quality of life, mental health and happiness in the succeeding years.

Before being sent home from the Austin again at Christmas, someone had recommended that, rather than take haloperidol (which I refused to go back on), I should visit a good psychoanalyst. Even with my doubts about how useful that would be, I submitted. Anything was better than more tablets with their untold side effects. This particular psychoanalyst was a calm, quietly spoken sixty-something with an established practice in a solid 1920s house in the suburb of Auburn.

Much to my discredit, I cannot remember his name. Suffice to say he was one of those avuncular types with the all-too-rare gift of timing who knows just when progress is possible. Halfway through our eighth hour together, and seeing that I was ready, he put the golden question: Would I like to go back to work?

I would love to sub-edit, I said, but if I went back to my old paper, the *Age*, where scores of my former co-workers knew me as an upright (I had initiated him into the jargon), what would they think on seeing me in a wheelchair? Wouldn't I have to explain my past, about which I remained hugely embarrassed, to each and every one of them?

'No,' he said. 'You will find people are very understanding.' And so they were. In the next four years, during which I worked every week on the newspaper's Sunday publication, not one colleague ever asked how I came to be in a chair. Given the insatiable curiosity of journalists as a species, it makes my hair stand on end just to think of it. But journalists can also claim a higher-than-average ratio of caring individuals within their ranks, and it is passionate caring that attracts many to the profession in the first place. (As a more aware individual now, it would amaze me if most of those colleagues didn't know, broadly speaking, how I came to be a paraplegic, but their consideration will forever be appreciated by me.)

Gaining access to the big red-brick building on Spencer Street called for a modicum of understanding on the part of security guards, who put out a ramp for me each Saturday, and other mornings as more shifts came my way. In the newsroom itself, new computer platforms were installed in 1993, with their own inclined edges which made it possible for me to work among, not apart from, the other sub-editors.

Apart from a love of the work itself, I knew why I was coming back, but never confided it to any of my colleagues lest they laugh out loud. Not only could I practise a craft I cherished, but the past two years had taught me in the harshest conceivable way that without the social outlet provided by work I would probably relapse into madness. The pit of insanity was one from which I might not clamber out a second time, and work, along with the social interaction that came with it, would keep me sane.

For the first time I thought how lucky, or providential, it was that my hands—with which I earn my living—had been undamaged. Had I been a footballer, or a dancer, the loss of my legs would have been a much more grievous blow.

Since those grim days of 1991 I have practised my craft in various cities of the world, from London to Hong Kong to Johannesburg.

I have to say that the disappearance of my mental problems about the same time as I resumed work remains as much a mystery to me now as it did then. I can think of no external reason why the oppressive weight of negativity, which had lingered months after the trigger event and right through to my second release from hospital after the haloperidol scare, dispersed just then like clouds vanishing before the dawn of a peerless new day. But it did, allowing me to look my new life in the face and relish the challenges of reconnecting with the community from which I had been isolated for almost a decade.

It was a mercy that, by the time my best friend found out what had happened to me, hospital visits were a thing of the past and I was on good terms with myself again. Nevertheless, I couldn't escape the knowledge that it caused great pain to Neil, whom I had known since we were eight-year-olds. True, we had drifted apart while I was overseas and it was he I had decided to spare 'the burden of seeing me as I now knew myself to be', helpless as I felt, on returning to Australia in September 1990.

Newly reintegrated into the community, it was in the back of my mind that one day I would probably run into him, his wife or their twins, in a shopping centre somewhere and there would be brief shock and embarrassment all round. Still, as I was not yet reconciled to my new life and felt a lingering stigma about being in a wheelchair, I was not going to take the initiative to get back in touch. Then, alerted through a mutual friend on Boxing Day 1993 that I was back in town, Neil rang me at work. We arranged to meet up for what would be the first time in almost ten years, although we had kept in touch by phone right through till 1988.

Our reunion took place in the first week of the New Year, 1994. An hour before he was due to come over, adopting that technique I would later use with my ex-employers in Bahrain, I rang to break the news as gently, and as close to the projected time of meeting, as I could. We adjourned to my local pub, where it took two hours to convey what had happened to me. As I came to the point of recounting the suicide attempt, Neil's eyes brimmed with tears (and he is not an overly emotional man), reminding me once again, as had been the case with family members, that I had caused grief and sadness. When that happens to people who matter to you, it is not a feeling you would wish upon anyone else.

From this point on, my best friend became part of my life again, for which I will always be grateful.

It would be foolish to recommend the wheelchair life to uprights, but it does have its moments.

Only people with similarly sick minds will relish the scene when, with one wheelchair just back from being repaired and another still on hire, I visited the local shops one day in 1995 while looking after Neil's twin sons during the school holidays. After Brad and I raced each other down to the shopping strip in the chairs, I explained to his brother, Ryan, what we were about to do. Then I told Brad to get up out of his chair, in full view of a mother and daughter just approaching us along the footpath, and walk into the bakery outside which we had parked our respective chariots.

As he did so, I turned to Ryan and shouted, 'That's amazing. The boy's never walked before. It's a miracle!' You should have seen the mother and daughter: they nearly keeled over with shock. As I say, this is a prank that it takes a truly sick mind to appreciate. But, oh, that's another benefit of being in a chair: when you're only 142 centimetres tall, people never expect you to grow up—and for my part I'm determined not to let them down.

Another time, I was playing backyard basketball and, in our heroic but unsuccessful attempt to complete a slam dunk, I cannoned into the garage, unable to put on the brakes or otherwise slow myself down after my mighty throw. A few days later, a taxidriver helping me into his vehicle and noticing my feet swathed in bandages commiserated, 'I see you're in a wheelchair because you broke your foot.' 'No,' I grimaced, 'I broke my foot because I'm in a wheelchair.'

By the mid-1990s the *Sunday Age* had developed its own brand image to the point where it received the ultimate accolade—dramatisation in a television series, *Mercury*. An ABC series, it took a revealing look inside a Melbourne Sunday paper's newsroom, and which one it was out of the two possibilities did not exactly come wrapped in thick disguise. The foreign editor in this series (one job I would love to have had, ironically) was a character in a wheelchair—based on guess who—and portrayed as rather headstrong.

Later that year I received an ultimate accolade of my own, winning a Walkley Award, Australia's most prestigious journalistic prize, for the best headlines published in a metropolitan daily newspaper that year. The awards ceremony was held at Brisbane's Hilton Hotel. A colleague who attended the ceremony and was at my table pointed out that the ceremony's organisers had contrived to get a ramp installed up to the stage. I smiled in recognition that this meant my chances of taking off the statuette looked promising, but was anxious not to jinx myself by reading too much into it. When my name was announced it came as one of the great thrills of my life, and I was up that ramp as quick as my wheels could carry me to shake the hand of Bill Hayden, the then Governor-General.

The award was not just gratifying in the normal way of such things. It also gave me an oddly humbling sense that, whatever had happened in the past, my second-life work was worthwhile, and that, after 1990 and all that, I had lived for something.

At the same time I felt due for a break, a change of pace, so, taking the view that it is always best to leave when you're in top form, I returned to Britain early in 1996. Six more months of sub-editing on Fleet Street newspapers followed. This time the main strings to my career bow were the *Sunday Telegraph* and the *Independent*.

Professionally, this was a restless time of life. My visa didn't permit me to stay in Britain for more than six months, so I returned to the *Age* to write editorials. But that, too, left me chafing at the bit, and in 1997 I landed a job sub-editing on the *South China Morning Post* in Hong Kong. A memorable year was in store, with the British colony reverting to Chinese rule that July under the terms of an agreement hammered out back in the 1980s between Beijing and Margaret Thatcher's government.

In 1998 I took to the road again. This wasn't the first time I had travelled in the chair. I'd been to the Philippines, then to South Africa and, in 1998, I visited ten countries in Southern and East Africa. For the second time in my life, I crossed Africa from east to west—from Zanzibar to Namibia—only to find that Livingstone had already achieved the feat.

This 1998 foray taught me that, far from solo wheelchair travel being too much of a strain, it inspires you to discover techniques for overcoming the most common impediments to a smooth trip. Africa offered the first proof for my conjecture that seeing the world from a wheelchair should not be insuperably more difficult than seeing it on foot, and confirmed that I had the personal resources to undertake another long-haul journey.

Like all good journeys, this was one of self-discovery, too, and I discovered that people almost everywhere are very accepting: they do see past the wheel casing and metal housing to the person. Seated with fellow travellers in a bar at the end of the day in some remote corner of Malawi, the consciousness of physical difference between us quickly seeped away. Sometimes I would find myself drawing attention to it, but only as part of that venting of humour which embraced many other topics.

'I'm glad to get here early in the evening,' I would say to them, 'because I'm paralytic when I arrive: you have to work at it all night.'

Or 'You know why my friends don't like playing cricket with me? Because when they get me out I refuse to walk.' (I play that one just for the look on people's face *before* the punchline.)

The way I look at it, fairly freewheeling humour is a boon that prevents us taking ourselves too seriously—and that is a snare to be side-stepped at all costs. Some of the funniest cracks came from colleagues on the paper. One of them, a sports sub-editor named Mark, on seeing me carry a precariously balanced tray of snacks and coffees up from the canteen, quipped, 'Here comes Meals on Wheels.' (I nearly dropped the tray, which would have served him right.)

Another time, when a stranger visited the office and asked, 'Where does Ken sit?', my workmate Seamus replied, quick as a flash, 'Everywhere.'

Considering what I have been through, there is no point in upholding some taboo that preserves a fear I have long since overcome. Political correctness as a sign that you care about other people's sensitivities is something I respect, but not the avoidance of certain words *per se*. For some people, 'cripple' is a no-no: well, not for me. Able to move most anywhere I want, by a perfectly good mode of personal transportation, I know who the real cripples are. They are those people bound up so tight by the fetters of their resentment at life's cruel twists that they are mean with themselves, and thus incapable of relaxing and giving of themselves to others. I feel sad for them.

Back home in 1999 I decided to use my international travel experience and media contacts to apply for work as a sub-editor wherever they would have me. Clearly, I felt no sense of alienation whatever country I went to work in, which is why I cast a wide net, but nevertheless it was greatly reassuring to have a 'pad' to come home to.

After some time, this round of applications yielded a bite: from Japan's *Asahi Evening News*, the English-language publication of *Asahi Shimbun*, which sold just eight million copies a day and was tearing its proverbial hair out because it was only coming second in its market.

First the *Asahi* management asked me to do a subbing test, which was faxed over and completed within the set hour before I faxed it back to head office. Upon being told, 24 hours later, that I had done well enough to be offered the job, I chose that moment to bite the bullet and mention my sedentary status. To say anything earlier might have led to there being no subbing test to sit or even to a rejection on grounds that I would forever suspect were paralysis-based rather than merit-based, but now was the time to pipe up. After all, if I got to Tokyo and the office were inaccessible, bad vibes would flow both ways.

The sound of an editor biting his lip across 8000 kilometres was quite unmistakable, if scarcely audible. But the Japanese don't pride themselves on courtesy for nothing, and Mr Asano sounded very concerned. 'Things will be difficult for you. How can we help you?' he said. Going onto the front foot, I pointed out that he need have no fears about my ability to move round the office in a wheelchair, provided the building itself and the toilets were accessible. If I could take an English-speaker along with me to the nearest real estate agent, that would be a great help, because finding lodgings was of prime importance. Then I could safely be left on my own to arrange for a taxi to bring me to work every morning.

Asano-san sounded sympathetic but still faced a conceptual problem with his management colleagues. And then, at two o'clock one February morning in 1999, he phoned back with an ingenious solution. Explaining that the paper was starting up an international division and had a guy filing sports copy from New York, he asked whether I would like to sub-edit from home. Every day, features and some news articles would be sent for me to edit and send back—all by email. When I asked how much work there would be, a minimum was set and *Asahi* honoured its word generously for the next two years. During that time I settled into the life of an open-collar worker, or e-lancer, and would sometimes smile to myself on realising that, had I not been in the wheelchair, the work would never have come in this form.

In April 2001, just before my Eurasian crossing, I was a guest speaker at a conference of the American Copy Editors' Society held in Long Beach, California. There I reprised my *Asahi* experience of telecommuting for the benefit of America's finest. Life No. 2 was still looking up.

Beware of those who would have you believe everything is rosier now that they are spinally injured. Good luck to them, I say, but let's not kid ourselves. And yet … I have often said that if a remedy for my paralysis appeared tomorrow I am not sure I would take the cure. If you genuinely don't miss walking, or rather see it as just one form of locomotion, why would you go back to it?

When I survey the past two years, and then the past fifteen, and even (whisper it) 50, and think how far I've come, and the wealth of things I have seen, suffered and done, I'm not mad enough to say I wouldn't have done anything differently. To take that view would imply an enormous love of suffering combined with an inability to learn from my mistakes. But I am generally happier with the way things in my life are now than I ever expected to be, while having acquired enough wisdom not to want to examine too closely just why this is so.

The breakdown didn't make me an all-round better person, but it did make me a more aware one, and that's an improvement in one direction. To be truthful, it is the only improvement I have been able to detect, and others must be asked about any reverses that offset it.

Recovering from the breakdown was neither smooth nor steady but fitful, with fully as many obstacles, speed bumps, 'Wrong Way—Go Back' signs and detours as wheelchair users confront every day. It took me two years after the descent until I felt good about myself and wholly at ease with my newly configured physique. (Fortunately, the old one was not so great that decades of mourning were called for.)

In the healing I received not so much wisdom as a stock of new insights, amounting to a better appreciation of what moves the world. Presumptuous and preposterous as it sounds, I cannot help wondering when people will come to see that the strongest forces in the universe are not weapons of mass destruction but abstract nouns: hope and fear, compassion and anger, pride and shame, love and hate. If we could control these, rather than the other way round, we would be right to consider ourselves masters of the universe, rather than the cleverest fish in this most beautiful of ponds.

Chapter 24

FINNISH LINE

O Fortune, variable as the moon. Always dost thou wax and wane. Detestable life, first dost thou mistreat us, and then, whimsically, thou heedest our desires. As the sun melts the ice, so dost thou dissolve both poverty and power.

LIBRETTO FROM CARL ORFF'S CANTATA *Carmina Burana*

EASTER 2003

FINLAND: 10–28 APRIL

In one of Monty Python's undeservedly lesser-known songs, Finland is pictured as such a boring place that it comes 'a poor second to Belgium when going abroad'. The unexciting truth about the land of Nokia is that for pristine natural beauty and polite unfussy people there are few places on Earth as calming to the soul. Add to that the most comfortable and efficient transport system in the entire journey and there are plenty of moments when I suspect the best has been left until last. Dare I say it, Finland is a nice place to live, but its remoteness explains why so few want to visit.

My route here would take me west from Helsinki to the seaside town of Turku and northward from there to the Arctic zone. When I reached Oulu, in the Gulf of Bothnia's upper reaches, the scale of my exploit defied the ability to comprehend it: that glassy sea was the far edge of the continent I had now crossed. The epic had encompassed one fifth of the land surface of the globe.

DAY 648 (11 APRIL): TALLINN TO HELSINKI

Leaving Estonia and its ferocious blizzards astern, the oldest ferry in the Tallink Express fleet shears its way relentlessly through great slabs of pack ice that Peary or Amundsen would have felt at home amid. By the time I've become acquainted with all that a ferry of this type has to offer—from cinemas to video parlours, restaurants, cafés, TV rooms, lounges and viewing decks—it's time to disembark.

My first choice of lodgings in Helsinki, the snazzy Eurohostel, is full and it takes three or four hours to find an accessible alternative. The bad news is that this alternative is a dive, a boarding house where, the manager warns me, one of the residents is a drunk *and* a kleptomaniac. (I lock and bolt my door.) The good news is that it is right in the heart of the city.

DAY 650 (13 APRIL): HELSINKI

Sixty degrees above the Equator, Helsinki, the most northerly of all capitals after Reykjavik, has its share of urban problems—and is up near the head of the world's-worst-practice league table when it comes to suicide and alcoholism rates—but the city itself is subdued, pleasant and orderly.

On Sunday morning the city artery called Alexanderinkatu (Alexander Street) is empty and windswept. Factor in tram tracks, and the sight is oddly reminiscent of Melbourne on a Sunday. Or am I just getting homesick?

I wander between landmarks, a snap-happy chappie. Helsinki is a photographer's delight, even if today is one of those grey-sky affairs. Onion-domed Uspensky Cathedral, which towers over the port, is packed with the Russian Orthodox faithful.

By way of contrast, I seek out Finlandia talo concert hall, the white Lego-like work of Alvar Aalto, Finland's most renowned (and controversial) architect. During his lifetime he worked on 200 000 designs and left 500 buildings behind for observers to admire, or loathe.

Temppeliaukio (the Church in the Rock, 1969) has become the country's most visited building. The idea of burrowing into the conic section of a hill so that your construction sits below ground level was adopted here years before Canberra welcomed its new Parliament House.

This being Sunday afternoon, a service is about to begin when I arrive, so I decide to swap my mobile pew for a fixed one. Well over a hundred worshippers are here (the church is multi-faith) and I hardly believe my ears when the American minister who is giving today's sermon compares the Jews' return from Babylon to Jerusalem with 'the liberation of Baghdad'.

A feisty woman of about 80 to whose side he returns afterwards (his mother?) then stands up and, turning to address us all, introduces a busload of male choristers from Oslo 'sent to us by God' who sing an Ethiopian hymn in Norwegian. Well, this is something different.

After the service, the minister ushers the old lady—yes, definitely his mother—into a car bearing diplomatic plates. Blessed be the speechmakers.

DAY 652 (15 APRIL): TURKU
On the bus here I noticed my rabbit-fur hat had 'walked'. Then I recalled with a shudder that, after locking my room door in Helsinki, I had placed it on a table in the corridor that was one of the light-fingered vagrant's usual haunts. Upon arrival at Turku, I ring the manager and ask him whether my hat is anywhere to be seen. Silly question, really.

This is the hometown of Paavo Nurmi, the great Finnish long-distance runner and Olympian from the 1920s. He is still running—albeit as a statue these days—near the stream that flows through Turku.

DAY 653 (16 APRIL): OULU
When you're staying at a luxury hotel, the temptation to venture outside isn't all that great, especially when the view from inside is a stunning panorama of the gulf as a field of ice.

With funds getting low, it had not been my intention to go upmarket. The likeliest-looking option here was Nallikari, a campground occupied by bungalows and chalets. Unfortunately, the only cabin I could have stayed in (the others having steps) was one the key to which was kept by the manager. And the manager, so the duty clerk informed me with averted eyes, had a strict rule not to open it to visitors out of season. So if I could come back in June I would be welcome to stay.

Where would the clerk suggest for tonight? 'Over there,' she pointed to the Kylpylahotelli Eden, where room tariffs begin at US$100 and skyrocket from there. If campground management was about as hospitable as an iceberg, the Eden's displays a refreshing flexibility. On seeing that I genuinely have no affordable alternatives (Finland, like all the Scandinavian countries, is extremely expensive), the receptionist agrees to reduce the room rate to US$40.

The waking part of my night is spent indulging in the myriad delights of cable television, eating a juicy steak and drinking on the terrace. For the other part of it, I sleep like a dream. My gosh, I think before pegging out, if I had stayed in hotels like this all along, I'd have had a ball—and gone home 21 months ago.

DAY 654 (17 APRIL): ROVANIEMI TO SOMEWHERE NEAR THE ARCTIC CIRCLE

Where Rovaniemi ends, just 8 kilometres south of the Arctic Circle as it says on the signboard, I wait for a bus to that old familiar dotted line. Waiting with me is a woman in her seventies (she was proud to tell me that, I would have guessed late fifties) who is steadying herself on ski poles planted in the grass verge. The Finns' habit of using ski poles to propel themselves along, even while out walking in summer, has occasioned the odd sly dig from foreigners. As if reading my mind, my prospective fellow passenger says in flawless English, 'People think we're silly, but it keeps us fit, and most of those who criticise us for it will be dead before we are.'

What an exciting ride this is: I've never been *above* the Circle before in all my meanderings and, if I'm ever denied the chance to plant a flag at the Pole itself, this will do for a substitute. When the bus pulls up, I am steeled for the sight of a little commercialism but here, in garish letters, we have Santa Claus Village theme park. (Don't they know he lives in Turkey?) A signboard immediately captures my attention: I am now 2648 kilometres from the North Pole.

At the service counter just inside the entrance, I hear a vaguely familiar accent: broad Australian. The voice belongs to Eva-Marie, a German-Australian formerly from Adelaide whose main stock in trade is selling certificates that enable visitors to make their friends envious that they have been to the Arctic Circle. But, on learning that I am an

Australian too, she comes clean, whispering conspiratorially, 'Did you know the Arctic Circle is no longer here?'

'I beg your pardon,' I counter, 'but the bus that brought me here had the destination "Arctic Circle" written on the front.'

'Well, it was here,' proceeds Eva-Marie, 'in 1887. But since then it's moved up the road 1.4 kilometres.'

'Then those lines out there in the yard are a fraud.' 'Certainly are,' she beams, like a schoolteacher who has just succeeded in imparting a difficult concept to a quizzical pupil.

But her enlightenment has left me in the dark. Outside it gives the latitude as 66°32'35"N. Over in Santa Claus's Post Office, where the workers wear ridiculous red-and-white bobble hats all year round, it is given as 66°33'7"N. And, if I recollect my schoolbook accurately, the line is actually parallel 66°30'N.

It is beyond my grasp how the line could have moved. Oscillation of the Earth? Changes in the magnetic field? And, if the Circle marks the southernmost latitude at which the Sun never sets on the longest day of the year, mustn't it be 66°30'N even if the North Pole gets up and relocates? By this time my head is spinning rather like the planet itself.

'Yes, it is a bit of a fraud,' Eva-Marie drags me back from my reverie. 'But we have a business to run.' She breaks off to prepare more precious certificates for a gleeful quartet of students all the way from China and says not a word to disillusion them. As they shuffle off to be photographed on the line, Eva-Marie completes her point. 'Nobody's going to go to the expense of moving the village all the time, so we don't usually let on.'

DAY 656 (19 APRIL): ROVANIEMI TO INARI, LAPLAND

According to my best estimate, the bus bearing me north is crossing the Arctic Circle right now at 12.15 pm.

It's 6 pm and here I am at the end of *my* road. *The* road goes further, over the border into Norway, but mine stops here.

Down I get from the bus, carefully transferring myself from the bottom step to my waiting chair, right in front of the Inari pub. The Inari pub is called the Hotel Inari, and rightly so, because it is the only one in Inari (population 550). From here, a point 300 kilometres indisputably beyond the Arctic Circle, and going north almost to Nordkapp, you would pass through the traditional land of the nomadic Sami, a people whose lives and general fate sound curiously familiar to someone from the Antipodes. From Nordkapp all the way down to the Gulf of Finland was once the land of the Sami, before they were driven to the edge by Finnish settlers.

It is Saturday 'night' and everyone in this Arctic equivalent of an outback pub is a bit over the top—some quite a bit. Technically, I suppose, 'night' doesn't really begin until the sun goes down, and at this time of year—in what will soon live up to its tag as the Land of the Midnight Sun—it does that at about half past eleven. But a mere four hours later, at 3.30 am, it reappears to scare the living daylights into those still at the bar.

A teacher, Nils Joks, sits by the bar-room window tonight, his hands locked in those of his Finnish girlfriend, Maria. Joks, who is a Sami and a Norwegian, feels no conflict about his dual heritage. You might say he has mastered the art of living on the edge. Others are still struggling, like the barman who frogmarches 'Michael'—another northern Sami in town for the weekend, and a man who could best be described as harmlessly drunk—out of the pub.

Michael is no more inebriated than some of the Finnish patrons sipping their beers undisturbed but, resplendent in his bright yellow-and-red traditional jacket, he is treated as a stranger in his own land. No, on second thoughts, the stranger in his land gets treated better. I have nothing to complain of.

DAY 657 (20 APRIL): INARI

Today is Beassazat, what the Christianised Sami call Easter, and I'm off to learn more about these aboriginal people of the Arctic. Despite its minuscule size, Inari is the site of a magnificent museum in their honour, crisply known as Siida.

At the end of the last Ice Age, around 10 000 BC, reindeer-herding Sami followed the receding icecap inland from the Atlantic and Arctic coasts of Scandinavia. Antlered animals remain important to the lives of their descendants today. On the way to the museum I pass a deerskin that has been left out to dry in the sun, the first step in an ancient Arctic-wide tanning process.

DAY 658 (21 APRIL): INARI

In ten days' time it will be two years since my plane trip to the other side of this continent, the first step in a long trek that I have now completed just a fraction over budget (for every A$40 of estimated expenditure, I spent A$41).

To gauge how the times have changed since that touchdown, I have only to consider that you can no longer jet into Karachi. The Pakistani government itself considers its most populous city too dangerous to visit. People talk glibly of the 'global community', yet every day people on the subcontinent live behind curtains as opaque as the one of iron that divided Europeans from one another not so long ago. Sooner rather than later, I hope and pray, those curtains will be rung down, too, and people everywhere will see one another in a truer light.

This Easter Monday, 69°N of the Equator, we are on the cusp of winter's miraculous transformation into spring. Fresh air tingles my nostrils, and my ears can almost hear the silence. The sun today is surprisingly strong—powerful enough to cleave the ice, unleashing waters long pent up, and their mighty rush is all that disturbs the stillness.

If you were here, you would see me pushing up the road in the direction of Norway. My arms feel ready to drop out of their sockets. Hunger starts to gnaw. At 5.30 pm, beside a wilderness trail, I pause to rest and reflect on how far I have come, and where I have been, these past two years.

Projected on the screen of memory are the highlights, and the lowlights, of this odyssey that has taken me further from home than I have ever been. I see it all, as if for the first time, and wonder how on earth anyone can say there is nothing new under the sun, no untrodden path waiting to be discovered. Then, warmed by the sunshine and steeled by that mental trove of memorabilia, I glance over my shoulder and turn my wheels for home.

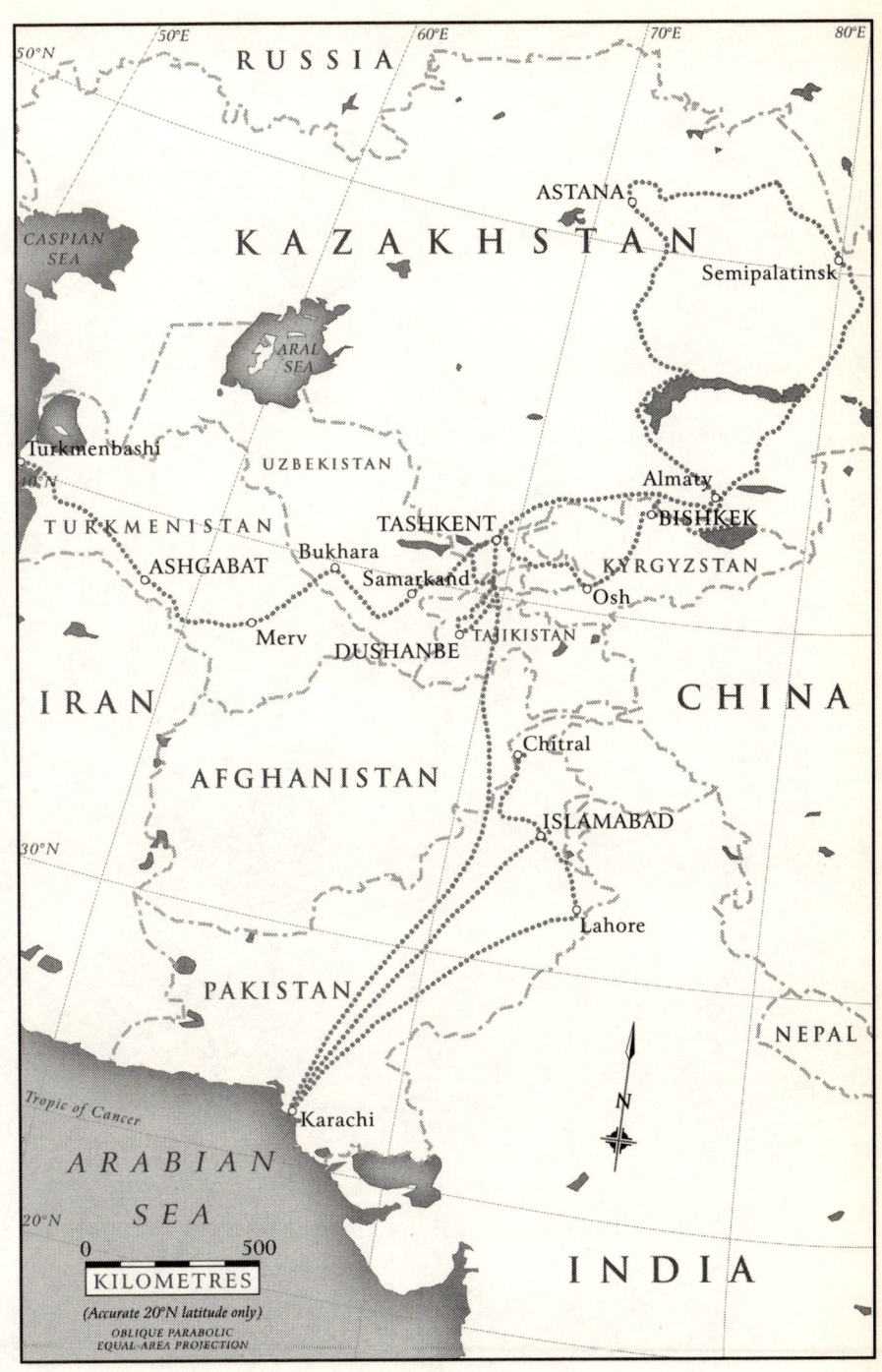

GREECE
BULGARIA
Varna
Sozopol
Gallipoli
Troy
Istanbul
ATHENS
Mykonos
BLACK
SEA
UKRAINE
RUSSIA
ANATOLIA
ANKARA
Budrum
Iraklion Marmaris
Crete
Rhodes
Karpathos
Kobuleti
GEORGIA
Gori TBILISI
Goreme
TURKEY
ARM Dilijan
Lake Sevan
YEREVAN
AZER BAKU
Tarsus
MEDITERRANEAN
SEA
NICOSIA
CYPRUS
Larnaca
Antakya
Aleppo
Apamea
Qamishle
Tabriz
CASPIAN
SEA
LEBANON Byblos
Tripoli
BEIRUT
Tyre Baalbek
ISRAEL
SYRIA
EGYPT
30°N
30°E
CAIRO
Ajlun
DAMASCUS
Suweimeh JORDAN
IRAQ
TEHRAN
IRAN
Madain
Salah
Ahwaz
Isfahan
Yazd
KUWAIT CITY
Failaka
Island
KUWAIT
Shiraz
Persepolis
Bushehr
SAUDI
20°N
RIYADH
BAHRAIN
QATAR
Doha
Dubai
Abu Dhabi
UAE
ARABIA
Muscat
Nizwa
N
OBLIQUE PARABOLIC
EQUAL-AREA PROJECTION
SULTANATE
OF OMAN
Tropic of Cancer
40°E
10°N
50°E
YEMEN
Salalah
0
KILOMETRES
(Accurate 20°N latitude only)
500
60°E

324

KILOMETRES
(Accurate 40°N latitude only)
OBLIQUE PARABOLIC
EQUAL-AREA PROJECTION

325

BIBLIOGRAPHY

Bibby, Geoffrey (1996) *Looking for Dilmun*,
Stacey International, London
Birenbaum, Halina (1994) *Hope Is the Last To Die:*
A Personal Documentation of Nazi Terror, Publishing House
of the State Museum in Oswiecim (Auschwitz), Poland
Bulgakov, Mikhail (1996), *The White Guard*,
The Harvill Press, London
Burton, Sir Richard (trans.) (1997), *Arabian Nights*,
Penguin Books, London
Carlyon, Les (2001), *Gallipoli*, Pan Macmillan, Sydney
Carver, Robert (1999), *The Accursed Mountains:*
Journeys in Albania, Flamingo, London
Dalrymple, William (1998), *From the Holy Mountain:*
A Journey in the Shadow of Byzantium, Flamingo, London
Eastwick, Edward B. (1976 reprint of 1864 original),
Journal of a Diplomate's Three Years' Residence in Persia,
Vols 1–2, Offset Press, Tehran
Hasek, Jaroslav (1974), *The Good Soldier Svejk*,
Penguin Books, London
Herodotus (1996), *The Histories*, Penguin Books, London
Hitchens, Christopher (1997), *Hostage to History: Cyprus from*
the Ottomans to Kissinger, Verso, London and New York
Hopkirk, Peter (1991), *The Great Game: On Secret Service*
in High Asia, Oxford University Press, Oxford
Hourani, Albert (1992), *A History of the Arab Peoples*,
Faber and Faber, London
Hudik, Pavol (ed.) (2002), *In Search of Homo Sapiens:*
Twenty-five Contemporary Slovak Short Stories,
The Publishing House of the Slovak Writers' Society, Bratislava
Jokai, Mor (2001), *The Man with the Golden Touch*,
Corvina Books, Budapest
Kaplan, Robert D. (1996), *Balkan Ghosts:*
A Journey Through History, Vintage Books, New York
Kapuscinski, Ryszard (1995), *Imperium*, Granta Books, London

Kinross, Patrick (1964), *Atatürk: The Rebirth of a Nation*, Phoenix, London

Klinge, Matti and Kolbe, Laura, (1999), *Helsinki: Daughter of the Baltic: A Short Biography*, Otava Publishing, Helsinki

Kundera, Milan (2000), *The Book of Laughter and Forgetting*, Faber and Faber, London

Lamb, Christina (1991), *Waiting for Allah*, Viking, New Delhi

Lawrence, T.E. (1926), *Seven Pillars of Wisdom: A Triumph*, Doubleday, New York

Lermontov, Mikhail (2001), *A Hero of Our Time*, Penguin Books, London

Loti, Pierre (2002), *Constantinople in 1890*, Unlem Basim Yayincilik, Istanbul

Maalouf, Amin (1995), *The Rock of Tanios*, Abacus, London

Mackintosh-Smith, Tim (2001), *Travels with a Tangerine: A Journey in the Footnotes of Ibn Battutah*, John Murray Publishers, London

Makdisi, Jean Said (1999), *Beirut Fragments: A War Memoir*, Persea Books, New York

Malcolm, Noel (2002), *Bosnia, A Short History*, Pan Books, London, Basingstoke and Oxford

Mansfield, Peter (1992), *The Arabs*, Penguin Books, London

May, Walter (trans.) (1999), *Manas: The Great Campaign*, Kyrgyz Heroic Epos, National Academy of Sciences of the Kyrgyz Republic, Institute of Literature and Arts, Bishkek

Milosz, Czeslaw (2001), *The Captive Mind*, Penguin Books, London

Nicholson, Reynold A. (trans.) (1950), *Rumi, Poet and Mystic 1207–1273*, Allen and Unwin, London

Ormanian, Malachia, Armenian Patriarch of Constantinople (2000), *The Church of Armenia*, Armenian Holy Apostolic Church Canadian Diocese, Montreal

Plutarch (1960), *The Rise and Fall of Athens: Nine Greek Lives*, Penguin Books, London

Pullerits, Albert (ed.), *The Estonian Yearbook 1927*, Government Printing Office, Tallinn

Purmonen, Veikko (ed.) (1981), *Orthodoxy in Finland: Past and Present*, Orthodox Clergy Association, Kuopio

Reid, Anna (1998), *Borderland: A Journey Through the History of Ukraine*, Phoenix, London

Said, Edward W. (1995), *Orientalism: Western Concepts of the Orient*, Penguin Books, London

Said, Kurban (1990), *Ali & Nino*, Robin Clark Ltd, London

Salehpour, Salehe (trans.) (1998), *Divan of Hafez*, Booteh Press, Tehran

Seal, Jeremy (1995), *A Fez of the Heart: Travels Around Turkey in Search of a Hat*, Picador, London

Sidhwa, Ervad Godrej Dinshawji (2000), *Discourses on Zoroastrianism*, Karachi

Skultans, Vieda (1998), *The Testimony of Lives: Narrative and Memory in Post-Soviet Latvia*, Routledge, London

Stark, Freya (2001), *The Valleys of the Assassins*, The Modern Library, New York

Thesiger, Wilfred (1991), *Arabian Sands*, Penguin Books, London

Thubron Colin (1986), *Journey into Cyprus*, Penguin Books, London

Thubron, Colin (1994), *The Lost Heart of Asia*, William Heinemann, London

Thucydides (1972), *History of the Peloponnesian War*, Penguin Books, London

Trinkunas, Jonas (ed.) (1999), *Of Gods and Holidays: The Baltic Heritage*, Tverme, Vilnius

West, Rebecca (2001), *Black Lamb and Grey Falcon: A Journey Through Yugoslavia*, Canongate Books, Edinburgh (reprint of the work first published by Macmillan, 1942)

Young, Gavin (1999), *Eye on the World*, Penguin Books, London

ACKNOWLEDGEMENTS

AUSTRALIA

First and foremost, Mum and Dad, whose moral support in uncertain times was matched only by their financial support. You got me from there to here.

My first guide to the publishing world, Teresa Pitt, who acted on an impulse: I hope this volume feels like your justification.

All the crew at Transit Lounge: Barry and Rhonda Scott, Tess Rice and Tim McQuiston. You took a wounded bird and made it fly.

Other publishing professionals who demonstrated and maintained faith in my work: above all, Siobhán Cantrill, Anouska Jones (you're revisionists, in the nicest sense); and Suzanne Falkiner, several of whose textual amendments I have incorporated with gratitude.

Brad and Ryan Warburton, who told me a decade ago that I should write a book. Well, I've kept my part of the bargain …

Neil: ready when you are.

Bruce and Els: for being there when I needed you.

The late Dr Gerald Ungar, Dr Terry Lim, Mr Doug Brown and surgical team (you know who you are): for bringing me back from the brink.

The nurses and specialist staff on Ward 13 and in rehab at the Austin: for seeing me through, and for all your help, physical and philosophical.

Terry Lane and Jon Faine, and Sarah Ashley, Jon's producer, the first to think my story might interest the wider world.

Garry Linnell: for reminding me why we write.

Michael Gawenda and Rod Wiedermann: for sending me to a tranquil corner.

Gideon Haigh, severely tested friend: your Bastille Day email liberated the book within.

Mal Schmidtke: for refusing to sell me short, even in a bearish market.

Gary Walsh: it was through your generosity, with just a tincture of forbearance, that 'Emails from the Edge' first saw the light in the travel pages of *The Age*.

Creighton Burns: for your calm and steady wisdom, combined with the soundest of advice.

Lucas, Linda and Joash Yong: thanks for doing your best to see the mail got through.

Jon and Jenny Cook: for looking after my home as if it were your own.
T. and D.: you know why.

Danny, Michael and all the crew at Mobility Plus: you were right about durability.

Lisa and Graham, Elsternwick Camera Centre.

ENGLAND

The late Gavin Young, and his 'sea anchor', Gritta Weil, for showing faith in works yet unattempted – in particular to Gavin for giving my voyage his benediction, in the first month of the millennium and the last of his life.

Stephanie Bunbury, for saving my life and for calling the professionals in. This book owes everything to you.

NAMIBIA

Craig Newby and Kris Pate: for making the computer do its job so that I could do mine.

Gwen Lister, founder and editor of *The Namibian*: for giving me time to write the book. And everyone else at the world's pluckiest newspaper who gave me the privilege of your company.

Viviane and Günther Scholz, in Swakopmund: for the gift of a family Christmas and, Viviane, for taking on the task of taming the Beast.

Graham Hopwood: for exercising the power o' the giftie, and keeping me more or less focused (as the need arose).

Werner Menges: for providing inspiration, and being one.

Christelle and Jaco Reed at Puccini: for giving me space to write the book.

SOUTH AFRICA

To *The Star* newspaper, especially *Saturday Star* executive editor Brendan Seery, chief sub-editor Francois Pienaar and my former travel-section colleague, Jenny de Klerk, for not being driven to distraction by it all. (Ah, but you were!)

Denis Beckett, for moral support and sound practical advice.

Jonathan Ancer: For selecting the title of Chapter 4.

Glenda and Shane Seagall at Chroma copying services, Norwood, Johannesburg.

UNITED STATES

Robert Frank and Carole Cheung: I was tired and true of heart. And also, you were tired and true of heart.

KAZAKHSTAN
Klara Duisengalieva, president, Hotel Zhetisu, Almaty: for outstanding hospitality and delegating staff to see me safely onto the northbound train.

UZBEKISTAN
Raisa Gareyeva, Azat and all my other friends at your travel agency, for unstinting hospitality, dependable companionship, generous use of your computers and guiding me through the postal and railway bureaucracies. May Allah preserve Bukhara!

TURKMENISTAN
Galina Yevgeniya, Mary: the world's leading authority on its least remembered massacre.

AZERBAIJAN
Fuad Axundhov, the most knowledgeable tourist guide in Old, or New, Baku.

GEORGIA
Zviad Mirgatia and Mark Mullen, National Democratic Institute for International Affairs: thanks for walking me through Georgia's politics on the morning of September 11, 2001. You were saying?

IRAN
Tom and Rebecca Hathaway, Tehran: in humble gratitude for your hospitality and long-suffering patience. Sorry if I got in the way.

Komeil Noofeli, travel guide, courier and drifter: for unbottling Shiraz and uncorking Persepolis.

OMAN
Rosemary Hector: for your hospitality and efficiency, taking me wadi-bashing and out to the bullfight, then letting me rest up at your home.

LEBANON
Ayssar abou Taif, super-receptionist at the Hotel Regis, Ain al-Mreisse, downtown Beirut: for doing as much as anyone to implant the idea of humanitourism in my brain.

GREECE
The generous soul who runs Santorini's best hotel, the Palladion.

Lou Economopoulos and Litsa Rovolis: for reminding me why we have a Greek word for the mood of fond recall. It was even better than the old times.

BULGARIA
Tsvetelina Ivanova (Vier Pfoten publicity director) and Ibrahim Garaliiski (at the park): for bearing with me.

YUGOSLAVIA (AS YOU WERE)
Ivana and Jelena, in beautiful Kotor, who wished me to 'remember us and our town and country with pleasure': wish granted.

CROATIA
Maya Petríc, managing director of Magnum Trade d.o.o.: your entrepreneurial spirit, and goodwill, gave me a wonderful first impression of Split – and it has lasted.

BOSNIA-HERZEGOVINA
Amelie Saríc and Professor Meliha Kulukchiha-Melly, Pavarotti Music Centre, Mostar: for building another mighty bridge. All donations to the work of the centre (pmc_org@cob.net.ba) are gratefully appreciated.

ROMANIA
Roberto Paulet, the master enamel-cup decorator and receptionist, Villa Helga Youth Hostel, Bucharest.

MOLDOVA
Sergei Mifodovski (romance_love_marriage@xaker.ru) and Vikki: for opening windows onto Moldovan realities. (Vikki, I hope you found your man, and happiness, wherever you're living now.)

UKRAINE
Janna Belousova and all the team at Eugenia: you lit up Odessa on the darkest days of the year.

GERMANY
Lotti Villinger, old friend and super-reliable in time of need: without you I might have given up and gone home early.

BELARUS
Oleg Loiko and family: the silver watch is treasured still. I hope you're all happy in Canada.

FINLAND
Father Deacon Vladimir (William Paul) Lysak, artist, baker, cook, iconographer, writer and Stavrophor monk at New Valamo Monastery: wouldn't have missed that aurora borealis for the (sublunary) world.

Santa Claus: go back to Turkey, the jig is up.

About The Author

Ken Haley is one of Australia's most widely travelled authors. To date he has visited 109 countries, 57 of these on his own two feet and 52 in a wheelchair. He became a paraplegic in 1991, but as far as Ken is concerned the only difference this has made is that he now observes the world from a sitting position. A journalist by profession, his experiences include stints on the foreign desk of *The Times*, *Sunday Times* and *The Observer* in London, the *Gulf Daily News* in Bahrain and the *Oman Daily Observer*. He has also worked at *The Age*, Melbourne, and as a newspaper sub-editor in Athens, Hong Kong and Johannesburg. He now lives in Melbourne.